THE PROMISE

Keith Ward

THE PROMISE

SPCK • London

First published 1980
SPCK
Holy Trinity Church
Marylebone Road
London NW1 4DU

Printed in Great Britain by
Lowe & Brydone Printers Ltd
Thetford Norfolk

ISBN 0 281 03748 5

Contents

Introduction

The Hebrew Bible – what Christians call the 'Old Testament' – is one of the greatest literary works in the history of mankind. Although it is made up of many different books – histories, poems, law-books and prophecies – together they form a continuous history of one people, the Jews, who believed God had chosen them for a special task. The story is a record of man's struggle to understand God, and – believers would say – of God's disclosure of his will to men. Throughout the ages, scholars and saints have meditated on its stories and symbols, seeking to discover new depths of meaning in the ancient texts, and understand its development and rich symbolism in new ways.

In our day, increased knowledge of the ancient world and of the original texts and languages has led to exciting new discoveries of ancient meanings. Many commentaries exist – too many for most people to read – and many new translations make the text easier to follow; but, as translations, they cannot bring out the full significance hidden in the text and explain its importance. What many people want is to be able to read the biblical story as a continuous narrative; to understand better the obscure passages that refer to obsolete customs or local traditions; and to see how the different parts of the history build up into one great design. Also, since the Bible is primarily a religious book, they want to see why each story was chosen and put in its particular place – the spiritual meaning which lies behind it. And they want to see something of the meaning that centuries of devotion and meditation have found in the stories.

These are the needs this book tries to fulfil. All the events recorded in the Bible are dealt with. They are not translated or even paraphrased. Rather, they are completely retold, in a way which attempts to bring out their spiritual meaning, to show their place in the total story, to explain references and terms which are often puzzling, and to incorporate some of the insights from Jewish and Christian meditation on them. But the whole is written so that it can be read as one dramatic story of symbolic power and beauty, which will live by its own power.

I have abstracted all the genealogies, putting them in the table following, omitting those names which have no further place in the Biblical narrative. I have also put the Law — the Torah — in an appendix, dividing it into subject headings, so that one can quickly see the laws by which ancient Israel tried to live, in systematic order. I have often used cross-references to other Biblical passages (as when Rahab, from Isaiah 51 and Psalm 89, is mentioned in the Creation account), or have adopted traditional interpretations not strictly warranted by the text (as when Cain's sacrifice is rejected by God because it was not of the best fruit). I have felt free to tell the stories in an imaginative — but I hope not too fanciful — way, to bring out their beauty and relevance. This is most pronounced in Gen. 1-11, where — uniquely — the nature of the material led me to some departures from the Hebrew text. In other passages such departures are minimal — as in the conflation of the three virtually identical stories of Abram and Isaac deceitfully concealing their marriages, or interpretations of such events as the crossing of the 'Red Sea' (the sea of reeds). But of course, for biblical accuracy, one must go to the Bible itself, and I hope this book may lead to a return to reading the Bible with renewed care and appreciation for its amazing subtlety and infinite power of inspiration. Nothing can ever replace the Bible itself; this book can best be seen as a literary meditation on a text which will always be irreplaceable.

THE ANCESTORS OF ISRAEL

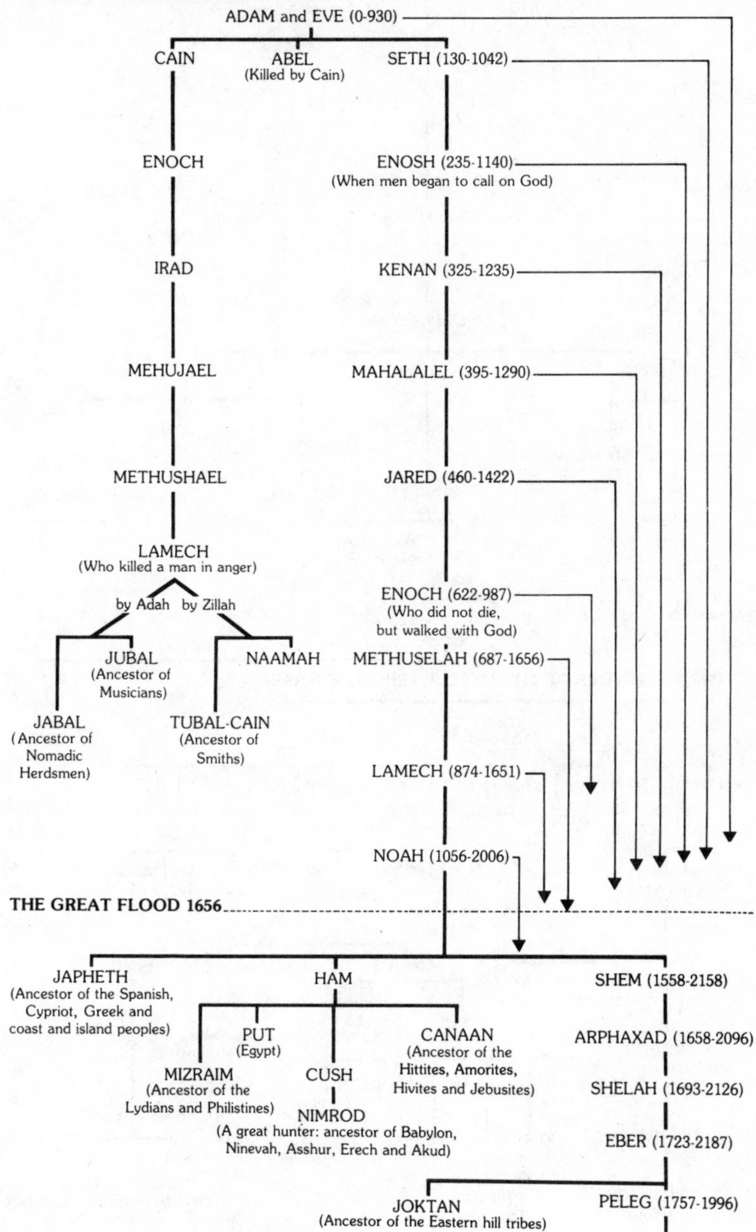

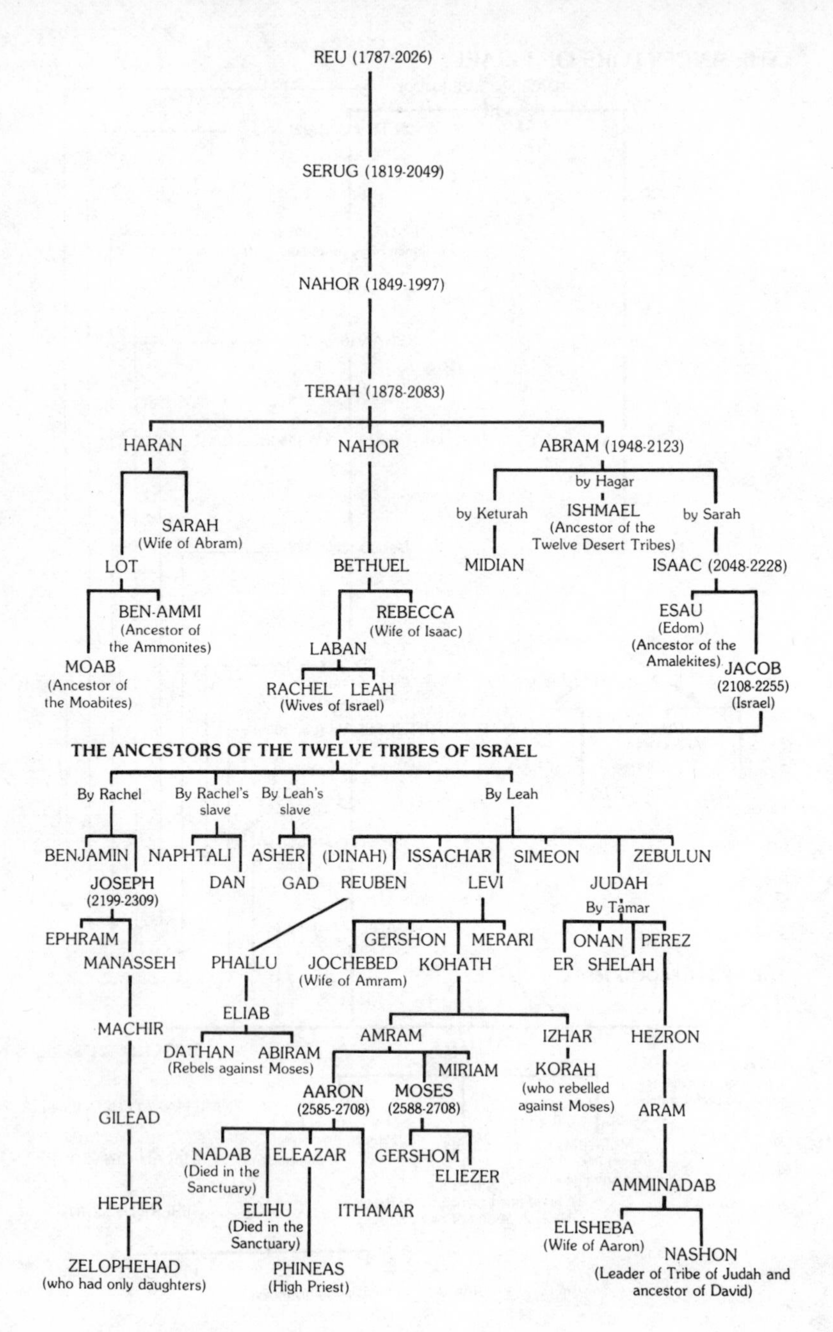
REU (1787-2026)
SERUG (1819-2049)
NAHOR (1849-1997)
TERAH (1878-2083)
HARAN
NAHOR
ABRAM (1948-2123)
SARAH
(Wife of Abram)
LOT
BEN-AMMI
(Ancestor of
the Ammonites)
MOAB
(Ancestor of
the Moabites)
BETHUEL
REBECCA
(Wife of Isaac)
LABAN
RACHEL LEAH
(Wives of Israel)
by Keturah
MIDIAN
by Hagar
ISHMAEL
(Ancestor of the
Twelve Desert Tribes)
by Sarah
ISAAC (2048-2228)
ESAU
(Edom)
(Ancestor of the
Amalekites)
JACOB
(2108-2255)
(Israel)
THE ANCESTORS OF THE TWELVE TRIBES OF ISRAEL
By Rachel
By Rachel's
slave
By Leah's
slave
By Leah
BENJAMIN
JOSEPH
(2199-2309)
EPHRAIM
MANASSEH
MACHIR
GILEAD
HEPHER
ZELOPHEHAD
(who had only daughters)
NAPHTALI
DAN
ASHER
GAD
(DINAH)
REUBEN
PHALLU
ELIAB
DATHAN ABIRAM
(Rebels against Moses)
ISSACHAR
SIMEON
ZEBULUN
LEVI
GERSHON
MERARI
JOCHEBED
(Wife of Amram)
KOHATH
AMRAM
IZHAR
KORAH
(who rebelled
against Moses)
MIRIAM
AARON
(2585-2708)
MOSES
(2588-2708)
NADAB
(Died in the
Sanctuary)
ELEAZAR
ELIHU
(Died in the
Sanctuary)
ITHAMAR
PHINEAS
(High Priest)
GERSHOM
ELIEZER
JUDAH
By Tamar
ER
ONAN
SHELAH
PEREZ
HEZRON
ARAM
AMMINADAB
ELISHEBA
(Wife of Aaron)
NASHON
(Leader of Tribe of Judah and
ancestor of David)

The Great Flood 1656

Israel went into Egypt 2238

Israel left Egypt after 430 years 2668

Moses gave the Law 2708

The Beginning

The Creation (Gen. 1)

This is the sacred story of the beginning of all things, guarded and handed down in the sanctuaries of Israel from times beyond memory.

At first there was only the great and formless deep. In its darkness there was no life or light; and over the surface of that deep, the wind of God's breath swept and stirred the waters of the limitless abyss. God said, 'Let there be light'; and immediately the deep was flooded with the radiance of his glory. So God limited the domain of darkness and divided it from the realm of light. The light he appointed to be Day, not measured by the sun or movement of the stars, but an aeon without measure, beginning and ending by his absolute decree. The darkness he appointed to be Night, the return of all things to formlessness and emptiness. But he decreed that the darkness should always be dispelled by the dawning of day. So that first unmeasurable night and morning marked the first day of creation.

On the second day, God made the sky, a firm and transparent dome, and placed it in the middle of the deep, dividing it in two, so that the waters above could be seen blue and clear through the dome. Thus Rahab, the dark dragon of chaos, was torn in two and disabled by the Creator's word, and chaos was confined by his almighty power.

On the third day, God drove back the waters under the dome of the sky, and gathered them into one place, so that the dry land appeared. By his word of command the surging deep was mastered, and the mountains and valleys of earth floated over the void. Around them the waters formed the oceans, calmed and controlled, their formless fury held by the hand of God. So the earth was ordered and the waters of chaos contained. Then God said, 'Let the earth produce life'; and at once vegetation covered the earth in uncounted forms of beauty, growing and reproducing until the barren soil was filled with the striving of luxuriant life.

On the fourth day of creation, God placed the sun and moon

and all the stars in the sky, to give light to men, to regulate the times for planting and for harvest, to order the passing of time and measure out the life of creation.

On the fifth day, God said, 'Let there be life to fill the waters and the sky'. He made the great sea monsters, which live and die at the limits of creation; fish to swarm in the sea and birds to soar over the earth below the dome of heaven. The stream of life flowed through the world, as it began to awaken from formless emptiness, to feel the urge to create, to come to consciousness and to explore, to delight in the beauty of the world God had made.

On the sixth day, God made all the animals, everything that moves and sees and feels on land. He sat on the throne of glory; about him, on his right and on his left, stood the hosts of heaven, the Elohim, clothed in light and calling ceaselessly, 'Holy; holy; holy is the Lord of hosts, infinite in majesty and might, everlasting without ending or beginning, unlimited in potency and power. Great are your purposes and mighty your acts; the whole earth is filled with your glory'. And they bowed before the throne and worshipped God. God saw the world that he had made, and said: 'Now all things have been prepared. Let us make mankind in our own image and likeness, and let us give him the power of understanding and judgement, wisdom and creativity, happiness and love. Let us give him power over the earth and all that lives upon it, so that he may be a god to all the creatures I have made, and they shall serve him'. All the hosts of heaven said, 'So may it be'; and it was so. Mankind was made, formed out of dust, and filled with the breath of God, to rule and subdue the earth and to fill it with his offspring, to the glory of God. God said to man: 'I have given you every plant and tree for food; and to the animals I give every green herb for food. There shall be no shedding of blood in all my creation.' So it was; God saw everything he had made, and it was completely perfect. That evening and morning was the sixth day.

On the seventh day the earth and the sky were completed; and on that day God rested from the work of creation; he thereby set apart every seventh day to be a remembrance and representation of the rest of the Eternal, in which all the work of creation is completed. For God is active without striving and remains changeless and untroubled in all the works of his almighty power. The last goal of all that he has made is the still centre of his own being, beyond joy and suffering, beyond action and inaction, the wordless rest which is the beginning and completion of all things. It is that rest which awaits the people of God, the end of all their striving, the completion of the promise which lies already at the first moment of the world's making.

The Garden (Gen. 2 and 3)

Once upon a time, God planted a beautiful garden, and called it the garden of bliss. He filled it with trees, bearing all kinds of fruit, with the most subtle and exotic flavours and perfumes, and a profusion of exquisite flowers. In the centre of the garden there were two trees, standing apart by the great river of clear blue water that flowed through the garden; one was the tree of life, which gives unending life to all who continue to eat its fruit; the other was the tree of knowledge. They stood by the river, great and graceful, their branches trailing peacefully in the water; all things in the garden seemed to lead to them and to live in their quiet shade.

God put man in the garden to care for it and said: 'All the fruit of my garden is for you to eat – all except the fruit from the tree of knowledge; do not eat that; for you are not yet ready for it, and if you eat from it now, you will certainly die.' Then God decided to make a partner for the man, so that he should not be alone. He brought before him all the animals and birds, and the man gave them names; but none of them could be his mate. So while the man slept, God took one of his ribs from his body and formed it into a woman. When the man woke, he saw her and said, 'Now at last I have found completeness. You are bone from my bone, flesh from my flesh. Now we shall find fulfilment in each other; we have been one flesh and in our children we shall become one flesh again'. So the first man and the first woman lived together and cared for the garden of bliss and all the animals in the garden, and found their delight in one another without shame or fear. In the time of innocence they walked with God in the garden, and all things gave praise to their creator.

One day the snake, cleverest of all the creatures God had made, said to the woman, 'Is it true that God has forbidden you to eat from any trees in the garden?' The woman answered, 'We may eat from any tree except one great tree by the river, whose fruit God has forbidden us to touch; if we do, we shall die'. The snake laughed: 'Of course you will not die. God knows that if you eat that fruit, your eyes will be opened and you will be like gods, able to know and do all things'. When the woman heard these words, she felt a strange excitement deep within her. To know and do all things, to be like gods, was that not enviable? Surely God would not kill them because of such a desire? Perhaps this prohibition was a test, to bring them to maturity; perhaps when they dared to grasp at knowledge, they would find the fulfilment of their destiny. Then they would be free, to know, to choose, to find for themselves the ways of good and evil, to be free and independent, masters of their future and of the world they lived in. The woman looked at the fruit of the tree of knowledge. It looked good to eat, firm and healthy, and it promised wisdom; she stretched out her arm, and took it in her hand, it felt fresh and soft, and it promised freedom; she placed it in her mouth; it tasted sweet and smooth, and it promised power. Excitedly she called the man, and they ate together. Then, as the snake had said, their eyes were opened; but the first thing they saw was their own nakedness, their own vulnerability and shame for they had disobeyed God. Pathetically, they stitched fig leaves together to cover their bodies, in the vain hope that their guilt would be concealed. The magic of their innocence was over.

When evening came, they heard the footsteps of God, walking in the garden, and they hid from him. God called, 'Where are you?', and the man said, 'I heard you walking in the garden, and I was afraid because I am naked; and I hid myself.'

'Why are you ashamed of your nakedness?', answered God; 'You have eaten the forbidden fruit when you were not prepared for it, and what it has showed you is your own guilt. Is that not so?'

'Lord,' said the man, 'the woman gave me the fruit to eat'.

'See the gifts your knowledge has brought', said God; 'Guilt, fear and now betrayal. What is this that you have done?' But the woman misunderstood him and said, 'The snake tricked me, and I ate'.

Then God said to the snake: 'Because of your deed you shall crawl on your belly in the dust; you shall be the woman's enemy; her children shall strike at your head, and you shall strike at their heel.' To the woman he said: 'In pain shall you bear children; you shall be dominated by your husband and be burdened with care for him.' And to the man he said: 'You shall gain your bread by the sweat of your brow, and the ground will bear thorns and thistles until you return to that from which you were taken. For you are dust, and to dust you shall return.' Thus knowledge sought in pride has its price. The price is that every man shall be set against his fellows, seeking mastery, finding slavery; that every man shall find his work a burden, seeking creativity and finding monotony; that every man shall find nature his foe, seeking plenty and finding famine; that every man shall find himself divided, seeking fulfilment and finding destruction; that every man shall seek for life without end, and find himself always on the way of death.

God made the man and his mate coats of animal skin and sent them from the garden of bliss; and at the east of the garden he placed the cherubim, with a whirling sword of flame, to guard the way to the tree of life. The woman and the man left the garden and walked out into the desert. The way ahead was rough and stony; the sun beat mercilessly down on the hard rock. Behind them the shaded trees shimmered in the heat; the flowers of the tree of life were full and their colours glowed in the light. But there was no going back; and as they walked on, the garden was soon lost to sight behind the desert hills. It was never to be found again, as long as man lived.

The Wanderer (Gen. 4)

There were once two brothers; one was a farmer and the other was a shepherd. At the time of the annual sacrifice, when men came to thank God for the gifts he had given them, Cain, the farmer, and Abel, the shepherd, came with their offerings. Abel took his finest young lamb, killed it and offered it to God as a sacrifice of thanksgiving; and God was pleased with his offering. But Cain did not really want to give up his best corn and grapes, which he had cultivated with such hard work and care. So he took some slightly blemished grapes and wind-blown wheat, and offered them to God in tribute to the creator. God was angry with Cain, and said: 'Did I not raise you from the dust of the earth, and give you everything that you have? And could you still not give me just one part of the best that you have? Take care; for evil crouches at your door, wishing to rule you; but you must overcome it.' Cain was ashamed; but he was also angry that God had criticised him in front of his brother; and he was jealous of Abel. This anger and jealousy simmered and grew inside him, until one day, when the two brothers were walking out in the fields, Cain picked a quarrel with Abel. They fought, and Cain hit his brother with a rock, and killed him.

Cain was afraid; he left his brother lying there, and went and hid. But God found him and said, 'Where is your brother, Abel?'

'How should I know?', answered Cain, 'Am I my brother's keeper?'

'I hear your brother's blood calling from the ground for justice', said God; 'From one small selfishness has sprung, in this short time, anger, shame and jealousy, lying and indifference; and the first shedding of innocent blood. Now I decree that you shall be a fugitive for evermore, wandering over the face of the world, a stranger to me and to the earth, pursued by your own guilt, homeless until the end of time'.

'This punishment is more than I can bear', said Cain; 'Without home or friends, I shall be at the mercy of anyone who finds me'.

'From this time on', said God, 'Men shall walk in fear and distrust of each other; each man a fugitive with no abiding home. Nevertheless if any man kills you, he will be punished seven times more severely than you'. And God placed a mark on the forehead of Cain, to protect him from harm. The mark was a mark of blood, in the form of a cross. 'The mark of Cain', said God, 'Will save the man who bears it, though he has shed the blood of the innocent; for it is the mark of my love, and it cannot fade.' So Cain left the presence of God, and became a stranger and a wanderer in the world.

The Flood (Gen. 6-9)

God looked down from heaven at the world he had made. He saw armies of men fighting in savage wars, treachery and intrigue in the courts of kings, poverty and oppression in the cities, violence and destruction in the country; everywhere the powers of evil walked the earth, and found followers to listen. Even the heroes were men of blood and deceit, and the priests turned to the dark gods of their own desires. In those days it was said that there were giants roaming the earth, the children of angels who had fallen from light, who coupled with those women whom they desired. So the dark powers of the courts of heaven stalked the earth, corrupting all things, lying in wait to master those who turned from God, and defacing the once flawless perfection of creation. God was sorry that he had created man, and he resolved to destroy all that he had made on earth. The waters of chaos from which the world had sprung would rise again, the womb of life would bring death to its offspring, and the breath of life would return to the one who gave it. So earth would be cleansed, returning to the silence of the waters of creation and destruction, where no man lives, only the unchanging deep.

But all was not loss. There was a man who had three sons, and lived with his family in an obscure town; his name was Noah. He was a just man and he walked with God. Through the virtue of this man the world was to be saved from utter destruction; his righteousness brought life to all the generations of men to come. God said to Noah: 'I have judged the whole earth, everything that I have made, and I have decreed destruction for every living thing, because of the corruption of my way upon earth. Everything that is upon the earth will die; but because you walk with me and keep my ways, all that you save will be saved.' So God chose Noah to be the father of men, and told him to build a gigantic ship of wood, and to take into it seven pairs of every ritually clean animal and one pair of every ritually unclean animal, and his wife and his sons with their wives, so that life on earth might be renewed.

Noah did all that God told him to do; he built the ship on dry land, and gathered together all the animals, and waited for God's word. God came to him again and said: 'You have walked with me in this corrupt land; now you will walk with me in a new world. Take your family and all the living things you have gathered, and go into the ship; for as in seven days I made the world, so in seven days I will unmake all living things.' Noah and his family and the animals of the earth went into the ship, and closed the doors. And after seven days, in the six hundredth year of Noah's life, in the second month and on the seventeenth day of the month, on that day it began to rain. For forty days and forty nights it rained, and the waters of the great deep rose and covered the earth, and no living thing escaped; all were destroyed. The great ship floated silently on the waters, high above the drowned world; nothing moved throughout the whole earth; only Noah remained alive, and those who were with him, voyaging alone towards a new creation.

Five months passed. God sent a wind over the wastes of water, and it began to return to the sea. The ship rested on a mountain, and Noah waited patiently. At length he took a raven and sent it out over the waters; strong-winged, it circled the ship, flying without rest until the waters left the earth. After seven days, Noah sent out a dove to seek out land. But the dove found nowhere to rest, and returned to the ship. Noah stretched out his hand and gently took her in. Seven more days passed, and Noah sent out the dove again; and at evening she returned once more, having nowhere to rest. But in her beak she bore an olive branch, the gentle bird of promise and of hope, and Noah took her joyfully into the ship. Noah waited seven days, and sent out the dove for the third time. Out from the ship of earth's salvation, cradled in the mountains under the clear stars, she soared, hovering with white wings spread over the silent fields, swooping with grace and power among the olive trees, calling her low soft song of life to come. The trees and valleys seemed to hear and rejoice as the warmth of her life ended their long waiting. Noah waited that day, but she did not return; he knew that she would not come to him again. So Noah and his family and the animals with him, left the ship on the mountain top, and life was renewed on the earth.

Noah built an altar, and offered sacrifice to God. And God said: 'Now I will make a covenant with you and with every living creature, from this time and forever. My promise to you is that I shall never again destroy all life on earth. As long as earth remains, seedtime and harvest, cold and heat, summer and winter, day and night shall never cease. You must be fruitful and increase and rule the earth. I put all animals into your hands, so that they shall dread and fear you; all living things shall live by killing and shedding blood. But you shall not eat flesh with blood still in it; for blood symbolises life, which shall be inviolate. He who sheds the blood of a man shall die, for man is made in my image. I will require satisfaction for the death of any man, whether from animals or men. Blood shall be prohibited to you, and set apart for me, as the life returns to the creator who gave it.' Then God set a rainbow in the clouds as the sign and seal of his promise, that he would preserve the earth and its life for ever.

The Tower (Gen. 11)

The story is told that long ago, men tried to build a tower to reach to heaven; but God confused their language, so that they spoke in many different tongues, and could no longer understand one another; and they scattered throughout the earth. The world was divided; men became strangers to one another, hating and fearing what they did not understand. So it has been from that time until now:

In the land between two rivers lived a King, in the greatest of all the cities of that land. The King looked at his armies in their ordered ranks, with flying pennants and with shining coats of mail; he looked at his palaces with their soaring walls, with shaded fountains and rich patterned furnishings; he looked at his villages and farms, set in their gentle fields by the long riverbank, and his heart was filled with pride. And yet he was not satisfied. On the edge of consciousness there lurked a fear, unnamed and un-admitted, gnawing at contentment, whispering that all this vast achievement still lay at the mercy of the uncaring powers of nature; the drought that could obliterate the fields, the fever that could decimate the armies or the merest tremor of the earth which could destroy the city at a stroke, and leave only a ruin in the desert, forgotten and unseen, swept by the scouring sands and the bleak winds. The suspicion of such a future gnawed into the present like a cancer, depriving it of significance and sense, turning joy to lassitude and pride to bitterness.

The King issued a decree; a great tower would be built on the wide plain beside the city walls, a monument so great that wind would not weather it nor sand erode; in its enduring it would outlive long generations of men, and speak for ever of the splendour of this city and its King. It would give eternity to this generation, and defeat the dark forgetfulness of death. The King would find eternal life in the work of his hands.

The building of the tower began. Thousands of men were conscripted to quarry stone and drag it to the site, to raise it with vast engines high above the plain. The tower rose up out of the plain like a sheer cliff; it soared, it seemed, as high as heaven itself. The King saw it and was pleased. Over the foundations thousands of workers toiled by day and night, and from the surrounding cities men came to see and admire this greatest monument of man, a tower to conquer time. Months went by; the rains came and went, the sun rose and fell in the sky; the tower grew, with the constant noise of hammering and cursing, the lines of workmen strung out along the roads and in the fields, bright torches lightening the night sky, fierce furnaces and kilns roaring and spluttering without rest. The King looked from his palace window, and saw the great tower rise above the highest pinnacle of the temple, and he was glad.

The months wore on; the tower grew higher; the city began to change. The merchants were taxed to provide ornaments and furnishings; the young men were sent to foreign lands to win slaves by war and conquest; the women were put to provide food for the workmen. There was murmuring in the streets and behind locked doors; the slaves, now far outnumbering their masters, grew insolent and restive; the guards, in turn, became cruel and harsh; and on the borders of the land, a growing league of plundered cities began to arm and train a larger force than had yet been encountered. In the shadow of the tower, the city grew dark, grey and diminished by its hungry child, and the confidence that began the task started to fail. Men questioned why they worked for an uncertain future while their present grew darker. The King sensed their unease; he sensed it in himself; and drove it out in fury with a more demonic will to shape and build. The city became a circle of oppression, ruled by the violent, riddled with the intrigue of the cunning. The King retired to his inner room, and did not look out on the tower again. Concealing from himself his own despair, he ordered work redoubled on the pain of death. The tower stood over the city; but it did not soar; it stooped with menace, heavy with despair, built on pride, clawing at the sky.

The end came suddenly, with harsh inevitable violence. Insurrection within, armed attack from without, indecision and corruption at court, uncertainty and fear in the streets. In one night the city fell, and in confusion the people were scattered throughout the land. The city which had been the envy of its enemies was burned and gutted; the tower was broken, stone by stone; and when the armies left, the desert crept over the broken ruins. What was built to storm the gates of heaven and survive the powers of nature was destroyed by stronger forces deep within, turning good to evil in the human soul.

In the land between two rivers, in the desert plain between their shadowed banks, where once a King had looked to find eternity, is a ruin blown by the sand, whose broken walls men call, without remembering why, the Tower of Confusion, in the city of the Unknown King.

The Journey (Gen. 12)

When the journey began no man can say. Beyond measured time and memory the wandering tribes had journeyed out of the deserts, driven by restless and obscure desire, seeking the unknown, the resting place. Moving from watering place to watering place, the harsh warriors urged the people on, laughing and drinking by the evening fire, proud and silent over desert ways, fighting for survival in the early dawn. Aggressive, hot-tempered, open hearted, hospitable to all, a people forged by the desert in ruthless simplicity, a loose unity of tribal groups and families, they moved over the land, following the call of the one they called their god.

At length they came to Babylon, a fertile land at the river's mouth, and there they settled in the city of Ur. For the barren desert scrub they now had green, well-watered fields; for the dry hills, they had the open wind of the sea; for goatskin tents, they had streets and walls of stone. But this was not to be the end of their heart's long searching; the voice of the god who would not let them rest in the desert was heard again in Ur, calling them out from prosperity and peace, Northwards to the unknown lands. Some of the tribes heard the voice of their god, the god of the mountain and the storm, calling them to find a land that would be their own, and they travelled North. Among them was one called Abram, who settled in Harran, at the edge of the wilderness, by the source of the two great rivers which ran to the sea. But he knew that his journey was not ended; and as he stood day by day looking out over the wilderness, he came to feel that he must again leave behind all that he knew and cared for, the possessions that bound him, the comfort and culture of the river valleys, the people who had come to know him. The call of the wastelands had entered into his life; the fierce glare of the sun and the wide horizons of solitude made the calm valleys seem confined and confining. He was a man of the desert, and his god was the god of the sun's fire and the star-spun sky, the desert storm and the highland hills. His god called to him in the wind over the trackless plain; and in that call Abram thought he sensed a promise, uncertain and obscure, of an end to all journeys and a land where desire would be content, of a Kingdom of peace and justice, where wars would end and every man would find the home his heart desired. Looking out over the wilderness where he was to go, he saw the beginnings of a vision which was to haunt his children's children to the end of history. He saw the desert flower and clear water flow over the parched soil, bringing life and rich vegetation where scorpions had scuttled under bare rocks. He saw a city, far away on a hill, shining white in the sun, high and alight with splendour; and he saw men of all nations, families, races, old women and children, camel trains and herds of oxen going to and from the city by a broad highway; he saw peace and prosperity and fruitfulness, the barren land renewed and transfigured with living water and the joyful labour of men.

What he did not, could not, see was the length of the journey to the city of his vision. All he knew was the need to find his own land, to leave the place of his birth and build a new city by a strange sea over the wilderness. And he knew, too, with an uncanny certainty, that by his obedience to this inward call he would find and found a new nation. If he stayed, he would remain one obscure shepherd among a thousand others, living and dying in his own unnoticed way. If he went, he would be the father of a people as numberless as the sand of the shore, a people who could renew the desert and transform the world. There was the hint of pride in this; in the belief that his was a special destiny. And there was more than a hint of absurdity; for he was a nomad and a stranger, of no account in the rich culture of Babylon, scratching a hard living on the very edge of the wilderness. Abram knew this, and sometimes laughed at himself for his dreams and visions. Yet he could not escape them; over the years they haunted him, until he could almost physically hear the voice of the desert calling him out, and see the city of his children, like a mirage on the far hills, and feel the ache in his body to find the land of promise.

At last Abram put aside his doubts, and gathered together his family and his nephew's family with their herds and possessions and those who followed him. In the early morning, before the sun's heat raised the desert haze, a small group set out over the desert to the West, to complete the long journey of their ancestors to the land of the heart's desire. The end of that journey, and the way it was to take, none of them could have foreseen.

The Land of Promise (Gen. 12)

The first glimpse of the river was like a miracle. After the long lifeless plains and scattered oases, the clear water of the Jordan gleamed in the Westward sun, and the wooded hills stretched away beyond the river in a succession of gentle fertile slopes, overlapping like the waves of the sea. As the people breasted the hill they saw the sun, dull gentle red, flooding the valley with a glowing golden light. The sweet smell of acacia and olive filled the still air; the shrill call of the cicada echoed in the shaded groves. Abram knew at once that this was the land of promise, the land of his dreams. Here, between Egypt and Babylon, between the desert and the sea, a new people would take root and build a great and prosperous nation; here he would find blessing for himself and the wandering tribesmen who were his people.

They crossed the river and followed the road of the sun into the mountains of Samaria, pitching their tents by night and moving the sheep and cattle slowly onwards in the cool mornings and evenings. They kept to the mountain regions and travelled by long winding mountain roads; for the country was the home of a great and cultured people, the Canaanites, whose walled cities dominated the valleys and whose villages stretched up into the foothills. The gods of the Canaanites were the gods of field and fertility, Lords of the land, and their rituals were celebrated in sacred groves and in the holy places where the hidden forces of death and rebirth were conjured and controlled. At Moreh, by the great walled city of Shechem, was a terebinth tree, standing alone in an oak grove, a sacred tree of mystery and power, where the arcane rites of initiation were held, at the dark times of the year. Abram came to the terebinth tree of Moreh; he went alone to the sacred grove, to seek the gods of the land he desired for his children, and to find their will. For three nights he stayed by the tree on the hilltop, and heard nothing but the soft rustle of leaves and the far-off cry of dogs in the valleys, and saw nothing but the moon rise and fall, and the clouds pass, and the stars brightening the darkness. On the fourth night, he saw God.

Men have sought the gods in many ways and seen them in many forms; terrible and bloody in catastrophe; smiling and benign in prosperity; merciless in judgement and comforting in grief. They have offered them their children in fear, and their finest crops and herds in gratitude; they have called to them for mercy and cursed their names in anger; they have trembled at their presence and despaired at their indifference. The god whom Abram saw by the sacred tree was familiar and yet unfamiliar, and his appearing showed that he had been known and yet not known. He was the god of the desert and of a wandering people, bearing water in the heat of the day, bringing harsh whirlwinds of sand in the raging storm, drawing life out of the dry ground, covering the sun-bleached bones of the forgotten dead. Seeing him, Abram knew now the voice that had called him on his far journey and set in his heart the vision of the city of light. No one walked in the oak grove

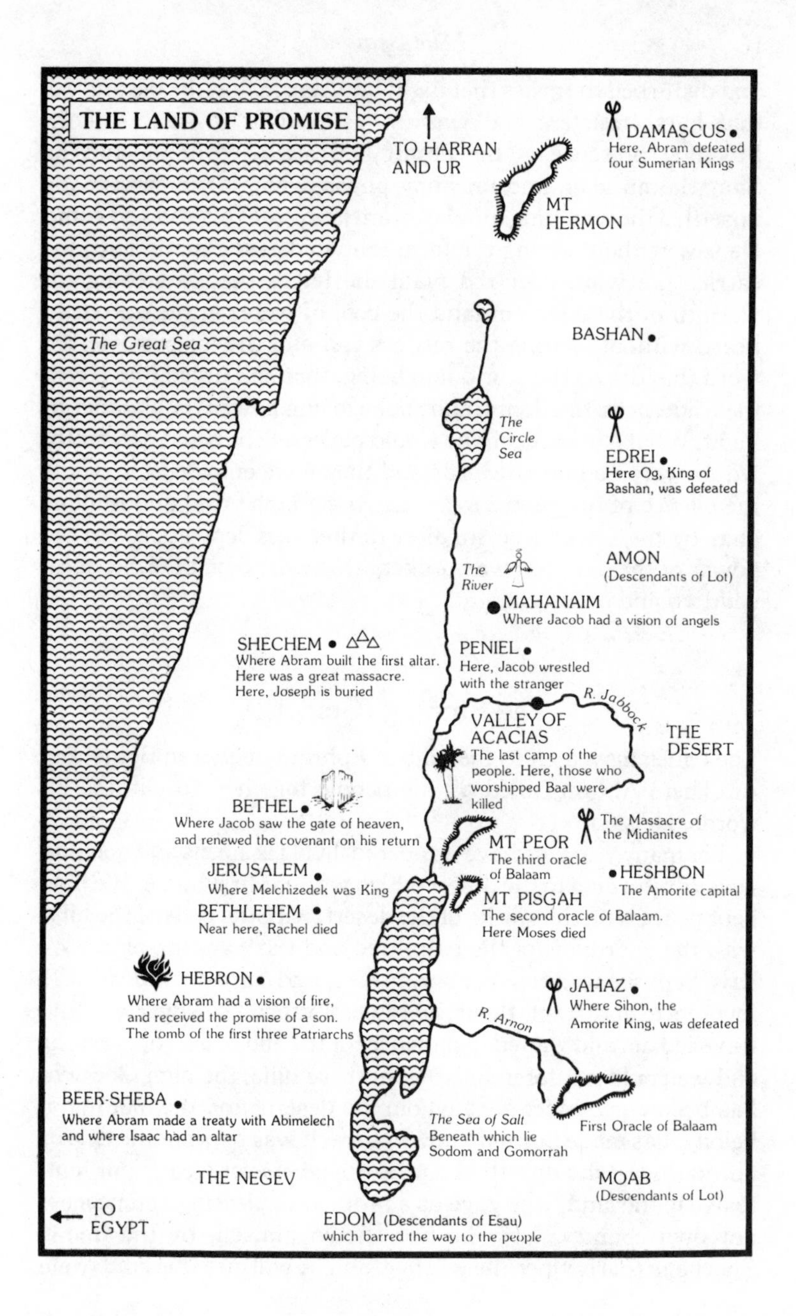

THE LAND OF PROMISE
TO HARRAN AND UR
DAMASCUS
Here, Abram defeated four Sumerian Kings
MT HERMON
The Great Sea
BASHAN
The Circle Sea
EDREI
Here Og, King of Bashan, was defeated
AMON
(Descendants of Lot)
The River
MAHANAIM
Where Jacob had a vision of angels
SHECHEM
Where Abram built the first altar.
Here was a great massacre.
Here, Joseph is buried
PENIEL
Here, Jacob wrestled with the stranger
R. Jabbock
VALLEY OF ACACIAS
The last camp of the people. Here, those who worshipped Baal were killed
THE DESERT
BETHEL
Where Jacob saw the gate of heaven, and renewed the covenant on his return
The Massacre of the Midianites
MT PEOR
The third oracle of Balaam
HESHBON
The Amorite capital
JERUSALEM
Where Melchizedek was King
MT PISGAH
The second oracle of Balaam.
Here Moses died
BETHLEHEM
Near here, Rachel died
HEBRON
Where Abram had a vision of fire, and received the promise of a son.
The tomb of the first three Patriarchs
JAHAZ
Where Sihon, the Amorite King, was defeated
R. Arnon
BEER-SHEBA
Where Abram made a treaty with Abimelech and where Isaac had an altar
The Sea of Salt
Beneath which lie Sodom and Gomorrah
First Oracle of Balaam
THE NEGEV
MOAB
(Descendants of Lot)
TO EGYPT
EDOM (Descendants of Esau)
which barred the way to the people

and disturbed the grass that night but Abram. Yet the presence of that harsh, austere god was unmistakeable; it was as if the brooding presence of the desert had settled over the hills of Samaria, an alien and uncanny power which filled the air and unsettled the watching mind. Abram knew that his god had come. He saw without seeing the form that shakes the mountains and carries the wind over the plain; he felt without touching the warmth of the noon sun and the cool of water in the desert; he heard without hearing the restless call and the far promise, the word that draws the world into being, that had urged him across the wilderness, that found and spoke to him now in the shuddering night. What Abram heard he would never tell; he could not, for the words were no human words and they were enfolded for ever in the silence of his heart. When dawn came, he rose and built an altar by the sacred tree, an altar to the alien desert god. For the power of the old gods was broken; this was to be the land of his children and of his god.

The Binding (Gen. 12)

The tribes moved on to the hills of Ephraim, between Bethel and Ai. There Abram called all his people together, to witness his words. He said:

'For many years we have wandered, living as aliens and nomads, always returning to the desert which was our first home. We have kept peace with the spirits of the desert, with the gods of the hills, with the guardians of the palm tree and the watering-place. We have kept the traditions of our fathers, and buried our dead with reverence and kept them in remembrance. Always we have travelled on, and waited in patience for the end of our journeys, an end we could not foretell. Now, in these hills, the high God who has been our protector, to whom the deserts and the mountains belong, has made himself known to me. It was he who called us on our journey, who unsettled our hearts whenever we left our tents to live in the land, who gave us a promise of blessing and peace in our own country. Now he has shown himself, by the tree of Shechem; this is where he will live, and he will give this land to our children, and they will honour him here for ever; this land shall be his temple.'

The people listened to Abram; and they built an altar on the mountain, and took the high God of the mountains to be their god. They offered a sacrifice from among their finest animals, and Abram called on the name of God:

'Lord God, Lord of the mountains, strong and immoveable, age-long and unchanging, let us live under your shadow and be shielded from the winds of destruction. Lord God, Lord of the storms, high and all powerful, bringer of life and death, protect us with your power and spare us from your anger. Lord God, Lord of the hosts of warriors, God of battles, strengthen our arms and hearts and give us victory over our enemies. Lord God Almighty, greatest of gods, be a strong father to your people, who have obeyed your call and trust in your promise, to whom you have revealed yourself, who hereby worship and revere you. Bring us good fortune in the land you have chosen for us; may we be bound to you, now and forever.' From that day, the children and the people of Abram were bound to God; and from that binding there was no release, until the world's end.

Doubt and Repentance (Gen. 12; 20; 26)

Abram and his people lived as strangers in the hill country, moving their tents from place to place, building altars and worshipping their god. Then, one year, there was a famine in Canaan. There was little rain; the rivers dried up; the cattle began to die of disease; the crops failed. It was some time since the vision by the terebinth tree, when the promise of a land of plenty had seemed so plain. Abram's people were still aliens in the land, and the land was failing them. The people began to grow restless, and to talk of the land of Egypt in the South, where, it was said, there was a great river and wide green plains in the delta, and room for many desert tribes in a hard year. Some of the herdsmen came to Abram and asked him to take them through the Negev to where they could survive the drought. Abram considered. Perhaps the drought would not last for long, and the land would flower again. Perhaps the Lord would sustain them if they obeyed his call to stay. But then Egypt was not very far, and they could soon return. Perhaps the promise in the oak grove had not been what it seemed. The vision itself was undeniable; but what of its meaning and its source? Had Abram misheard the demand that was made? Had the object of his vision the power to give what it promised? Was this really the land of promise? And was it so important that he stayed, and did not turn back? Abram did not really doubt either the call to stay or the promise to bless; and yet no new vision had come, no vision now commanded him to stay. Was staying loyalty or stupidity? Was going prudence or unfaithfulness? In either case, things were so finely balanced that one could not be blamed, whatever one's decision. Abram went alone to pray; but only his own thoughts whirled fruitlessly in his head. He offered sacrifice, but the ritual was empty and mechanical. He consulted the stones of the oracle; but they were silent. The next day the people took their tents and belongings and set out for Egypt.

Abram's wife, Sarah, was very beautiful; and as they drew near to Egypt, Abram began to be afraid that the Egyptians would take her by force and kill him. So he asked her to say that she was not his wife, but his sister – which was, in a sense, true, since she was the daughter of his father by another wife. They came into Egypt, and before long it was just as Abram had feared. Fame of Sarah's beauty spread throughout the country, and came to the ears of the King himself. The King sent for Sarah, and he desired her, and took her into his palace, to be among his wives. There was nothing Abram could do. He even had to show pleasure as the King courted his wife, and gratitude as the King gave him presents of slaves and camels, sheep and cattle in payment for her attentions. Abram became a wealthy man in Egypt, building wisely on the gifts of the King, owning gold and silver and precious stones. But all the time he had to endure the knowledge that his own wife, the most beautiful woman in the land, was given to be a courtesan at the King's court, with his own blessing.

There came a time, however, when an infectious fever raged in the court of the King, and he called his magicians and fortune tellers to find the cause and save his people. It was not by magic that they discovered Sarah was Abram's wife; but they found by divination that it was because of that deceit and breaking of the marriage laws that the epidemic had come upon the King's family. The King called Abram to him and said:

'Why have you brought these things upon me and my family? Why did you not tell me Sarah was your wife? You have the reputation of a prophet, but you have brought only deceit and distress to my country. Here, then, is your wife; take her and go. Pray to your god to take this fever from my family and leave us in peace.' There was nothing Abram could say. He traced the moment when doubt crept into his mind in Canaan; when fear came to him on the borders of Egypt. He saw how, by almost indiscernible steps, he had come to prize honour less than survival, how faith and confidence had been replaced by doubt and anxiety. He had reaped what he had sown. What he most loved was taken from him, his own people mocked or despised him; he was forced into dishonesty and dissimulation, his very wealth was built upon his wife's dishonouring. From the first moment of weakness, he hurt or corrupted those whom he met; his heart hardened as he learned to cope with his own contempt and resentment; the memory of the vision faded as he increased in wealth and began to rule by fear and not by loyalty. Now he stood before the King, silent in shame. The soldiers of the King took Abram, his wife Sarah, his nephew Lot and all their people and possessions to the desert border of Egypt and expelled them from the land. They journeyed towards Canaan, and after many days they came again to Bethel, where Abram had first called on God by name. Abram, sad and disillusioned, rebuilt the altar on the mountain, and remained alone there for two nights. On the third night he returned to his tent, and called for Sarah his wife. Gently he kissed her on the cheek; without a word, they embraced. Abram had discovered repentance.

The Parting (Gen. 13)

The journey into Egypt had unsettled the tribes under Abram's command. They had brought many slaves with them; they had more possessions to quarrel over; they had exchanged the settled security of the Nile for the constant wandering in Canaan; they had seen Abram's leadership undermined and his faith fail. Many of them began to turn from the god of the binding at Bethel, to return to their old familiar gods of city and field and household. Fighting broke out between those who followed Lot and those who remained with Abram. At length Abram summoned a meeting of the clans, on a high hill overlooking the Jordan valley. 'We have grown too large to live together, and strife has broken out between our people', he said. 'But we are kinsmen, and there is land enough before us. Let us then part in peace, and let us divide the land between us. If you choose the left side, then I will take the right. Or if you choose the right side, then I will go to the left.' Lot looked down from the hill over the countryside. On his right, to the west, were the hills of Canaan, a beautiful but hard country, a high but often barren land. On his left, to the east, was the plain of Jordan, a green and broad river valley with townships scattered over it and prosperous cities in the plain. As Lot looked over the plain, it was like a memory of Eden, the legendary garden of the Lord, beyond human reach, the lost land of innocence that haunts every man who dreams of childhood. It was as fertile as Egypt and as beautiful as Babylon. Lot's heart was captured by the remembrance of past happiness, by the desire for security and the comfort of familiarity. He chose the plain; he pitched his tent near one of the two great cities, and made treaties with the citizens and offered sacrifices to their gods. The name of the city was Sodom, a city whose government was corrupt, where murder and theft were commonplace, and every perversion of cruelty and sensuality was practised openly. Lot had chosen the easy way and the old way; but the end of that way was to be destruction and death.

Abram was content to take the way that was left to him, and as he turned west to the highlands of Canaan, he felt that God's promise of this land was confirmed. He vowed he would not leave the land again, but take possession of it and establish it for his children. He came to Hebron, and there, by a sacred grove, he built an altar and prayed to his god. He grieved at the parting with Lot; but he saw that on his journey there would be many partings; that God would show himself in strange ways and hide himself even from those who sought him desperately; that those who followed the vision would always be few; and, as Abram painfully knew, that even they would falter and turn aside. So, on this first of many partings, his own kinsman had chosen the backward glance to a land that could not be recaptured, the path of ease and security which would turn out to be a way of no escape. The harder way was to be true to the vision that always calls forward, to work in hope for a promise grasped in faith, to follow the call to an unknown journey's end. Abram, feeling suddenly alone and afraid, prayed for courage and humility; and, like a warm enfolding cloak, there was borne into his mind the thought that, though many friends would part, though he himself would die at the journey's beginning, the journey would not end. What he had been chosen to begin his children would continue to its unimaginable completion. And after many partings, perhaps the innumerable ways of the children of men would meet again, and they would tell strange tales of their far journeyings; and, with tears of joy and sorrow, would find themselves together inheriting the blessing of the children of Abram, as numberless as the dust of the earth and the stars of the sky. So Abram prayed, and so God gave him comfort, at the sorrow of the first parting.

The Battle of the Kings (Gen. 14)

The overlords of the cities of the plain of Jordan were Kings from beyond Babylon, who exacted tribute from the cities of the plain for twelve years. In the thirteenth year the Canaanite cities rebelled, seeing that their masters were far away and occupied with their own internal quarrels. They formed a league of city states, each with its own King, to live in peace and freedom. And so they lived, for one year. Then there came out of the East a swift and terrible retribution. Four Kings of the Sumerian cities marched over the wilderness with their warrior bands; they were armed with axes and swords of bronze, and with them they brought horse-chariots, swift and light. As they met the armies of Canaan, their charioteers wheeled and circled around the heavy carts, drawn by slow-witted asses, and the low foot soldiers drawn up in line before them. Their swords of bronze sheered through the copper axes and clubs of the Canaanites, and left them weaponless in disarray. They massacred the helpless and bewildered defenders almost without pausing in their march through the land from North to South. Killing and burning, they swept down to the Southern wilderness; in their savage wake, Karnaim, Ham, Kiriathaim and Seir were desolate ruins, women and children aimlessly wandering in the dead streets. Laughing and triumphant, laden with treasure, the four Kings turned for home; and as they passed through the land they put to death every living thing and burned the crops and villages. No one could stop them in their terrible strength, the strength of the sword of bronze.

The Kings of the five cities of the plain of Jordan watched the approach of the invincible hosts, and heard the tales of their ruthlessness and strength. They heard of the strange new metal that cut through copper like a knife through cheese, and were afraid. They heard of the crying of widows and the massacre of children, and were enraged. They saw smoke rising from burning fields over the horizon as the armies approached, and knew that there was no escape from the conflict to come. Torn between defiance and despair, they called together all the men of their cities who could carry arms, and formed a united army in the valley of Siddim, between the hills of Judea and the wilderness. There they waited for the enemy to come; five Kings against four, in the valley where Lot had made his home.

The four Kings rode from the East bearing death; and Lot felt suddenly the futility of all he had sought for. He had chosen the plain for its fertile fields and rich pasturage. The cities, though corrupt and violent, offered excitement and the prospect of advancement. The chances of material gain seemed high; and, if the price of luxury was compromise, conscience could be appeased by charitable giving. Lot had flourished; his tents were of silk brocade, his herds were fat, he ate well and enjoyed his affluence. Now the sun burnished the distant hills, and under a brilliant sky the armies of the Kings stirred restlessly, watching the distant columns that approached along the river, pennants raised, drums and trumpets filling the air with menace. Lot looked over the fair valley, shimmering with an unearthly beauty, the Eden he remembered from his first moment of choice. Before the night came, that still ground would be strewn with the bodies of men, its beauty become agony, its brooding quiet shattered with execration and entreaty. The scene stood in his mind with sharp-edged intensity, as if this was the last edge of life before oblivion. And in that desperate grasp of beauty, Lot regretted the pleasures that had separated him from simplicity, and made his life an unending search for diversion. That had been a way of self-forgetting; but, in emptying the self, it left a vacuum, a hollow space, whose futility could only be faced by turning away to distraction. But it was too late for regret; it was too late, even, for the fear of pain and death, for despair at the cruelty of men, for recognition of the emptiness of human endeavour.

The armies of the nine Kings faced each other across the valley; the long lines of soldiers – shields upright, lances glistening in the sunlight, drums beating together, orders called with cool precision, bowmen at the ready – roused in the soul a primitive nobility, the heroes' deadly lure. Hearts leaped with tension and excitement; the meekest man saw for an instant the glamour of combat; the flags were raised, the trumpet called, its sharp and urgent voice echoing from the hills, and with a terrifying delirious roar the battle joined. The vast armies surged and wheeled over the plain, armies of human avarice raging in their futility, hiding their insecurity by aggression, battling to the death for a heap of gold. All day the battle lasted, soldiers wearily killing until their arms ached and the blood ran over them like sweat. But the outcome was not in doubt; the superior numbers of the Canaanites could not withstand the mysterious swords and chariots of the invaders. Slowly and ineluctably they fell back; they were forced towards the bitumen pits in the valley of Siddim; and there the Kings of Sodom and Gomorrah fled and fell. Their allies fled into the mountains, leaving the cities to the four conquering Kings. The Kings took Lot and his household among their prisoners, and all their goods, destroyed the foodstocks in the cities, ransacked the treasuries and departed for their homeland.

Lot had chosen to belong to the world of greed and desire; the powers of that world had taken him captive, and deprived him of all he had worked for, even of what he had first brought with him. Only his life remained; and that was the life of a slave. Lot's way had reached its end.

The Blessing of the King (Gen. 14)

Abram was living in the highlands of Judea when news came to him of the battle of Siddim and the capture of Lot. At once he called together a small company of hand-picked men, three hundred and eighteen of them; and, together with the warriors of the confederate tribes in the area, he travelled North to the aid of his kinsman. They travelled light, resting in the heat of the day and skirting the main trading routes. The army of the four Kings moved slowly, hampered by the flocks, herds and provisions they had taken. Victory had made them careless, and they spent the nights in drinking and taunting their prisoners. Abram's company had caught up with them by the time they reached the northern shores of Galilee. In the night they surrounded them silently in the hills. Abram took a handful of his best men and, running soundlessly through the darkness, they despatched the armoury guards one by one, and armed their companions with the feared weapons of bronze. Before the alarm was raised, they walked through the camp which was noisy and bright with celebration, into the great tents of the Kings. There, without word or warning, each King was stabbed to death where he lay or stood. A trumpet was sounded, and the men from the hills attacked. In the darkness and confusion, leaderless and unprepared, the Sumerian armies were decimated; they broke and fled to the North by whatever means they could find. The Highlanders pursued them as far as Damascus, and then let them go. The Kings who had set out to beat the cities of Canaan into submission would never return. Abram and his people brought back Lot and his family and possessions, and all the treasures that had been taken, to the plain of Jordan.

As Abram came to the valley of Shaveh, the new King of Sodom came out to welcome him. With him there was a tall man, dressed plainly in white and mounted on a pure white horse, and following them, a great throng of people, shouting in welcome. Abram dismounted and waited as they approached. The face of the stranger fascinated him; it was lined and weather-beaten as though it had endured for centuries, with a rock-hard quality of firmness and strength; yet the eyes were young and alive with light, filled with a youthful joy and innocence at once piercing and deep, inviting and impenetrable. He seemed to Abram like a kinsman, nearer than the brother he had lost in Ur so long ago; yet he knew they had never met. Familiar and yet unfamiliar, friend and stranger, Abram looked into his eyes and felt that in some unutterable way his destiny was bound to the life of this man. He knew this to be a King, though he wore no crown; naturally and without hesitation he knelt before him, while the King of Sodom stood apart, dark and resplendent in the gold and brocade of his office.

'My name is Melchizedek', said the unknown King, 'My city is Jerusalem. I am the priest of El Elyon, the most high God, God of Gods and Lord of Lords, the one who owns the heaven and the earth'. His voice was soft, yet it carried a note of authority Abram had heard only once before; it was like the expression of the inward call that had so often driven the tribes from beyond the river; and Abram knew with a sudden uplifting of his heart that the God of whom he spoke was the God whom Abram had taken for his own, the God of Shechem and Bethel. The stranger took bread and wine, and blessed and offered them; he laid his hand on Abram's head and said, 'Blessed be Abram of the most high God, possessor of heaven and earth; and blessed be the most high God, who has given you the victory of faith, and overcome your enemies.' Abram did not understand all that the King did, nor all that his words meant; but he took the bread and wine that were offered him, and he worshipped the most high God in the fellowship of the King. Then he rose and gave the King tribute from all that he had captured. As the King departed with those who had come with him, Abram felt a strange sense of loss, and a hope that one day the King would return to bring the blessing of God to the land of Abram. But they were not to meet again before death. Of that King there are no records, anywhere in the land of Canaan; and of his tomb there is no trace.

The King of Sodom came to Abram and said, 'Take all the treasures for yourself; you have won them by your valour. Return to me only my people, that the city may live again'. But Abram said: 'I have worshipped the most high God, who owns all things in heaven and earth. He gave me victory, and his priest has blessed me and set me apart to be faithful to him for ever. I will not take for myself even a shoelace, lest you should say, "I have made Abram rich". For these are possessions gained by oppression and won by violence, and I may have no part of them. I will take only what the warriors have eaten, and my allies shall have their share. My nephew has his freedom; now I will return to the hills, to follow the way of my god.' So Abram renounced the treasures of Sodom and returned to the hills; but Lot remained behind in the city.

The Vision (Gen. 15; 17)

Abram worshipped his god in the hills of Judah. He spent long nights in prayer, and kept fasts and vigils in the hills, by tumbling streams under the distant stars. He sought for the god to whom he had bound himself, like a man seeking water in the desert. He searched for omens in the stones and in the entrails of animals. He wandered through the shrines of Canaan, the sacred trees and pillars and mysterious groves where hidden powers were felt. He talked with priests and holy men of what they knew or guessed as guardians of the sacred shrines. But always he travelled on from place to place, haunted by remembrance of the vision he had lost, seeking to break the silence of the god he sought, catching a glimpse of comfort and of love, giving obedience when his heart was cold and bored. He watched a thousand dawns break over the valleys, some cold and sad, drawing the mists out of the dark earth; some bursting over the mountain tops in brilliant splendour; some gently drowning the valleys in quiet gold. He felt the wind screaming through the bare wastes of the Negev, the water of new rain bringing life to the fields, the warmth of the sun unfurling the summer bloom and bathing the hills in sleep. He learned to trace the rhythms of time in the dawning and dying of the days, to read the signs of summer in the cold spring wind. He learned to love the land with passionate intensity; and through the years he came to feel in those familiar hills a presence always hidden, yet incalculably near. This was the land he longed for, and it was a land hallowed to the presence of his god, where wandering could cease and the heart rest. He could almost hear aloud in the rustle of pine trees on the hillside, in the stillness of the night, the calm compelling voice, 'I am your shield and your reward. I will shade you from all evil and bring you to myself. I will be your god, and this shall be my dwelling place and the place of my people'. But how could it be? For he was leader of a small wandering tribe, an alien in a land not his own, whose goods he had renounced, whose ways he could not follow. And he was childless; with him his name would die and he would have no enduring reward in his posterity. So Abram searched to find some answer to his questions. He could not deny the presence in the hills and the strong insistent urging that he had been called and chosen, that his whole life was a wavering response to a will beyond his own, that the high mountain god had brought him to this land and would protect him there. Abram believed, but he did not understand; and so he searched and puzzled to discover the hidden ways of his god.

Then the vision came. As he prayed by a sacred grove, he fell into a trance, as he often did, and the spirit within him urged him to make ready the covenant-ritual and then wait. Without understanding why, he felt an inward compulsion to perform this act; he took a cow, a goat and a ram, a dove and a pigeon; he killed them, cut the animals in half and laid the pieces side by side, in accordance with the custom of the time. When men took a vow or made a treaty, they walked between the pieces, signifying that the oath was made in blood and bound them to the death. When Abram had laid the pieces out, he waited beside them all that day, driving away the vultures and the carrion crows which circled near. As night came, a deep sleep overwhelmed him; not an ordinary sleep, but an abyss of unconsciousness, a vast darkness that seemed outside of time, endless and endlessly deep. Abram was seized by terror, but he could not move. As if far away, he saw the carcasses lying on the ground; as in a dream, he saw a pillar of fire and great clouds of smoke passing between the split bodies. The mountain god of smoke and fire bound himself in covenant with Abram on that night. And in his sleep Abram heard the voice of his god: 'From the border of Egypt to the Euphrates, from Egypt to Babylon, I give this land to your people. Your people, sprung from your own loins, will be as numberless as the stars of the sky; they shall inherit this land. I, El-Shaddai, god of the mountains, promise this.' So the strange promise was made, and bound by the vision of the pillar of fire. From that day he was called by a new name, Abraham — the father of a multitude — and he dedicated all his people to God, setting them apart to follow his choosing. Those who would not bind themselves left the tribe of Abraham; but all who accepted God's call were circumcised, from the oldest man to the child of eight days old. Abraham took a knife of flint and severed the flesh of the foreskin of every tribesman and every slave who belonged to the tribe, on the same day. Thus circumcision became the sign of the covenant which God made with Abraham at the time of the vision of the smoking flame and the torch of fire, that Abraham would be patriarch of an innumerable host, that the land of Canaan would be theirs for ever, and that God would be their everlasting shield and enduring reward.

Hagar (Gen. 16)

Abraham walked in love with God, and trusted in his promises. But Sarah and Abraham were now growing old; indeed, Sarah was already past the age of child-bearing, and she had no child. In those days the prowess and honour of a man were measured by the number of his children; and the greatest wish of every tribal Sheikh was to end his life in his own tent, surrounded by his children, passing on his name and patrimony from generation to generation. It was a shame and a reproach to Sarah that she had borne no heir to her husband, and a sad regret increasingly overtook her that she would never be the mother of children of her own. Abraham had won honour as a warrior and respect as a prophet of the god of the vision; yet he was still an alien in the land he claimed as his own, and he who had taken the name, 'father of a multitude', was yet without an heir. One day Sarah came to him and said, 'It is not the Lord's will that I should be the mother of your children. Take my slave girl; perhaps I shall have children by her'. It was the custom of the time that if a wife could not bear children, she could give her personal slave to her husband; if the slave bore her child on the knees of her mistress, then the child was counted to be the offspring of husband and wife. So

Abraham considered what Sarah said. He had waited long for the fulfilment of the promise, with patient trust. He was, despite his daily vow of faith, puzzled and disappointed by the continued postponement of the promise. As he grew older, his faith was touched with a resigned sadness that he would not share with his wife, his chosen companion, the fulfilment he looked for. He had prayed that she should bear him children; the days passed; and now it seemed that it would not be as he longed for. So he listened to Sarah, and took her slave girl, Hagar, whom she had brought with her out of Egypt, as a concubine.

In time, Hagar became pregnant; and as the months went by, Abraham began to feel a new joy and expectation as he thought of the son who would bear God's promises. He looked on Hagar with tenderness and cared for her every whim and desire. From being an unnoticed slave, Hagar found herself now the object of respect and affection; and as Abraham showered her with attention, she found herself beginning to despise Sarah, the barren mistress, the one who could not grant her husband's greatest wish. She began to be haughty and aloof, even openly deriding her old mistress, whose place she had now taken, and flaunting her pregnancy before Sarah with undisguised arrogance. At last Sarah confronted Abraham with her discontent:

'You are the master of the house and you must be the judge in this', she said, 'I gave you my slave girl and now that she is with child, she openly despises me. She has flaunted right and custom; may the Lord see justice done.'

'Your slave girl is in your hands', said Abraham, 'Deal with her as you will'. From that time Abraham returned to his wife, seeing that her complaint was just. Hagar was deprived of her rights as Abraham's concubine, and returned as a slave to Sarah, and Sarah began to ill-treat her. It was not long before Hagar ran away. So Abraham and Sarah's attempt to claim God's promise out of impatience and frustration ended in acrimony and a confused breaking of old and loyal relationships.

But God did not leave Hagar to her own devices. As she made her way through the wilderness towards her old home, she came to a well in the desert. Dispirited and tired, she sat down to drink and lie in the shade of the oasis. In the silence and solitude of the desert, she fell into a troubled sleep; and at that place God appeared to her.

'Hagar, maid of Sarah', he said, calling her softly by name, 'Where have you come from and where are you going?' Hagar trembled; for she recognized the god of her master Abraham, who found her even in the wilderness, and knew all that she had been and was yet to be, who claimed her even as she fled from him.

'I am fleeing from Sarah my mistress', she said; and she knew that this god saw even the depths of her mind, yet that he pursued her in love and not in anger.

'You must go back to your mistress and submit to her', said God, 'That is the destiny I have planned for you. And for you I also have a promise: from you will descend a great and numerous people, from you and from your son. He will be a proud and free man, a Bedouin of the desert, at odds with all but yoked by none. His sons will people the wilderness; they shall be Kings of the desert lands.' So Hagar returned to her mistress, bearing in her heart the promise of El Roi, the god who appeared to her by the well and showed her his will. In due time she bore a son, and she called him Ishmael – 'God hears' – because the god of Abraham heard her distress, and healed her sorrow by the vision of his presence in the wilderness.

Annunciation (Gen. 18)

Abraham and Sarah remained in Hebron, by the sacred grove where he had seen the god of the mountains in a vision of fire, where he had taken a new name and his people had bound themselves to God's covenant by circumcision, where his son Ishmael, his only heir, had been born, and where the years passed in peace and happiness as they followed God's way. Abraham sat at the door of his tent in the heat of the day, musing, as old men will, on the long course of his life. He had tried to remain true to his god, and slowly an unshakeable faith had been formed in patience and a deepening love. It was no longer a faith that looked for miracles or for a sudden unmistakeable vindication. Rather, it was a quiet undemonstrative trust that the purposes of God would work for good, and his promises would find fulfilment, perhaps in ways quite unexpected and unlooked for. The land and the people of the promise were the constant centre of his prayers; and while he became less sure of when they would be given, and of how the strange repeated promises would be fulfilled, he never wavered in his conviction that somehow the god who had called him out had prepared a special destiny for his family and would bring this chosen people to their own homeland, in his own way. So Abraham sat in the door of his tent, and the sun brought sleep to all living things, both animals and men, as it burned the sky in fiery splendour.

Suddenly he started, unaccountably, and raised his eyes. Before him, some distance from the tent, three men were standing. He had not seen or heard them approach, and they seemed to be alone, without camels or servants. They did not walk or speak, but just looked steadily towards Abraham. He shook his head and passed his hand over his eyes, as if to dispel the remnants of a dream; but still they stood there, silent and unmoving. Without considering who this might be, or what he should do, Abraham found himself running to meet them with an eagerness he was quite unable to explain. As he came up to them, he bowed to the ground and said: 'My Lord, do not pass by your servant; but, if you will, let me have water brought to wash your feet and rest for a while under the tree in the sacred grove. I will find some bread for you to eat, and after that you shall continue your journey.' The tallest of the three strangers bowed his head gravely, and they approached the tent. Abraham ran into the tent ahead of them and woke Sarah. 'Quickly,' he said, 'Make some fresh cakes of flour; travellers have come by our camp'. Then he ran to where his herds were kept, and selected a fine young calf and gave it to a herdsman: 'Kill this and make ready a meal', he said. He took butter and milk, and the bread and meat which had been prepared, and set it before the travellers under the tree, and stood with them as they ate. The sun picked out the colours on the fields and hills, flooding the air with an almost painful brightness; but the tree beneath which they sat, branches concealed in layered leaves, cascading to the ground, cast its cool shade over the small company. For centuries the tree had stood in the sacred grove, centre of rituals of regeneration from beyond man's memory, symbol of the new life that sprang yearly from its withered winter limbs, a place now set apart for the altar of the god of Abraham, a place for the remembrance of past vision and the rekindling of future hope, for the sacrifice of obedience and the binding of the heart; a place for endings and beginnings, for the ordered celebration of eternity. At that place, and under that tree, the three strangers sat with Abraham and broke bread and ate with him.

Abraham did not know what he said, or what was said to him. He seemed to be both filled with joy and overcome with an intense sorrow at the same time. Joy was at the heart of it; the convivial sharing of that fellowship brought a delight not known before or since, reaching out to every part of life and transfiguring it with gaiety. Yet sorrow was there too. He did not know how or why, but as he looked at the tallest of the three, he seemed to see a deep grief, dark in the eyes and etched on the drawn lines of the face. The face haunted him, yet he could never remember or describe it; and the sorrow he saw there was suffused with an accepting calm and an inner serenity which gave it a meaning he seemed to grasp, but could never express. There was another quality, too, a harsher one, muted by the mealtime fellowship but present nonetheless, a quality which aroused a certain fear and awe in him, a quality of stern command and implacable purpose. These feelings flowed and merged as the four ate together, and there seemed a constant communion and sharing, a coming to light of all one had never dared to express, a drawing out for the first time of all that was best and most intensely felt. But what words were uttered there, if indeed any words were uttered, Abraham could never say.

At the end of the meal, the strangers said, 'Where is your wife Sarah?'

'She is in the tent', Abraham answered, not surprised that her name was already known.

'Next year I will return', said the tall stranger, 'and Sarah shall have a son, and he shall inherit the promise made to you'.

Sarah was standing inside the door of the tent, and she heard these words and laughed to herself, a laugh of incredulity, regret and even of slight bitterness; for she was old and past the age of child-bearing, and her hopes of conceiving an heir for Abraham had long since vanished.

The tall man said to Abraham, 'Why did Sarah laugh? Is anything too hard for the Lord? I will return, and she shall have a son'. Sarah came out of the tent door, and said, 'I did not laugh'; for she was confused and afraid. The tall man looked at her and said, 'You laughed', and his eyes seemed to penetrate every hidden wish and longing in her heart. She tried to look down; but something held her eyes fixed on his, until the shame and confusion and embarrassment dissolved away, and she knew herself known for what she was, and yielded up herself to his gaze, and found herself embraced by the total understanding of his love. After an endless moment, she opened her mouth to speak again; but the strangers had gone as silently and completely as they had come, and in any case there was nothing left to say. Sarah tidied the place where they had sat; and as she worked she began to sing one of the songs of her youth, quietly under her breath.

The Prayer (Gen. 18)

Abraham stood on the heights east of Hebron, looking over the plain to Sodom and Gomorrah. Beside him stood the three strangers, looking silently towards Sodom; and Abraham heard the voice of his god: 'In Sodom they have built a city; its walls are strong and beautiful and its gardens are cool and fair. But the city is built on ugliness and the weakness of men, and its beauty and strength will be obliterated from the earth. For I, the Lord God, require truth and rectitude, compassion and equity. Those who obey my will in these things, I will bless with happiness and prosperity. Those who fail in these things, I will destroy. From Sodom a cry for judgement has come to me; and the time for judgement has come.'

Abraham trembled with fear as he heard these words, and fell to the ground. If the Lord was the judge of men, who could survive? As he looked up, two of the strangers turned away and went towards Sodom without a backward glance. He lay motionless for a time, considering the terrible words he had heard. Would God indeed destroy the cities of the plain, good and bad alike, the innocent with the guilty? Out of his terror and distress, he spoke to the stranger who remained beside him. 'Lord', he said,

'Will you destroy the good together with the bad? Perhaps there are fifty good men in the city; will you destroy them also? Shall not the judge of all the earth do what is right, and spare the city for the sake of fifty good men?' The man replied, 'If I find fifty good men in Sodom, the city shall not be destroyed'.

Then Abraham continued to speak in agony of mind: 'Lord, I was formed out of the dust of the earth; dust I am, and to dust I shall return. Yet you gave me a tongue to speak and a mind to think; therefore I dare to speak to the one who made me and holds me in life; perhaps there will be only forty five good men in the city; will you destroy it for the lack of just five men?'

And the stranger said, 'If I find forty five good men there, I shall not destroy it'.

'Perhaps', said Abraham, 'there will be only forty'; and the man said, 'I will not do it, if forty are there'.

'Lord, do not be angry with your servant', said Abraham, 'But it may be there will be only thirty men'.

'Then I will not do it'.

'And if there are twenty?'

'I will not destroy the city'.

'But Lord, what if there are only ten good men in all the city?' asked Abraham.

'I will not destroy it, if there are even ten good men', said the man; and he departed, leaving Abraham alone. Then Abraham saw that the life of even one just man could save the people; but he also saw how hard justice was to find in a world of corruption, and how inexorable was the judgement of God on all the ways of men. He saw what the justice of God required, and said no more, but returned to his tent without another word.

The Destruction of Sodom (Gen. 19)

It was dusk when the two strangers came to the city. The men were gathering by the gateway, as they usually did in the evening, to talk or just to sit in the shade and watch people come and go. As the strangers drew near, they aroused a special interest among those who saw them. They were young men, with flowing golden hair and clear blue eyes; their skin was light and almost seemed to glow with some inner warmth; their dress was simple, yet as clean and elegant as the most expensive kaftan; and as they walked, they moved with a grace and dignity which were both regal and yet entirely without affectation. It would hardly be too much to say that they walked as gods amongst men, and the citizens could not disguise their envy and admiration. Abraham's nephew, Lot, was sitting in the gateway, and he went forward to meet the strangers, bowing low to the ground. 'Come and rest at my house', he said, 'Wash your feet, and eat with me; and sleep in my house until you are ready to continue your journey'. 'No', they answered, 'We will spend the night in the street'. But Lot insisted, with some urgency, and so at last they came to his house, where he prepared a meal and baked unleavened bread, and they ate together.

The men of the city, however, were gathering together by the tower gate, where they talked excitedly of the two strangers; and as they talked, they found themselves in the grip of a strange and strengthening compulsion. It was the time of the rites of Baal, when the natural powers of procreation and birth were conjured up by erotic rituals and secret ceremonies of sadism and depravity. The men were intoxicated with the mystic drugs which the priests prepared from old and carefully guarded formulae; and when the two fair strangers came among them like gods, their unearthly beauty aroused their sexual passions and drew their minds inexorably to thoughts of desire and lust. As the night wore on, the men formed into a mob and roamed the streets of the city, shouting and cursing, stopping only to drink or vomit in the streets. They came to the house where Lot sat with his guests, and stopped. Lot was an unpopular man who never joined the festival of Baal, who took no bribes and did not curry favour with those in authority. His wealth had protected him from injury, but now the mob were filled with a venomous hatred, and they hammered on the door of his house.

'Where are the men who came to you tonight?', they shouted, 'Bring them out, and let us have them'.

Lot was pale with anxiety. He had known that the strangers brought danger, coming at the festival of Baal; and he, too, sensed something in their beauty and bearing which was more than human. But whereas their effect on the men of Sodom was to inflame their hatred and desire beyond the bounds of reason, they brought out in Lot a courage he had almost lost in the tangled ways of the city. He went out to the crowd, and stood in the street, closing the door behind him.

'My brothers', he said, 'I beg you not to act so wickedly. Look, I have two daughters, both virgins; let me bring them out to you, and you can do what you wish with them; but do not touch these men, for they have come under the shelter of my roof.' Even in his courage Lot compromised; he somehow knew the strangers must be protected above all else; but in offering his own children to the drunken mob, he betrayed his fear and moral uncertainty. His desperate words had no effect.

'This man has come here as a foreigner, and now he takes it on himself to be our judge. Stand aside, or we will treat you worse than them', they cried. They crowded about Lot and made to smash the door down. The strangers pulled Lot inside the house and barred the door. The mob outside continued to shout; but suddenly the tone changed from belligerent anger to one of confused bewilderment. As the strangers looked at them they began to be afflicted with violent hallucinations and giddiness, and spasms of blindness. At once angry and fearful, the whole mob moved off in confusion, staggering through the streets to fall into a drunken stupor or mumble incoherently until sleep overcame them. By midnight the streets were silent.

The strangers said to Lot, 'Have you anyone in the city who belongs to you, sons or daughters or anyone else? Get them out of this place, because we are going to destroy it in the morning. The outcry against its people came before God, and he sent us to pronounce judgement on its ways. In this night the people have judged themselves; their thoughts have been brought into the open and made plain to all; now therefore the judgement is pronounced: the cities of the plain will be destroyed, and not a trace of them will remain after this night.'

Lot went out quickly into the city and found the young men who were engaged to his daughters. 'Rise quickly and leave this place', he urged, 'For God is going to destroy it'. But the young men laughed in their sleep, and would not leave.

The night passed, and dawn came. The strangers urged Lot to

hurry and take his wife and daughters out of the doomed city. But Lot had lost his will and hesitated, lingering in the city which he had made his home, afraid and yet reluctant to leave or to entrust his life to the strangers. They took him by the hand, and dragged him out into the countryside. 'Flee for your lives', they said, 'Do not look back or stop anywhere in the plain. Flee to the mountains or you will be overwhelmed with the destruction that is coming'. But Lot still vacillated and temporized. 'My lords, you have shown your servant great favour and have saved my life in your mercy; but I cannot reach the mountains before disaster overtakes me. Let me make for the village of Zoar; it is small and nondescript, and I will be safe there. It is near enough for me to reach'. Afraid to stay and afraid to go, seeking security but unable to respond to the help he was offered, Lot was a pitiable sight, as he cringed and pleaded before the strangers. 'Go', they said, 'We will not destroy Zoar; but hurry, for the time is at hand'.

Lot hurried on. As he entered Zoar, the sun rose full over the horizon, and the world exploded in fire. The earth shook and split open, with a low rumbling roar that echoed from the hills and seemed to fill the air. From out of the earth huge clouds of sulphur and asphalt were thrown into the sky and ignited in a holocaust of flames which destroyed everything in its path. The god of flame, the god of judgement and destruction, obliterated the cities of the plain on that day. There is now no trace of where they were, but only the still salt waters of the Dead Sea and the desolate rocks of salt where no life survives.

By the grace of God, Lot escaped from death; but his wife lingered in the plain behind him, looking back to see the earthquake and the fire. As she watched in fascinated horror, she was overwhelmed in a rain of salt and asphalt, and died where she stood, buried in the salt rocks. So Lot lost all that he had, his wife and his possessions, except for his two daughters. He stayed with them for a short while in Zoar, but became increasingly obsessed with fear of judgement and the memory of the fire of destruction; and he moved up into the hills, where he lived with his daughters in a cave. There he remained until his death, a solitary and broken man, a man who had left God's way and could not find the strength to accept his grace. Lot's daughters each bore a son to him, by drunken and incestuous unions, and so his degradation was complete. They were to be the tribal ancestors of the Moabites and Ammonites, traditional enemies of future Israel.

On the morning of the cataclysm, Abraham rose early and went to the place where he had stood in the presence of God. From the hill top he looked down over the valley of Sodom and Gomorrah, remembering his conversation with God. As he looked down over the plain, in the distance, where Sodom lay, he saw only a cloud of thick black smoke rising from the earth, staining the blue sky. Silently, he turned away.

The Child of the Promise (Gen. 21)

Sarah remembered the words of the Lord and held them in her heart. For long and patient years she had loved Abraham, and bound her life to his. Out of Ur and through the wilderness, forsaken in Egypt and travelling the hills of Judah, she had loved the dark warrior prophet who was always driven onwards by the vision of his god. She had been loyal and faithful, and her beauty had not faded with age; but the greatest gift of all had not been hers to give her husband. Throughout the long years she remained childless; a barren woman, tree without fruit and seed without flowers. Inevitably, sorrow had entered into her heart; and as her husband talked of the promise of his god, of the homeland given to his children, of the destiny shaped for his offspring, she remained silent and despairing. Abraham's eyes glowed as he talked by the evening fire of the children of god's promise who would live in the city of light, and as she heard the hope in his voice, Sarah wept soundlessly in the shadows of the tent.

Yet now, at last, beyond all hope, long after the age of child-bearing, she felt the trembling movement in her womb, and she recalled the words of the stranger, 'Is anything too hard for the Lord?' As the months passed, and she felt the swelling life within her, she was filled with a deep exultant ecstasy. After the long waiting, the breaking of God's silence brought a wonder and expectancy which was almost unendurable. Day after day, Sarah felt the child within her and laughed aloud – not now in bitterness, but in joy. She was the bearer of God's promise; within her body, taking life from her own blood, was the one marked out by God for his own and born by his will. Still she felt, half consciously, the anxiety and fear of pain or loss; but she could welcome pain if by it she could become the mother of Abraham's dream, mother of God's people.

Her time came. From the pain of her body a new life was forged and brought to being; for a time the whole world seemed to wait around the tents of Abraham; he prayed alone, helpless before the mystery of motherhood; no one moved throughout the camp. Then came the unmistakeable protesting cry as the first breath seared unused lungs; Abraham heard the shouts of jubilation and ran stumbling to the tent, scattering goats and chickens in his path, quite forgetting his prophetic dignity; Sarah had borne a son. God's promise had been fulfilled; when the possibility of hope had passed, then God had kept his covenant and renewed the life of his people. On the eighth day Abraham circumcised the boy and called him Isaac, the child of laughter, God's surprise.

God's Choice (Gen. 21)

When Isaac was three years old, the time came for him to be weaned, and Abraham gave a great feast. Fondly he watched his two sons as they played together; Ishmael was now sixteen, and Abraham laughed with joy to see the sons of his old age making up solemn children's games. But Sarah took a different view. She still bore the bitterness of her old jealousy, and she saw how much older and stronger Ishmael was than her own son. So she took Abraham aside: 'Cast out this slave woman and her son', she said, 'The son of an Egyptian slave shall not be heir with Isaac, my own son'. Abraham was angry and tried to argue with her, but she was immovable. In deep distress he went apart to pray to God. 'Lord, that Ishmael my son may live before you', he said, 'He too is my son, flesh of my flesh; shall he not inherit your promise?' But as he prayed, he remembered that Isaac was indeed the child of the promise, born by the will of God; but Ishmael was the child of doubt, born by human desire. Between these two there must be rivalry and conflict; and they could not live for long in peace together. 'Lord, why should you choose Isaac?' asked Abraham; but God was silent. Abraham remembered his own choosing, called out of Ur to be a wanderer in search of God; and he could find no reason for that choice either. God chose those whom he willed to choose and asked only for obedience from those he set apart to follow him. Now he chose Isaac, as heir to his promise and keeper of his covenant. There was no more to be said. 'Lord, what will become of Ishmael, my son?' Abraham asked. 'Those whom I do not call, I also bless', said God.

Early the next morning, when the feast was over, Abraham took bread and a skin of water and gave it to Hagar, and sent her out from the camp with their son. He showed no sign of the deep emotion he felt as he looked at his son for the last time; he turned quickly away and busied himself with the affairs of the day. Hagar made for the southern wilderness, drawn instinctively towards her old home; but as she travelled on, she lost her way in the trackless wastes, and soon found herself surrounded by hills and unending plains of arid scrubland. For days she wandered on, but she came to no familiar landmarks or oases; only the hills, indistinguishable one from another, and the sun distorting the air, cracking the dry earth, and a solitary bird high above, waiting. Ishmael was the first to fall. The water was finished, and they had not eaten for many days. Hagar dragged him under the sparse shade of a bush, and went to sit some distance off, where she would not see him die. She sat, a lonely despairing figure in the bare hills, her mind empty, waiting for death.

It was then that she heard the voice, half forgotten yet immediately familiar: 'Hagar, what troubles you?' She wept with relief; the god of the vision had returned to her in her need. 'Do not be afraid; God has heard the cry of your son. Go to him, lift him up and hold him in your arms. For I will make him the father of a great people, as I promised before his birth, by the well of the vision'. Hagar remembered the promise, so long past and overlaid by the years of service and submission, and hope returned. She rose and walked a little way, and there she found a well filled with water. Quickly she filled the skin with water, and ran to Ishmael to let him drink. From that time, God was with them. They lived in the wilderness between the Jordan and the Nile; Ishmael became an expert bowman and took an Egyptian wife, and they rode with the desert Bedouin, hunting and raiding on the borders of civilization. Far from the land and people of the promise, they remained always under the care of God.

Abimelech (Gen. 21; cf. 26)

At this time Abraham was living a nomadic life on the borders of the Negev. He was a very wealthy man, with great flocks and herds and many servants. He was feared and envied by the city kings of southern Canaan, and there were frequent skirmishes and disputes about pastures and watering places for the animals. In particular, the people of the land would seize the wells which Abraham dug and fill them with earth. Abimelech was King of Gerar, a city in the South by the sea; he watched with alarm as the foreigners from beyond the Euphrates moved through the land. They spoke of a strange god who had called them to a nomadic life, who bound them to belong to him, and who had given them a promise to keep and pass on to their descendants. The gods of Gerar were the gods of the sea, and Abimelech was worried by this god who had no place, but claimed to possess the lives of men. He came with Phicol, the commander of his army, to talk with Abraham.

'Your god is with you in everything you do', they said; 'Let us make a treaty together. We have not attacked you, and have done you nothing but good. Swear by your god, who has surely given you good fortune, that you will not do us harm, nor our descendants, in the country where you have come to live as an alien'. Abraham told him about the wells which had been seized, and Abimelech promised to leave them in peace. So Abraham and Abimelech made a treaty together, and exchanged gifts of sheep and cattle, and held a great feast. Abraham called the place Beer-sheba, the Well of the Oath, because there Abimelech acknowledged the power of god, and gave Abraham the right to live at peace as an alien in the land. Abraham planted a tamarisk tree by the well at Beer-sheba, and he invoked El Olam, the everlasting god, without end or beginning, who throughout endless time brings his purposes to fulfilment in all the things he has made.

The Sacrifice (Gen. 22)

Abraham camped by the well of Beer-sheba, and worshipped his god by the sacred tamarisk tree. Occasionally he thought sadly of Ishmael, the son who had unknowingly caused envy and conflict; and of Lot, his brother's son, who had escaped the earthquake only to live now in a cave like a wild animal. Both men had left the tribes of Abraham, and God guarded them still in wild and desolate places; but both had left for ever the company of the promise, which was Abraham's alone, to bear and bequeath, under the eye of God. Abraham thought, too, of Terah his father, who had taken him out of Ur and died in Harran, who had taken him from his home and begun his long wandering towards the land of promise. Now his own life was nearly at an end, and all his hope and love were centred on Isaac, the little child of laughter who had been born by God's will to bring joy to his old age.

Yet as Abraham prayed, day by day, a shadow came over his thoughts. For it seemed that God required of him something which at first he could not bring himself even to think. Again and again he thrust it from his mind in horror, breaking off his prayers and pacing the ground in agitation and dismay. Again and again it returned, against his will, until it took clear shape and irresistible intensity. His conduct became moody and irritable; his air was one of abstraction and torment; he took to watching Isaac with a fascinated concentration as the child played. He told Sarah nothing of his thoughts, and she sensed his deep uneasiness, but there was nothing she could do to reach him. Abraham spent more and more time in the sacred grove; as he struggled with the terrifying demand that came to him so firmly and insistently, he began even to doubt his sanity. The whole of his life stood on the edge of ruin; all that he had known and believed, all that he had fought and striven for, all was now in question. Was it not the almighty and eternal god who had called him through the wilderness? Had he not delivered him in battle, and given him prosperity and happiness? Had he not bound himself in covenant for ever with the house of Abraham? Had he not sealed his promises with the birth of a son when hope was dead? This was the god to whom

Abraham had given his life, on whom he had staked all his future, for whom he had renounced his past. Yet this same god – what other could it be? – now asked of Abraham something so cruel that it could not be spoken.

It was not, indeed, unheard of; for in Canaan it was the custom of the people to offer the first fruits of the harvest to the gods, and first born animals were sacrificed to celebrate and assure the friendship of the gods and the gifts of their fertility. And for special favours, or to wipe out great wrongs, or to show utter devotion, there was a sacrifice which was named with dread and esteemed with shuddering admiration, as the ultimate offering to the dark gods who oversee the lives of men. The sacrifice of the first born son, the most precious fruit of the body to wipe out for ever the sins of the soul, was the last and greatest sacrifice. By this terrible oblation, man surrenders the object of his deepest love, renounces the future of his family, and thereby throws himself utterly into the arms of God, bound to him in irrevocable agony.

This was the sacrifice God asked of Abraham, the sacrifice of Isaac, child of promise, as the final test of faith. Yet this God who required so much was the god of covenant and promise; he had bound himself by oath to Abraham, to make his offspring great, give them their own land and bring them to a destiny dimly foreseen but deeply cherished. By God's will, Ishmael had been cast out; now Isaac was the first born of the promise, only son, and on him all hopes depended. How, then, could God demand his death? The gift was his, to give and take; and yet this seemed the end of all his promises, the end of hope. Abraham prayed with tears and agony; and he remembered how his god brought life out of despair, and how his call into the unknown was upheld by the secure sustenance of his presence. Slowly he found a response arising in his heart to the insistent demand of God, and as the words took form, he repeated them over and over again: 'Commit your way to the Lord; trust in him, and he will act'. Slowly, out of his agony and doubt, a deep unshakeable trust was forged, not now in joy and exultation, but in his grief and bewilderment, in the silence after all questions end, the silence of the soul held firm by God. God would be true to his promise; as he had brought life from the barren womb, so even from death he would raise up the life and hope of his people. So Abraham committed his way to God, and obeyed his word.

In the early dawn he took two of his men and cut wood for sacrifice. He said nothing to Sarah, but roused his son Isaac; he saddled his ass and rode from the camp before the others woke. After three days, they came to a mountain in the wilderness, and Abraham knew that this was the place of sacrifice. He said to his men, 'Stay here with the ass; the boy and I will go over there and worship, and then we will return'. Abraham took the wood and placed it on Isaac's shoulders; he himself carried a flaming torch and the knife for sacrifice, and the two walked to the mountain together.

Isaac said to Abraham, 'Father'; and he said, 'Yes, my son'. Isaac said, 'We have the fire and the wood, but where is the lamb for the sacrifice?' Abraham said, 'God will provide the lamb for sacrifice himself, my son'. And they walked on in silence, father and son, to the lonely mountain top.

Abraham built an altar on the mountain and placed the wood in order; he bound Isaac, his son, and laid him on the altar. Then he stretched out his hand to take the knife, and he prayed to God that through the acceptance of this obedient sacrifice, the life of Isaac would in some unimagined way be given back to his people, to renew their life. His hand touched the knife; and in the wind sweeping over the hills he heard the whispered name: 'Abraham, Abraham'. 'Lord', he said, 'Here I am'. The voice went on, gentler than the wind yet with the power of the storm, overwhelming the mind and will of Abraham, leaving him shaking with terror and relief, drained of emotion yet trembling on the edge of hope: 'Do not touch the boy. Now I know that you fear God, for you have not withheld your son, your only son'. Abraham fell to his knees, and for a long while he could not think or speak; the world seemed an insubstantial vision, far away; there was only the wind on the mountain, and the altar of God with the flaming torch of sacrifice, and the young child, hope of all the world, softly beginning to cry. At last Abraham raised his head, and as he looked up he saw a ram with its horns caught fast in a bush of thorns. He went and took the ram and offered it in sacrifice. So Isaac the son of Abraham was redeemed by the offering which God provided; by

Abraham's obedient faith the promise was renewed, by which all the nations of the earth were to be blessed. Abraham called the place, 'The Lord will provide', but he never revealed the place of that terrible testing, and it remains unknown to this day. Abraham took Isaac by the hand, and they went back to his men; they returned to Beer-sheba, father and son, and only God knew what had passed between them and him that day.

The Grave (Gen. 23)

As the tribes were camped near Hebron, Sarah, the wife of Abraham, and the companion of his journeys, died, in the place where the Lord had promised her a son in her old age. Her body lay in state, and Abraham went in to mourn her death, to remember their life with gratitude and commend her in love to the mercy of God. At length he rose and left the tent, and went down to the city of Hebron, to talk with the elders at the city gate and to find a plot of land to bury his wife. 'I am a stranger among you', he said; 'Let me buy a little land to bury my dead, that the body of my wife may not rest in foreign soil, but in land that belongs to me and my descendants'. The elders of Hebron looked wryly at one another. They did not wish to give this nomad from the East any of their land; but on the other hand, he was a very wealthy man, and no mean warrior, not a man to cross. They decided what to say.

'My lord, you are a mighty prince of God, honoured among us. We would be honoured if you would bury your dead in the best of our graves', they said; 'None of us will withhold his grave from you, or prevent you burying your dead'.

Abraham knew that they were trying to avoid selling him land, and his resolve hardened. He had brought Sarah out from her own land and people to follow the way of the promise; that promise was of the land of Canaan, and Abraham was determined that, though she had not seen the fulfilment of the promise in life, in death she would at least lie in land that was her own by right. 'If you are willing that I should bury my dead', he said, 'Then hear me, and ask Ephron that he may sell me the cave of Mach-pelah, which he owns, as a burial place, and I will pay him the full price for it, in your presence'.

Ephron was among the elders; he rose and said to Abraham: 'No my lord, hear me. I will give you not only the cave but the field also, in which it stands, to bury your dead.'

Abraham was in no mood to bargain. 'No, but you must let me give the price of the field, and accept it from me'.

Ephron said: 'My lord, the land is worth only four hundred shekels of silver; what is that between you and me? Take it and bury your dead.' The price was exorbitant; but Abraham weighed out four hundred shekels of silver then and there, and took the field and the cave of Mach-pelah in Hebron, as his legal possession for ever. There he buried Sarah his wife; so that in death she entered into God's land of promise; that was her final homecoming, the last strange gift of the god of fire.

Rebecca (Gen. 24)

Abraham was now very old, and the Lord had blessed him in all that he did. There was one more thing he had to do. Isaac was a young man, and all the hopes by which Abraham had lived now rested on him. Already, Abraham had given presents to the sons of his concubines and sent them away to the East; now all that he had he bequeathed to Isaac, child and bearer of the promise, laid on God's altar and given life by him alone. He called his High Steward to him, who had charge of all his possessions and had served him many years.

'Place your hand under my thigh', he said, 'and swear by the Lord, the god of the whole world, that you will not take a Canaanite wife for my son, for he must remain true to the god who took me from the land of my father and who swore to me that he would give this land to my posterity. He must keep the covenant of circumcision; he is the inheritor, by God's choice, of the vision and the promise and the hope of my people. He must treasure it and hand it down in safety, from one generation to another, so that this people will be bound for ever to God. This guardianship will not cease, whether for good or ill, until faith becomes sight, and all the families of the earth possess the blessing of our god. You must go to my own country, to my kinsmen, to find a wife for my son Isaac; then my posterity will flourish and my descendants be as many as the stars of the sky.'

The Steward said, 'What if the woman is unwilling to come with me to this country? Must I then take your son back to Mesopotamia?'

Abraham said, 'If the woman is unwilling to return with you, then you are released from your oath to me. But you must never take my son back there; for this is the land of the promise, and from it there is no going back. The Lord will be with you and go before you in your journey, and he will guide you and give you success'. So the Steward placed his hand under Abraham's thigh and swore to do what his master asked.

He took a caravan of ten camels and many splendid gifts, and set out for Harran, in the upper Euphrates valley, the city of Abraham's brother Nahor. He came to the city at evening, at the time when the women come to draw water from the well, and let the camels kneel to rest, but he did not let them drink. He said: 'O Lord God of my master Abraham, give me success in my quest today, and show your care for my master. As the women of this city come to draw water, let the girl whom I ask for water, and who shall say, "Drink, and I will water your camels also", let her be the one you have appointed for your servant Isaac. By this sign I shall know your will for my master'.

As he was praying, a young girl who was very beautiful came to the well, carrying her water jar on her shoulder. She descended the steps to the spring, filled the jar and came up again. The Steward ran to her and said, 'Please give me a little water from your jar'. At once she lowered the jar into her hand and gave him a drink. As he drank, she saw the camels kneeling quietly, weary and dusty from their journey. 'I will draw water for your camels, too', she said, and quickly she emptied the jar into the water trough, and refilled it at the spring, until all the camels had drunk their fill. All this time the Steward watched her in silence, seeing his prayer answered with growing excitement. When all the camels had been watered, the Steward took a gold ring and two golden bracelets, and gave them to the girl. 'Tell me your name, and whose daughter you are', he said. She answered, 'I am Rebecca, the daughter of Bethuel, son of Nahor'. The Steward could hardly conceal his surprise; this was the daughter of Isaac's cousin, the grandaughter of Abraham's own brother; God had led him to the house of his master's kinsmen. 'Is there room in your father's house for us to stay tonight?', he asked. 'Yes', she said, 'We have straw and provisions and room for you to stay'. The Steward bowed to the ground and prostrated himself before God. 'Blessed be the Lord, the god of my master Abraham', he said, 'For he has not failed in his care and love for my master; he has gone before me, and guided me to the house of my master's kinsmen and given me success in my journey'.

The Betrothal (Gen. 24)

Rebecca ran to her mother's house to tell them of the rich caravan and the distinguished stranger who had given her the ring and bracelets of gold. Laban, her brother, went out to the well to meet the Steward, who was still standing by the camels. 'Sir', he said, 'Clearly the Lord has blessed and prospered you. Come with me, for we have prepared rooms for your company'. So he brought the Steward to the house, unloaded the camels and provided straw and fodder for them, and water for him and all his men to wash their feet. Then he placed food before them, but the Steward said, 'I will not eat until I have delivered my message'.

Laban said, 'Let us hear it'; so the Steward told them how Abraham, Nahor's brother, had become a powerful and wealthy man in Canaan, with many slaves and possessions, all of which he had bequeathed to Isaac; and how Abraham had sent him to his father's house and family to find a wife and arrange a marriage for Isaac, as was the proper custom. 'Abraham has lived in the presence of the Lord', he said; 'and the Lord has blessed him; the Lord has gone before me now to give me success; when I bring back a wife for Isaac, I will be released from my oath; or if the family will not let her go, I shall still be released'. He told them of his prayer at the well, and of how Rebecca had answered his prayer. 'Now', he said, 'the Lord has showed me whom he has chosen to be Isaac's wife; he led me by the right way to take my master's kinswoman to be the wife of Isaac. If you accept this as the Lord's will, and wish to deal loyally with my master, tell me; if not, say so, and I will turn elsewhere'.

Laban and Bethuel answered, 'This thing comes from the Lord; we can say nothing for or against. Here is Rebecca; take her and go, and let her be the wife of Abraham's son, as the Lord wills'. When the Steward heard this, he was overcome with joy, and he prostrated himself again before the Lord in the presence of all the family. Then he brought out gold and silver jewellery and robes and gave them to Rebecca to seal the marriage contract; and he gave many costly gifts to her brother and her mother. Shyly the girl put on the robes and headdress. The jewels sparkled in the firelight as she stood before them, and there was a sudden moment of silence as they looked at her; a warm light seemed to surround her, a brightness from within that made all who saw her see for an instant, with the eyes of innocence, a beauty and grace that time had overlaid in all their lives. The young girl of simple kindness and charm was transformed into the Princess of the tribes of Abraham, the mother of the people of the promise, God's chosen bride.

Then the moment passed; the men shook their heads as if to clear the remnants of a dream; the women whispered excitedly, admiring the cut and styling of the robes, the richness of the jewellery; Rebecca was again the shy young village girl, arrayed in all her wedding finery. That night the Steward and his men ate and drank and spent the night in festivity. The next morning, he rose and said, 'Now let me return to my master'. Rebecca's mother and brother said, 'Let the girl remain here for some days, ten at least, and then she shall go'. But he said, 'Do not detain me, because the Lord God has given me success, and I cannot delay in doing his will; I must return to my master, for he is old, and the time is short'. They said, 'Let us call the girl, and see what she says'. They called Rebecca and asked her if she would go at once with the Steward, and she said, 'Yes, I will go'. So they blessed Rebecca, saying, 'You are our sister; may you be the mother of myriads; may your sons possess the cities of their enemies'; and Rebecca, her nurse and her maids went with the Steward towards Canaan.

Isaac was living in the Negev, near Beer-lahai-roi. He went out from the camp, as his custom was, to meditate in the open country in the evening; and he looked up and saw the camel caravan coming towards him out of the desert. Rebecca saw the man walking to meet them, and got down from her camel. 'Who is that man walking to meet us?', she asked the Steward. He answered, 'It is my master'. So she took her veil and covered herself. Isaac and Rebecca met for the first time by the well of the vision of the living god, and Isaac brought Rebecca to the tent of Sarah his mother. There he took her, and she became his wife. As the months passed, he grew to love Rebecca, and was comforted after the death of his mother, and God blessed them with happiness. The future of the promise was assured.

The Death of Abraham (Gen. 25)

Abraham lived in the presence of God and trusted in his promises for many years; and he was a very old man when he died in peace, in his own tent and among his own people. His sons Isaac and Ishmael buried him in the cave of Mach-pelah with Sarah his wife.

Long years before, he had followed the haunting call of the desert god into the western land between Babylon and Egypt; there he had wandered all his life, seeking his god in the mountains and among the green valleys, calling on his name with prayer and sacrifice. His people had followed him and bound themselves by solemn rite to keep the way of his god; they had flourished, and God had given them good fortune in the land. In the vision of fire and on the nameless mountain of sacrifice God had sworn to Abraham that his children would be a great people, numberless as the stars of the sky; but when Abraham died, Isaac, the child of his old age, was his only heir. God had promised that Abraham's people would inherit the land of Canaan; but when Abraham died, the only part of Canaan that he owned was a grave. God had promised that all the people of the earth would be blessed because of Abraham; but when he died, he was an alien in a foreign land, unnoticed by the great Kingdoms of the fertile crescent. So he died in faith, not having received the promises of God, but having seen them from afar and held to them in hope. For he knew that when God touches human lives, the barren womb becomes fertile; the sacrificial death is given back in life; the grave becomes the way to the city of light. Seeking that city, man is a stranger in the world, a wanderer whose heart is fixed on the far country of God's promise. Abraham put his faith in God, and thus he founded the company of the covenant, who bear for ever the promises of the God of Abraham and keep his laws. In all his sorrows and his failures, in all his joys and his successes, he was the friend of God. It is because of this that when men think of him, they see the father and the pattern of their faith, and pray, 'May we be blessed as Abraham was blessed'.

The Hidden Life (Gen. 26)

Isaac, the child of the promise, took the god of Abraham his father to be his god. He inherited all that Abraham had, and he in turn became a prosperous man, with many flocks and herds and slaves. He moved around in Canaan with his herds, staying long enough in one place to sow barley and wheat for his herds, skirmishing and making treaties with the townsmen and farmers of Canaan. The Lord appeared to him, as he had to his father, and said: 'Fear nothing, for I am with you. I will bless you and give you many descendants, and give them all this land, and all the nations of the earth will pray to be blessed as you are blessed. So I shall fulfil the covenant I made with your father Abraham, because he obeyed me and kept my covenant.' Isaac built an altar at Beer-Sheba and worshipped the god of his father there, by the sacred tamarisk that Abraham had planted. As he offered sacrifice through the years he sometimes thought of the windswept mountain long ago, and the ram whose offering had given him life, and the silent tears on his father's face as they walked on the mountain path. He thought of his brother Ishmael, whose children became princes of the desert, who had been driven out of his father's camp and saved in the wilderness by God. They had only met once, to bury Abraham their father, and they had little to say, the shepherd of the plains and the Bedouin warrior, and what each felt the other never knew. He thought of Sarah his mother, who had loved him with the passion of age; and with gratitude of Rebecca whom God had sent to love and comfort him. He considered the ways and the promises of God; but in his life he saw no fulfilment of the promise which he faithfully bore; he received no clear commanding call, no new overwhelming vision to proclaim. Yet he was the child of God's choosing, and he worshipped God in his heart and walked in his way. He was once offered on God's altar, by the Lord's command; and his life was then and always will be hidden from the world, the secret history of a soul and its creator.

The Birthright (Gen. 25)

When Abraham died, Isaac had no son, and he prayed to God, as his father had done, for an heir to the divine promise. Rebecca conceived twins, and they struggled in her womb; she was afraid and went to consult the oracle at the sacred shrine by the well of the vision. She offered sacrifice, and the priest of the shrine took the entrails of the beast and declared this oracle: 'In your womb there are two nations, two peoples going their own ways from birth. One nation shall be stronger than the other, and the elder nation shall serve the younger.' Rebecca was comforted, but she wondered what the oracle signified, and what sort of enmity would grow between her children. When the twins were born, the first born was red and covered in hair, and they called him Esau. The second was born with his hand clutching his brother's heel; they called him Jacob, and Rebecca loved him from the first.

As the boys grew, Esau became a hunter, riding the open plains, living the wild carefree life to the full. He would go for days into the hills with his hunting party, pursuing wild beasts and game, sleeping under the open sky; when he returned, the camp rang with his laughter, and he would drink and entertain his companions with open-hearted generosity. Isaac saw in him, perhaps, an echo of his brother Ishmael, and he loved him for his simplicity and freedom. Yet Esau was a man of the earth, a man who did not care for the gods, who had little time for prayer or piety. He was not grasping or ambitious or arrogant; but he was happiest with the world he could see and touch, the thrill of the hunt, the pleasures of convivial company; and so he left the practices of piety to Jacob, his younger twin. Jacob was intoxicated with the story of his father's god. He heard with awe and fascination, the tale of the call from Ur, of the vision of flame and of the promise of the land, and he craved the vision and the blessing of the god of Abraham and Isaac. He lived as a shepherd, an ordered and cultured life, loving the land promised to the people of the covenant, offering the sacrifices and remembering the Lord God. He loved his brother; but it grieved him to see him neglect the way of the god of his father, he who was by right of the first born son, guardian of the covenant and head of the family. One day he was in his tent boiling soup when Esau returned from the hunt, empty handed and exhausted. 'Give me some of that red soup', he said, 'for I am starving'. Jacob determined to test his brother, and said, 'First you must sell me your rights, as first born son, to inherit a double share of the estate, to be head of the family, to receive our father's blessing and to be the guardian of the promise of the god of our fathers'.

Esau was tired and hungry, and he said, 'What do I care about my birthrights? I want for nothing, and it matters little to me which of us rules the family; give me the soup, for I am dying of hunger.'

Suddenly, Jacob saw his chance to possess the birthright he so strongly desired; he would care for the commands of God with a passionate love, and take from Esau only that which mattered little to his brother. He said, 'First you must swear to me on oath'. So Esau swore, and sold his birthright to Jacob that day. Then Jacob gave Esau bread and the lentil soup, and he ate it quickly and left without a word. Thus in one moment of carelessness Esau sold his inheritance of the blessing for a bowl of soup; for at that time he thought little of the blessing which God gives to those whom he chooses. There was to be no release from his oath, though he sought it later with tears.

The Blessing (Gen. 27)

Isaac was an old man; he was confined to his bed, and had gone blind, and he thought that his death was at hand. One day he called Esau his elder son to him and said: 'My son, I am old and near death. Take your quiver and your bow now, and hunt game for me out in the open plains, and bring back something good to eat, just as you have always done in the past. Then I can eat and be strong again, and give you my blessing before I die.' So Esau took his quiver and his bow, and left the camp to hunt the game which his father loved to eat.

But Rebecca his mother heard what Isaac said to Esau, and she remembered the oracle at the well of the vision, and how Jacob had told her of the sale of the birthright many years before. Moreover, Esau had taken two Canaanite wives, who openly derided the way of the god of Isaac, and worshipped their own household gods. Thus Esau had taken little heed of the instructions of his grandfather Abraham, and did not hold sacred the way of his god, as Jacob did. So Rebecca went to her son Jacob and said: 'Your father has asked Esau to hunt game, and prepare a meal so that he might be filled with the strength of the land and give Esau his blessing. The blessing is yours by the birthright which he sold to you on oath. But your father is weak; he has always loved Esau. So now do as I say. Bring me two kids from the herd, and I will make savoury meat for your father; then you shall take it to him, so that he may bless you before the Lord.'

But Jacob replied, 'My brother Esau is a hairy man, and I am smooth-skinned. Perhaps my father will feel me; then I shall seem to be mocking him, and he will curse me, not bless me'. Rebecca said, 'May the curse fall upon me, my son. Just do as I say and bring the kids'. Jacob went and got the kids and brought them to his mother, and she made a savoury meal. Then she took Esau's best clothes and put them on Jacob; and she prepared the skins of the kids so that they felt like hairy human skin and put them on Jacob's hands and neck. She gave him the stew and some bread and sent him into his father. So Rebecca's great love for Jacob and for the promises of God led her to deceive her husband and corrupt her son. She was prepared to suffer for her action; and she did.

Jacob went in to his father and said, 'My father'.

'Who is that?' asked Isaac.

'I am Esau your firstborn', answered Jacob. The die was cast. 'I have done as you told me. Now sit up and eat the game I have prepared, that you may bless me in strength and not in weakness'.

But Isaac said, 'How have you found game so quickly, my son?' Jacob saw that his father was suspicious, and he felt his heart pounding. 'Because the Lord your God gave me success', he said lamely.

Isaac frowned: 'Come near that I may feel you, my son, to know whether you are really my son Esau or not'.

Jacob went over to his father, and Isaac felt his hands and said, 'The voice is Jacob's voice, but the hands are the hands of Esau. Are you really my son Esau?'

Jacob said, 'I am', and his voice quavered. Isaac was confused and perplexed; 'Bring me the meat, that I may eat and bless you', he said.

So he ate, and the meat tasted to him like the game that Esau often brought him. Jacob gave him wine to drink; then he said, 'Draw near and kiss me, my son'. Jacob came and kissed him; and he smelled Esau's clothes, and was reassured.

'The smell of my son is like the smell of the open plains which the Lord has blessed, and the land which he has promised', he said, and he gave his blessing to Jacob. 'May God give you the dew of heaven and the richness of the earth, corn and wine in abundance. May tribes serve you and kingdoms bow down to you. Be Lord over your brothers; may your mother's sons bow down to you. A curse upon those who curse you; a blessing on those who bless you.'

So Isaac gave the blessing to his son Jacob; but it was a blessing obtained by deceit, and though he was to be wealthy and powerful, Jacob was to be denied the things he most desired and to die in exile from the land he loved.

Almost as soon as Jacob had left his father, Esau returned from the hunt. He too prepared savoury meat, brought it to Isaac, and said, 'Come, sit up and eat the game I have prepared for you, that you may bless me'.

'Who are you?' asked Isaac.

He answered, 'I am your son, your firstborn, Esau'.

Isaac recognized his voice, and guessed at once what had happened; his voice trembled with anger and agitation and he said, 'Then who was it that hunted game and brought it to me? I ate it all before you came in. I gave him my blessing, and that blessing must stand'. Esau gave a loud and bitter cry and said, 'Give me your blessing also, my father'. But Isaac said, 'Your brother came deceitfully, and he has taken away your blessing'.

'He is rightly called Jacob, the supplanter', said Esau, 'For he has supplanted me twice. He took away my right to be head of the family and now he has taken away my father's blessing. Have you not kept any blessing for me?'

Isaac answered, 'I have made him your lord; I have given all his brothers to him as servants; I have prayed that he may have corn and wine in abundance. What is there left that I can do for you, my son?' Esau said to his father, 'Have you then only one blessing? Bless me too, my father'; and he wept bitterly.

Then Isaac laid his hands on his son's head and said, 'You shall live far from the richness of the earth, far from the dew of heaven above. By your sword shall you live and you shall serve your brother; but the time will come, when you shall break loose and break his yoke from your neck.'

So Esau, even with tears and bitter regret, was not able to escape from his youthful oath to Jacob, and his father's strange blessing, reluctantly confirming the oracle of God, set the destiny of the tribes of Israel and Edom for generations to come. For the Edomite country of the South is mountainous and barren; and the warrior tribes of Edom were to be subjugated by King David, only to recover their independence in Solomon's reign. Esau hated Jacob because of the blessing his father had given him, and he said to himself, 'My father is ill and he will soon be dead. Then I will kill my brother Jacob'.

Flight to Beth-El Gen. 28)

Rebecca heard of Esau's threat to kill Jacob, and she called Jacob to her and said, 'You must go at once to Laban my brother in Harran and stay with him until your brother's anger cools. When it has subsided and he forgets what you have done to him, I will send for you and bring you back. If you stay he will kill you and, by the law of the tribe, he too will be put to death, and I shall lose both my sons in one day'. Rebecca went to Isaac and said, 'Our son Jacob must not take to wife a Canaanite woman, with their immoral gods and superstitious practices. Let him go to the house of Bethuel my father and take a wife there who will be true to the way of your god'. So Isaac called Jacob and sent him to Harran with his blessing to find a wife. Thus Jacob turned his back on the land of promise, which he desired so intensely, at the command of his mother. Rebecca watched him leave the tents of Beer-sheba in the early dawn, and knew in her heart that she would never see the son she loved again. The consequences of their deceit were beginning to work themselves out.

Jacob travelled North all that day, through steep, rocky valleys and over the wooded hills, scented with olive and palm. Far on his right, the great river Jordan glinted occasionally in the sun; and to the left the wide plains disappeared towards the sea. The sun rose until the heat shimmered on the ground like spray on the water; it descended on Jacob's left hand as he rode on, flooding the hills with golden light and casting long shadows over the fields. As night came, he rode up into the highlands, leaving behind the few scattered villages and tents which he had skirted on his journey, picking his way over the hilltracks, and by rushing mountain streams. The hills were black and desolate, worn into tortured crags and deep ravines, pale and translucent under the yellowing moon. He rode on, only the sound of his donkey's hoofs echoing against the rocks, and the short sharp cry of an unseen animal, hunting or hunted, breaking the silent air. The rock walls rose around him as he climbed, his mind imprisoned in the dark circle of his thoughts – the passionate desire to serve his father's god; the envy of his brother's impulsive freedom; the anger at his careless disdain of the divine promises; and then the cunning bargain, the calculating deceit, and exile and remorse, the unknown future in a foreign land. He rode on silently, unseeing and uncaring through the barren hills.

Suddenly, his donkey stiffened in alarm. Jacob shook himself and looked up. At the end of the mountain path they had come out onto a wide plateau, scattered with huge rocks, some standing, some strewn about the ground. The stones stood like a still and ghostly army, the broken remnants of a giant's battle. A cloud uncovered the moon, and there was an almost tangible feeling of shuddering awe, as the night wind whistled and sang around the stones; and the sudden pale unearthly light made them appear to move, like the forgotten dead rising from a frozen sea. The hairs at the back of Jacob's neck tingled for a moment; and then he laughed softly. Fatigue and hunger had roused his imagination; there was nothing but the moon on the far mountain peaks. But he had travelled far enough, and it was time to rest. Wearily he dismounted and unsaddled his donkey; he took a little of the food he had brought, and fed and watered the animal. Then he wrapped himself in his cloak against the cool hill winds, and settled down to sleep.

As he slept, he had a dream, a dream that was to stay with him for the rest of his life. He saw, quite clearly, the high mountain place where he slept, and the mountain peaks falling away on either side to the river and to the sea. But there were no broken stones scattered over the ground; instead, there was a temple-tower standing in the centre of the plateau, more beautiful than the Zigurrats of Babylon, its sides smooth and glistening in the moonlight. It rose from the plain in perfectly sculptured terraces of stone, almost half a kilometre broad at the base and rising slowly to a pyramid peak. There was no entrance to the tower, where an image of a god might be set, and priests stand ready to discern oracles or offer sacrifice. But up its sloping sides ran a broad stairway, ascending endlessly it seemed, to the tower's far tip, so high that at the top the stairs could no longer be clearly seen. Jacob gazed in awe at the enormous construction, so unlike anything he had seen before. And, as he looked, he saw that there was movement on the stair way, a continuous, ceaselessly active motion of light, weaving and throbbing, the whole length of the stair, something too fast to be seen and yet just within the edge of vision. He looked again, and it was as though the movement was slowed down for him to see. He began to make out shapes in the pulsating light, shapes of endless variety, ascending and descending the stair, spreading throughout all the earth and returning to their hidden source. It was as though these were messengers of light, bound on errands beyond his knowing, bringing knowledge from the farthest bounds of the world back to their origin. He looked towards the top of the stair, far above. At first he could see nothing, it was so far and high; but then he saw a pure flame, cold and clear, perpetually in motion, forming and reforming itself; yet somehow still and changeless, burning without consuming or being consumed. From it came all the forms of light, and to it they returned, and whether they were parts of the one flame or individual beings he could not tell. As he looked at that pure unending flame, Jacob knew that he was seeing beyond time and space, as if there were some great rift in the universe, and here eternity and his time met. The stairway was a stairway out of time, and the peak of the pyramid tower was not in any space that he could reach by walking. As he stared at the flame, space and time and all the things and people in them became unreal, like scenery blown down by the wind, and there was only the flame, placeless and eternal, and the myriad hosts of light streaming through all spaces and times and returning to their still centre. Jacob knew that he was seeing the Lord Almighty, and that these were the hosts of God; and he was afraid. This was surely the god he had desired; whose promise he had inherited by deceit; from whose land he was fleeing in exile. Was this god of flame now coming in the fire of destruction, to turn the blessing to a curse? The flame grew, until the hills and the plateau glowed whiter than at noon yet cold as night. Jacob threw himself to the ground in terror; and then he heard the voice:

'I am the Lord God of Abraham and Isaac. To you and to your offspring I will give this land where you lie. I will multiply your offspring, so that they shall spread throughout the world like dust in the wind. In you and in your offspring all the families of earth shall find blessing. I am with you and will keep you wherever you go, and will bring you back to this land; I will not leave you until all my promises are fulfilled.'

Jacob awoke, covered in perspiration, still terrified. The plateau was dark and empty; the great rocks were scattered on the ground; the moon was hidden behind a cloud. 'The Lord is in this place', he said, 'and I did not know it'. The rest of the night he spent in prayer, to the god of his fathers, who had confirmed his promises even as Jacob turned his face from the land of his desire; fleeing from the shame of his deceit. Now he knew, at the very moment of despair, that God would go with him; that he was the bearer of the promise still; that his god would be with him in strange lands, and would bring him safely home at last. When dawn broke, Jacob took one of the great pillars of stone and dug it into the earth so that it stood upright. He anointed it with oil, dedicating it to God, and he made a solemn vow:

'Lord God of my father and my father's father, hear me now; if you will be with me and keep me in this way that I am going, and give me food and clothing, so that I may return to my father's house in peace, then you will be my god also. This pillar, which I consecrate to you with oil, shall be called Beth-El, the house of God, for it marks the very gate of heaven and the place of God's appearing; it shall mark your sanctuary in years to come. And I vow that of all that you give me I shall give a tenth to you.' So Jacob bound himself to God by a three-fold vow; yet even at the height of his devotion, touched by the vision of the living God, his vow sounded almost more like a bargain than a prayer. He had seen the hosts of God; but he was Jacob still.

The Deceiver Deceived (Gen. 29)

After some days' journey towards the east, Jacob came to a well set in open country. There was grass on the hills and green trees growing along the valley. Sheep grazed quietly around the well, and as he came nearer, Jacob saw that there were three separate flocks, each with a small group of shepherds lying in the shade under the trees. The countryside did not have the rich beauty and enchantment of the land he had left; but after the monotonous stone and scrub of the desert, it was a welcome enough sight. Jacob greeted the shepherds courteously: 'My friends, what is your country and city?'

'We are from Harran', they replied. Jacob smiled with pleasure; he had arrived at the place he was seeking; the Lord was indeed with him.

'Do you know Laban, the grandson of Nahor?' he asked. They answered, 'We know him'.

'Is he well?' asked Jacob; and they said, 'He is well; and here is his daughter Rachel coming with his flock'. Jacob looked up; he had seen the little flock coming towards the well, but he had not noticed that a young woman led them, heavily veiled, but walking with grace and dignity. This was his cousin, the daughter of his mother's brother; perhaps the woman who would be his wife. He turned excitedly to the group of shepherds.

'The sun is still high', he said, 'and there is ample time to graze the flocks before they must be folded. Why do you not water them now and take them off to graze?'

'No; we cannot', they replied, 'for it is not permitted to move the stone which covers the well until all those who have rights to this water have gathered together. Thus we can ensure that there will be no disputes in this matter'. So the shepherds would not go, to leave Jacob alone with Rachel. He watched her approach and saw that she carried herself proudly, and her eyes sparkled with life and beauty. On a sudden impulse, he ran to the well and, with a huge effort, he rolled the stone, which was as big as a man, away from the well. Then he took an urn, and filled the water troughs with fresh spring water, so that Rachel's flock could drink from them. The shepherds watched, surprised at his strength, waiting to see what he would do. Jacob came up to Rachel, and he could see that, veiled though she was, she had the charm and grace of his mother. All the confused emotions of the last few days welled up in him — guilt, remorse, resentment, despair, regret and the fearful hope of Beth-El — and he burst into tears as he kissed her gently on the cheek.

'I am your father's kinsman and his sister's son', he said, 'although I am the younger son, I have obtained my father's blessing by deceit; and now I have left my own country, fleeing from my brother's anger; I hope to live here for a while with my kinsman, and, if God wills, find a companion for my exile'. At once, Rachel had pity on him; and she ran to tell her father. When Laban heard her account, he hurried to meet Jacob and embraced him, kissed him warmly and welcomed him to his home. Jacob told Laban the whole story, and Laban said, 'You are my flesh and blood. Stay with me'.

So Jacob stayed with Laban his uncle and worked for him as a shepherd. One day Laban said to him, 'You must not work for me for nothing, simply because you are my kinsman. Tell me, what shall your wages be?' Jacob had now fallen hopelessly in love with Rachel, and he desired her for his wife; so he decided to make Laban an offer he could not refuse. 'I will work for you for nothing for seven years', he said, 'if you will only give me your younger daughter Rachel to be my wife'. Laban was indeed surprised at such an offer, but he considered carefully as he said, 'It is better that I should give her to you than to anyone else; stay with me'. Jacob did not pause to consider the guarded phrasing of Laban's words, but at once struck the bargain. He worked seven years for Rachel, and they seemed to him like a few days, because he loved her.

When the seven years were completed, Jacob said, 'I have served my time. Give me my wife so that we may sleep together'. So Laban gathered all the men of the tribe together and gave a great feast. Now Laban had two daughters; Rachel was the younger, and she was graceful and beautiful; but the elder was called Leah, and she was plain. After the feast, when Jacob was fairly drunk, the men brought Laban's daughter, heavily veiled in her wedding garments, to Jacob's tent; she went in and they slept together. But when morning came, Jacob found when he awoke that he had slept with Leah, the elder daughter. Furious with anger, he rushed to find Laban and said, 'What have you done to me? Did I not work for Rachel? Why have you deceived me? But Laban and his men laughed, and Laban said:

'I have broken no promise with you, for I made no promise. In our country it is not right to let the younger usurp the elder, to give the younger sister in marriage before the elder. Nevertheless, if you go through with the customary seven day feast for your marriage to Leah, which you have already consummated, then I will give you Rachel also, in return for a further seven years' work.' Jacob looked at the mocking faces around him, and realized with bitterness that Laban was repaying him in kind for his own deceit. He had usurped his elder brother's privilege by appealing to a long forgotten bargain; now, by appeal to just such a bargain, Laban was reminding him in the most forcible way of the nature of his usurpation. God's retribution was working out with almost mathematical precision. Jacob was angry and humiliated; but there was little he could do. He still wanted Rachel; and he could have her in another seven days, if he stayed to work for Laban. So he agreed to Laban's terms; and when the week was completed, he took Rachel for his wife, and stayed in Harran for another seven years, still far from the country of the promise he desired.

The Tribes of Israel (Gen. 30)

Jacob stayed in Harran and worked for Laban, and in time Leah his wife bore him four children – Reuben, Simeon, Levi and Judah. But he did not love Leah; he was infatuated with the beauty of Rachel and loved her with all his heart. Rachel, however, remained childless, and she became jealous of her sister Leah. At last she came to Jacob and said, 'If I cannot give you a son and heir, I shall die. Take my slave girl and sleep with her, so that she can bear her sons on my knees and I can found a family through her'. So Jacob slept with the slave girl, and she bore him two sons, Dan and Naphtali. Leah, not to be outdone, gave her slave girl to Jacob, and by her Jacob had two more sons, Gad and Asher. About that time, Reuben found some mandrakes in the fields, and brought them to his mother Leah. Mandrakes were believed to increase fertility; and Rachel said to Leah, 'Let me have your mandrakes, that I may bear children for my husband'. But Leah said, 'Is it not enough to have taken away my husband, without wanting to take my motherhood also?' Rachel replied, 'Let me have the mandrakes, and Jacob shall sleep with you tonight'. Jacob did so; and thereafter Leah bore him two more sons, Issachar and Zebulun; and she bore a daughter, called Dinah. All this time Rachel was barren, and nothing she did brought her children; yet Jacob still loved her more than Leah. Then at length, when hope was almost gone, she conceived and bore a son and named him Joseph. These are all the tribes of Israel, except one; and in this story of tangled jealousy and love is hidden the history of their origin and growth. So God wove his mysterious will; and from the interplay of human hope and disappointment he formed the nation through which all the world would be restored.

Jacob in Exile (Gen. 30)

When Jacob had served Laban fourteen years for his two daughters, he said to Laban, 'Now I wish to return to my own country. I have served you well for fourteen years; now give me my wives and children and let me return with them'. For it was the custom that a man's wife should remain with her own father's family if her husband left the clan. Laban said, 'I have indeed prospered while you have been with me; and I have learned by divination that God has blessed me because of you. So name your wages and I will give you them'. Jacob saw that this was not a direct answer, and that Laban did not intend to let him go with his family. So he devised a bargain which Laban would not be able to resist. Jacob said, 'I do not want any pay. Instead, let me stay and work for you yet longer, and let me take for my own only the black and multicoloured sheep and the multicoloured goats which are born of your flock, as you shall decide. Moreover, I will today remove all such sheep and goats from the flock; I will not claim them for my own'. Laban replied, 'Let it be as you say'; but he himself took the precaution of removing all multicoloured goats and black and multicoloured sheep from the flock. He gave them to his sons, and sent them three days' journey from Jacob, so that Jacob was left with only white sheep and uni-coloured goats in the flock which he tended.

Over the next six years Jacob grew very rich as a result of this unprepossessing bargain, for the Lord was with him. He would put branches of poplar and almond in the watering troughs, with the bark peeled in strips, in the belief that the sheep and goats would produce offspring striped like the objects they saw at the time of conception. Whether or not this magical technique worked, some black and multicoloured sheep and goats were born; Jacob kept these animals apart, and mated the stronger animals with them. So Laban's flock grew weaker and Jacob's grew stronger; and though Laban continually changed Jacob's wages, sometimes saying he could have the striped animals, sometimes the spotted; whatever he did, Jacob's flock grew larger. Within six years, by God's help, Jacob was a man of substance, with many slaves and camels and donkeys. So God gave Jacob many sons and great wealth in his exile, and was with him even in a strange land, protecting the child and guardian of the promise until the day of his return.

The Return (Gen. 31)

The sons of Laban began to grow discontented and said, 'Jacob has taken away our father's wealth, and has it for himself; all his riches he owes to our father'. And Laban began to look on Jacob with disfavour. It seemed to Jacob that the Lord was now guiding him to return to his own country, after twenty years in exile. One night he dreamed that God's messenger stood beside him and called him by name and said to him: 'The Lord God says this to you: I am the god of Beth-El, where you consecrated the sacred pillar and made your solemn vow to me. Now arise and leave this country and return to your father's house; and I will be with you'. So Jacob called Rachel and Leah into the fields where he worked with the flock and said to them:

'It seems to me that your father is no longer favourably disposed towards me. But you know that the god of my father Isaac has been with me; I have served your father with all my strength, and whereas he had little when I came, now he is a prosperous man, through my work. Moreover, he has changed my wages many times, yet God did not permit him to harm me; indeed, God has taken his cattle and given them to me, for he caused to be born each year the animals which your father promised me for my wages. Now God has called me to return to my homeland. Will you come with me, or will you stay?'

Rachel and Leah said, 'Is there any inheritance left for us in our father's house? Does he not regard us as foreigners? For he has sold us for the price of your labour, and used for himself the dowry that should have been ours. So all the wealth that God has taken from our father is now ours and our childrens', and we owe him no loyalty. Now therefore let it be as your god has told you; we will leave our father's house and come with you.'

Jacob waited until the time of sheep shearing, when Laban had gone three days' journey away to see to his flocks. Then he took all his sheep and cattle, and sons, his wives and all his household, crossed the Euphrates and drove towards Canaan as fast as he could. It was three days before Laban heard of his flight; then he was filled with anger, and gathered together his kinsmen and pursued Jacob. After seven hard days riding they came within sight of Jacob's slow moving herds of sheep and cattle in the hill country of Gilead. But something held Laban back from taking Jacob by force; he had seen how Jacob's god had blessed him and been with him; and now God appeared to him in a dream and said, 'Take care that you do not harm Jacob; he is under my protection'. In any case, Jacob was now on the borders of his father's country, and his kinsmen were close at hand. But Laban had a grievance; not only had Jacob taken his daughters and grandchildren and flocks, which still belonged to Laban as head of the clan by tribal law, without consent or warning; but, unknown to Jacob, Rachel had stolen her father's household gods, the sacred property of the clan. So when he overtook Jacob, Laban came up to him and said, 'Why have you cheated me and carried away my daughters like captives? If you had told me, I would have sent you away with feasting and singing; but you did not even permit me to kiss my sons and daughters farewell. You have done foolishly, and it is in my power to do you harm; but your god has protected you in this. No doubt you longed to return to your father's land; but why did you steal the gods of our clan? That is a matter which merits death.' Jacob answered, 'I was afraid that you would take your daughters from me by force; therefore I fled secretly. But as for your gods, I know nothing of that. I swear that anyone with whom you find your gods shall not live. In the presence of our kinsmen point out what I have that is yours, and take it'. Thus Jacob condemned Rachel, the wife whom he loved above all, to death at her father's hand. Laban and his men searched through the tents of Jacob and his company but found nothing; then they came to Rachel's tent. Rachel had taken the household gods to establish Jacob's right to an inheritance in Laban's wealth; but her plan had gone disastrously wrong, and she was afraid. She took the gods and put them in the camel's saddle, and sat on them. Laban searched the tent, but found nothing; and Rachel said, 'Do not be angry that I cannot rise before you, father, but the way of women is on me'. By tribal law, a woman in menstruation was ritually unclean; she had to be separated for seven days, and whoever touched her or anything she sat upon became unclean also. So Laban let her be, and did not find the gods; and Rachel escaped death.

Now the tables were turned, and Jacob said to Laban, 'What now is my offence, for which you have pursued me? You have searched all my goods, but what have you found that is yours? Set it here before my kinsmen and your kinsmen, that they may judge between us. Twenty years I have been in your house; I have served you fourteen years for your two daughters and six years for your flock, and you have changed my wages time and again. I have cared well for your flocks and herds; the ewes have not miscarried; I have not taken your rams to eat, as I was entitled to; I have not brought to you lambs torn by wild beasts, as I could by law have done, but I have borne the loss myself. You required all stolen animals to be replaced, whether taken by day or night; I served you in the heat of the day and cold and sleepless by night. And if the god of my father and of Abraham had not been with me, even now you would have sent me away empty handed, without flock or family. But God has seen my sorrow and my care; it was he who last night rebuked you.'

Laban saw that his kinsmen were moved by this speech, and that their sympathies were now more with Jacob. He said petulantly, 'The daughters are my daughters, the children are my children, the flocks are my flocks, and all that you see is mine. But', he shrugged, 'What can I do to my own daughters or to their children? Come, let us make a covenant, you and I; the Lord watch between you and me, when we are absent from one another. If you illtreat my daughters or do not protect them or if you take other wives to supplant them, then, though no man is present, God is witness between us'. Jacob and Laban took stones and built a cairn, and they erected a pillar of stone also, as a witness and reminder of their covenant. They agreed that neither would pass over the cairn or the pillar to do the other harm; and they swore by the god of Abraham their father and the god of Nahor and the Fear of Isaac. Jacob offered a sacrifice on the mountain, and they held a feast all that night.

In the morning Laban arose, kissed his grandchildren and his daughters and blessed them, and returned to his home. Jacob continued on his way; as he walked towards the South the sky seemed to shimmer and tremble, and the hills became alive with light. Before him, a great flame burned in the sky; and all around him, streams of light pulsated with energy. There was a sound, strange and unearthly, filling the air, a sound of glory and of joy. Jacob's heart leaped, and his eyes shone, and he remembered the voice from long ago: 'I will keep you wherever you go, and will bring you back to this land; I will not leave you until all my promises are fulfilled'. He looked around him; his wives and children were walking on unseeing and unhearing, unable to apprehend the glory that surrounded them, suffusing them in light. But Jacob knew that he was met by the angels of God, the messengers of light, enfolding him in a love which was boundless and without end. He stopped and made camp, and called the place Mahanaim, the camp of the hosts of God. He went apart to pray, and as he knelt, he took some soil from the ground and held it high in his hands, letting it scatter over his head and shoulders. He laughed aloud, and the hosts of light around him shimmered and scintillated, as if in a great chorus of joy and welcome. Even as he laughed, great tears ran down his cheeks, streaking his face with dirt, the dirt of the promised land. His exile was at an end.

Jacob's Prayer (Gen. 32)

As Jacob and his company came into Canaan, he sent messengers to Esau his brother, who was camped south of Beer-sheba, with this message: 'My lord Esau, your servant Jacob has lived with Laban the Syrian until now, and has become a wealthy man, with oxen, donkeys, flocks and slaves. Now he returns in peace, and hopes to find favour in your sight'. The messengers returned to Jacob and said, 'We have met your brother Esau, and he is already coming to meet you with four hundred men'. Jacob was afraid and distressed, for he remembered well Esau's threat to kill him because of his deceit over their father's blessing. He divided his people into two companies, thinking that if Esau destroyed one, the other might escape. Then he took animals from his flocks and divided them into groups, two hundred and twenty goats, two hundred and twenty sheep, thirty camels and their colts, fifty oxen and thirty donkeys. He put each group in charge of a slave, and sent them off at intervals, as a present for his brother Esau.

He instructed the first slave to say to Esau, 'This is a present to my Lord Esau from his servant Jacob; and he is following behind'. And he told the second, third, fourth and fifth slaves to say the same thing. 'Thus', he thought, 'I may appease Esau with these presents; and when I at last come to him myself, perhaps he will be reconciled to me'.

Then he went apart and prayed: 'O God of my father Abraham and of my father Isaac, O Lord who said to me 'Return to your country and to your kinsmen and I will bless you', I am not the least worthy of all the steadfast love and all the faithfulness which you have shown to your servant. For I crossed the Jordan with only my staff in my hand; and now I return with two companies. For all these mercies, which I have by no means deserved, I give you thanks, O Lord. But now I am afraid, and face the future with fear. Deliver me, I pray, from the hand of my brother Esau, for I am afraid that he will come and destroy us all, the mothers with the children. Lord, remember your promise, to bless me and to make my descendants as numberless as the sand of the sea. Lord in your mercy remember me for good.' Thus Jacob committed his way to the Lord; and perhaps for the first time he did not try to bargain with God, but implored him for help, relying on his promises.

The Night Struggle (Gen. 32)

When night came, Jacob sent his wives and children, the two companies of his people and all his animals across the ford of the river Jabbok. He remained alone, in the dark gorge where the river ran down over shallow rapids between high gaunt cliffs on either side. The night was dark and moonless; the sound of rushing water echoed from the rock walls, with a thousand sounds of hissing, swirling, tormented battering of water ceaselessly etching away the rock, sweeping along the small stones in its deepening downward path. Shapes moved among shadows, there for an instant and gone again in the constant moving surge. Jacob stood by the water's edge; and the dark fears and deep desires and ancient hopes of his youth merged with the roar of the current, drowned in the patterned web of water, hurled from stone to stone, always pressed round and on by the stream above. As he stood there, a shape formed out of the shadows in the gorge, the shape of a man, dark and menacing; he waited, trembling, and the shape solidified and darkened, moved inexorably nearer, blocking his way across the river to where the children of his loins and the country of his boyhood longings lay. The shadow lay across his path; and Jacob knew in his heart that he must fight here for his life and future, fight the shadow of his fear and guilt. All that night they struggled, locked together by the dark stream in silent striving, until the dawn began to break. More than once Jacob would have retreated, as the strength of his opponent seemed unbreakable. But, even as he weakened, he remembered the vision of Beth-El and the hosts of light of Mahanaim; and as he thought of them, the darkness seemed to lighten around him and he felt his strength renewed. Only once did he give way to weariness and despair; and as his will began to break, the antagonist threw him to the ground and touched the hollow of his thigh, dislocating his hip. Pain flooded Jacob's mind; but somehow that very pain broke down the barrier of weariness and gave him new courage. It was as though he needed to be broken before he could find the power to overcome his adversary. His enemy had injured him, but not destroyed him; and at that moment Jacob knew that he would survive. As the sky began to lighten in the east, he fought with a new savage strength, and slowly he began to gain the upper hand. For the first time in that long night, the adversary spoke: 'Let me go', he said, 'For the day is breaking'. But Jacob, broken and weeping, said, 'I will not let you go, unless you bless me'; for he knew that his opponent was no mortal man, but perhaps an elemental spirit, whose supernatural strength could be bound and caught; and he determined to gain for himself something of that occult power.

The adversary said, 'What is your name?' Almost against his will, Jacob found himself answering, and as he said 'Jacob', he knew that his whole nature, all that he was, his lies and his deceits, lay exposed to view.

The man said, 'Your name shall no longer be Jacob but Israel, prince of God. For you have struggled against God and against men, and you will overcome'.

Jacob was amazed; 'Who are you?', he asked, 'What is your

name?' The adversary said, 'Why do you ask my name?'; and there, as the grey mists of morning began to form over the river, he blessed Jacob silently and disappeared; where he had been, there was only mist in the morning light.

Jacob walked slowly across the river, his mind numb and confused. 'Last night', he thought, 'I fought with a man until the breaking of the day. But what was it I fought? My own fear? A demon of the river? Or was it the one who knows me through and through, who has given me a new name and his blessing, who calls me to pursue his promise and follow his way? Could it have been God himself, whom I have seen face to face, and yet my life is preserved? Or was it just a dream?' As he crossed over the river, the sun rose above him; he walked slowly towards his wives and children; and they saw that he was limping as he came.

The Meeting (Gen. 33)

As soon as Jacob had crossed the river Jabbok at Penuel, he saw Esau his brother coming towards him with four hundred men. He had ridden past the first company, which Jacob had sent on ahead, and was pressing on towards the second company without stopping. Hurriedly, Jacob divided the children between their own mothers. He put the slave girls and their children in front, followed by Leah and her children, and Rachel last of all with Joseph, so that perhaps those at the back might escape Esau's anger. Then he went on ahead of them to meet his brother and to face whatever might come. Had he not already faced up to God in the long night struggle, who had met him face to face as he wrestled with his fears and guilt and hesitation, and blessed him with the rising of the sun? Now that he had faced up to God what did he have to fear from men? Indeed, he knew that, as he had dared to meet with God and work out anew his relation with him, however painfully, so this must in turn lead to a renewal of his relationships with his fellow men, and a working out of old wounds and present fears and enmities. So he walked alone towards Esau, as the four hundred men, silent and purposeful, rode towards him.

Suddenly the horde stopped and Esau urged his camel forward, a magnificent beast with graceful neck and gleaming reins and saddle. There he stayed, as Jacob walked up to him, bowing low to the ground seven times, in the formal manner of a slave approaching his King. Esau watched him, silent and unmoving, his camel as still as the desert rocks, his hand resting lightly on his sword. For a long moment they both stood motionless, each regarding the other as if to read what was in their minds, and the people fell silent, waiting for one of the brothers to make a move. It was Esau who made the first move. With a flourish of his cloak, one swift graceful movement of his body, he dismounted. Then he ran towards Jacob, his hands outstretched, and embraced him. He threw his arms around him and kissed him, and they wept together. Jacob was overcome with relief and joy; his prayer had been answered; God had delivered him and prepared the heart of Esau for forgiveness, in a way that Jacob could hardly have dreamed of. Jacob gave thanks in his heart of God his deliverer; he had committed his way to the Lord, and God had been faithful to his promise of blessing.

'Who are these with you?', asked Esau, seeing the women and children who followed Jacob his brother. 'The children whom God has graciously given to your servant', Jacob replied. The slave girls came near with their children and bowed low; followed by Leah and Rachel and their children, who bowed low also. Esau said, 'What was the first company of yours that I met on the way to you?' Jacob did not want to say that he had been afraid of his brother, and so he replied, 'It was a gift to win your favour, my lord'. Esau said, 'I have more than enough. Keep what is yours, my brother'. Jacob knew that if Esau accepted such a great gift, he would be placed under a virtually unrepayable obligation to the giver; but to reject a gift would be a form of insult; so he had placed Esau in the difficult position of either retracting his declaration of friendship or of publicly placing himself in his brother's debt. He said, 'No, I insist; if I have your goodwill, then accept this gift from me; for truly to see your face again is like seeing the face of God, you have received me so favourably. Accept this gift which I bring you, because God has been gracious to me, and I have all that I want'. Thus Jacob urged him; and Esau accepted the gift.

Then Esau said, 'Let us set out on our way and I will journey with you'. But Jacob was still not completely sure of his brother's mind, for Esau had always been an impulsive man, generous and open-hearted, but changeable and violently passionate too. So he said, 'You see, my lord, that the children are small; the flocks and herds are suckling their young; and I am concerned that if they are driven too hard, even for one day, they may die. I beg you, my lord, to go on ahead of your servant, and I will follow slowly, at the speed of my cattle and children, until I come to my lord in Seir'. Esau said, 'Then let me leave some of my own men with you to escort you'. But Jacob replied, 'There is no need for such kindness; we will be able to find our own way without troubling your men'. So Esau returned that day to Seir, with all his men, and the many gifts that Jacob had brought. But Jacob did not follow him; instead he journeyed a few miles Westward to Succoth, where he settled with his children and cattle and flocks. From that time, Jacob and Esau lived apart; the sons of Esau became the Kings of Edom, and Jacob stayed in the land of the promise, to follow the way of the god who had been with him in a strange land and had safely brought him home.

The Massacre at Shechem (Gen. 34; cf. Gen. 9)

After some time, Jacob moved on to the city of Shechem, where his grandfather Abraham had built his first altar to the god of the desert, in the sacred grove of Moreh. He bought the land on which he camped from the citizens for a hundred sheep, and he set up an altar. There he used openly for the first time the name which would leave its mark on human history forever from that time, and which would irrevocably change the course of man's destiny, the name of Israel. In taking that name, he also took the god of his fathers to be his own god. No longer was his god only the Shield of Abraham or the Fear of Isaac; now Jacob had met him face to face; he had been changed in that meeting, and given a new name and a new relationship to God. Now he belonged to God, and God was Israel's God, bound to his people forever by his own word of covenant and promise. So he built the altar, and solemnly dedicated it to El-elohe-Israel, God the God of Israel; a name which was to sound in the world from that time to the end of time, and dimly mark the goal to which all mankind, reluctantly or eagerly, with surprise or joyful hope, was bound.

Israel's sons grew to be skilful herdsmen and strong warriors. The nomadic highlanders of Israel became feared in the surrounding countryside, for they fought off those who tried to plunder them and rode boldly and unhindered through the cities of the Canaanite plains. Israel's mother had died while he was in exile, but he took her old nurse into his camp and looked after her and he re-established contact with his father Isaac, who was now very old and was living in Hebron. The city dwellers of Shechem feared and hated the uncouth highlanders, who grew rich on the open country around the city, who acknowledged no law but their own tribal customs and worshipped an alien god with no image who frowned on inter-marriage with the Canaanites.

One day Leah's daughter Dinah was visiting some local women when Shechem the son of Hamor the King and his retinue came upon her. He stripped off her veil, uncovered her thighs and raped her. Afterwards, when he discovered who it was, he was overcome with remorse and promised to take Dinah as his wife. Hamor his father came with Shechem to Israel's camp to discuss the matter; but when Israel's sons came in from the country they were overwhelmed with anger and grief.

Hamor said, 'My son is in love with this girl: I beg you to let him have her as his wife. He will deal honourably with her, and we can ally ourselves in marriage. Our countryside is open to you, to make your home in it, to go where you wish and acquire your own land. Settle among our people and we shall give our daughters to each other in marriage'.

Shechem also said, 'I am ashamed of what I have done; and I will give you whatever you ask to make amends. Fix the marriage present and the gift as high as you wish and I will give it; but you must give me the girl in marriage'.

Israel's sons listened to what they said, but they were unmoved; the rape of their sister was intolerable to them, and they could not forgive it. Hamor's offer of a marriage alliance only made the offence worse, for the tribes of Israel were a proud people who kept apart from the Canaanite city dwellers. They were horrified at the sexual profligacy of the Canaanites; and an old tribal story told how Ham, the ancestor of the Canaanites, had defiled his own father Noah while he was drunk, so that Noah had cursed his descendants and foretold that they would be slaves to the children of Abraham. So the brothers laid a trap for the Shechemites and said, 'We will agree on one condition; if all your men are circumcised then we can live together and be one people, and you can take our sister in marriage without disgrace. Otherwise, it is not possible'. Hamor and Shechem gladly agreed to his proposal, as it seemed a way to avoid the revenge of the Israelites and to gain a favourable alliance with the nomads. They put the proposal to all the citizens; and all agreed to be circumcised so that they would be one people with the Israelites and would gain access to their herds and riches in return for allowing them the freedom of the country.

Two days later, when all the men of Shechem were still in great pain from the circumcision, Simeon and Levi, Dinah's full brothers, came to the city with a band of armed men and killed every able-bodied male. After that, their brothers plundered the city, seizing all the livestock and treasures of Shechem and taking into captivity all the women and slaves. When Israel heard of the massacre, he called Simeon and Levi and said, 'You have brought trouble on this house by your rage and violence. Now I will be odious to the Canaanites; and if they join together to attack me, I shall be overwhelmed, both I and my people; for we are easily outnumbered. For this deed you will be scattered and dispersed, because your anger has been so ruthless and terrible'. But Simeon and Levi merely replied, 'Is our sister to be treated as a common prostitute?'

So human pride and anger and intolerance brought bloodshed and weeping to the first shrine of Israel; and the people who belonged to God left their mark in blood on the city walls of Shechem. So it would be throughout their history; violence, given or received, would never be far from the people of Israel; and yet within this complex interweaving of good and evil in the human heart, God's purposes were slowly to unfold and his promises were gradually to be made clear, until that far day when peace would come at last to Israel.

Journey's End (Gen. 35)

After the massacre of Shechem, Israel called his people together and said, 'We must leave this place, before the Canaanites come to take their revenge for the terrible thing my sons have done. Now my God calls me to return to Beth-El, where he first appeared to me in majesty, as I was fleeing from my brother. He heard me in the time of my distress and he has been with me wherever I have gone. He has given me food to eat and clothes to wear; he has protected me on my journey and brought me back in safety to my father's house. Now I must return to honour the vow that I made to him then, that I would build an altar and a sanctuary there and give to him a tenth of all I possess. Now, therefore, rid yourselves of all the foreign gods which you have brought with you, purify yourselves and change your clothes, and let us make pilgrimage to the God of Beth-El, the everlasting God of Light.'

So the people handed over to Israel all the household gods they had in their possession, all the sacred charms and images and rings, and he buried them under the terebinth tree at Shechem. They washed themselves, according to the ritual traditions, and put on new clothes and set out for Beth-El. The people of the Canaanite cities watched them pass, but they did not attack, for they were overcome with a strange fear of the awesome God of Israel. So the silent caravan moved through the land unopposed and their alien god, the god who had no name or image, overshadowed and protected them.

When they came to Beth-El, high in the mountains to the west of Jordan, the people made camp, and Israel built an altar and a sanctuary where god had first appeared to him. There he kept vigil, remembering his long wanderings and his passionate desire for God's blessing and the treasured promises his father had handed on. Israel offered a drink offering on the sacred pillar of Beth-El and made sacrifice to God and fasted for three days and nights. Then God appeared to him in a vision and said:

'I am El-Shaddai, God Almighty, God of enduring strength and might. Your father called you Jacob, but I name you Israel – may God rule – for you shall announce to all the rule of God. Be fruitful and increase, fill the earth and subdue it. Many nations and many Kings shall spring from you and be born of your people. And to you and your descendants I give this land, which I gave to Abraham and Isaac.'

Israel heard the words that God spoke; but he knew that they contained some meaning he could not grasp, something much more, hidden from him, but given for him to hand down to his descendants until the meaning became clear. But the words themselves were definite and sure. God had revealed himself by name, the everlasting and almighty one. He had blessed and chosen Israel, from all the people of the earth. He had commanded Israel to be true to him and keep his covenant. And he had promised Israel that he would father a great people in their own land. These things Israel could treasure and hold fast to; for all the unfathomable mystery of God's purposes for men, and all the inscrutability of his ways, Israel could never escape that word of vision, given at Beth-El, and echoing for ever in the hearts of his people: 'I am God Almighty. I name you Israel. I am your God and you are my people, inescapably and forever'.

When the tribes had renewed the sacred covenant at Beth-El, they moved southwards towards Bethlehem. There, on the road to Bethlehem, Rachel died in childbirth. As she died, she bore another son for Israel, and with her last breath she called him Ben-oni, son of ill luck. Israel renamed him Benjamin, son of good fortune, so that he would not have an unpropitious name. He buried Rachel by the road to Bethlehem, set up a sacred pillar by her grave and journeyed on. God's blessing did not save Israel from sorrow; and the death of Rachel, whose love and grace had made his long exile bearable, was the greatest grief he had yet faced. He had hoped to share with her the new country of the promise, to see their sons grow and prosper in the land, and to give thanks to God for his great gifts. But sorrow was to be the companion of Israel's last years, and even his sons were to bring him little happiness. That was a gift God's promises to Israel did not include.

At last Israel came to Hebron, where Abraham was buried and where his father Isaac lived. There he stayed with his twelve sons until his father died and was gathered to his people at a very great age. Esau and Israel came together to bury him in the sepulchre of

Machpelah, with his parents Abraham and Sarah and his beloved wife Rebecca. Israel's wanderings in the East had ended, by the grave of his fathers. 'Here I will stay, in the land my father has settled', he said; 'And here, with my fathers, I will be buried in God's own time'. So he swore; but he could not see the way that God had marked out for him. Israel's long journey was not to end till death, and no one could have foreseen what God was yet to do for the people of his choosing.

The Favourite Son (Gen. 37)

Israel camped in Hebron, near the land his father Abraham had bought, with his twelve sons. But of all his sons he loved Joseph best, the first son of Rachel, and the last to be born in exile. He made Joseph a long, sleeved robe, the robe of a prince and a man of leisure, and Joseph walked proudly among his brothers, the pampered son of his doting father. As he flaunted the signs of his father's favour before them, his brothers came to hate Joseph and could hardly bring themselves to speak peacably to him. To make things worse, Joseph brought bad reports of his half-brothers, the sons of his father's concubines, to his father. But the brothers' jealousy and dislike became almost unbearable when Joseph told them of a visionary dream which he had. The dream was that all Israel's sons were binding sheaves of corn in the fields, when Joseph's sheaf rose and stood upright, and all the other sheaves gathered round and bowed down before it. His brothers said, 'Does this mean that you will one day become a King and rule over us? Is that how to interpret your dream?' and they laughed at him. But secretly they feared him and their jealousy increased.

Then Joseph dreamed again and told his father and his brothers: 'Another dream has come to me in the dark hours of night. In my dream, the sun, the moon and eleven constellations of stars came and bowed before me'.

At this, his father rebuked him: 'What does this dream mean? Do you suppose that Leah and I and your brothers shall indeed come to bow down before you?' The brothers hated Joseph all the more for his arrogance; but Israel could not forget the dream, and it stayed in his mind.

When Joseph was seventeen, his father sent him to the country near Shechem, where his brothers had taken the flocks for the summer, to see how they were faring. When he arrived there, however, he found that his brothers had left, and he wandered through the countryside in search of them. After a while, he was told that they had gone further North, to Dothan, so he set off to find them there. His brothers saw him coming in the distance and said to one another:

'Here comes the dreamer, the one who prophesied our subjection to his rule, who walks in arrogance and luxury while we perform the hard labour of tending the flocks, our father's favourite. Let us kill him and throw him into one of the water storage pits, where no one will ever find him. Then we shall say that a wild beast killed him, and we shall see what will become of his prophecies.' But Reuben came to his defence and said, 'Do not take his life; let us shed no blood; put him into the pit, by all means, and leave him to die in the wilderness, but let his blood not be on our hands'. He then went off to see to his flocks, intending to return when the others had gone, to save him and restore him to his father. So the brothers agreed together; and when Joseph came up to the camp, they stripped the long sleeved robe from him and threw him into a nearby water cistern, a large bottle-shaped hole in the ground for storing water throughout the summer. But the cistern was empty of water; so Joseph survived, shaken but unharmed, in the dark prison of his brothers' hatred.

Some time later, the brothers were eating a meal when they saw a caravan of merchants coming down the trade route to Egypt from the North, carrying medicinal drugs and perfumes. Judah said to his brothers, 'What do we gain if we kill our brother and conceal his death? Let us sell him as a slave to these merchants; then we shall be rid of him without being responsible for his death — for he is our brother, our own flesh and blood'. So Judah, too tried to save Joseph's life, not knowing what had been in Reuben's mind. The brothers agreed and they took Joseph out of the pit and sold him for twenty pieces of silver to the traders, who went on their way South towards Egypt. When Reuben came back to the pit later, he was horrified to find that Joseph was not there. He tore his clothes and returned to his brothers and said, 'The boy is gone;

and I, where shall I go now?' They told him what they had done, that Joseph had been taken South to be sold as a slave in an unknown land. He and Judah were overcome with remorse, as they realized that their separate plans had frustrated each other; but there was now nothing they could do. So the brothers agreed to say that Joseph had been killed by a wild animal. They tore his long sleeved robe and smeared it with goat's blood and took it to their father as proof of his son's death. Israel recognized the robe and was convinced that Joseph had been killed. So Israel was deceived by his own sons and his favourite son was displaced, just as he had deceived his father and usurped the place of Esau his brother. As he passed on God's promise to his children, so his failures and deceits brought suffering upon his family, and they were caught up in and multiplied in themselves the consequences of their father's sin. Israel tore his clothes, put on sack cloth and mourned for his son for many days. His sons and his daughters in law tried to comfort him, but he was inconsolable and said, 'I will go to my grave mourning for my son'. And he wept bitterly.

Tamar (Gen. 38; cf. Deut. 25)

Judah left his brothers and went into the South, to the Canaanite plain with his flocks. There he married a Canaanite woman and had three sons; and in time he found a wife for his eldest son; her name was Tamar. But the eldest son died soon afterwards, and in accordance with tribal law, Judah gave her in marriage to his second son, Onan. The law was that when one brother dies without leaving a son, it is his brother's duty to marry the widow and give her a son. Thus he can perpetuate the dead man's name so that his family line will not be lost to the tribe. But Onan had no wish to give his brother an heir; though he married Tamar and had intercourse with her, he always spilled his semen on the ground so that she would not conceive; thus he cheated his brother and his widow. Soon, however, he too died. Now Tamar was bound to marry Judah's third son. But Judah was afraid that by some magical power, Tamar was causing the death of her husbands, so that his third son would die like the others. He said to Tamar, 'Remain as a widow in your father's house until my son grows up'; so she did. Time passed; Judah's wife died and his son grew up; but still he did not call Tamar back to give her in marriage.

Now she was in an impossible situation. She could not marry outside the family, while her husband's brother lived; nor could she stay with her father, by the tribal law. She decided on a desperate course. Hearing that Judah was on his way to the feast of sheep shearing at Timnah, she took off her widow's clothes, veiled her face and perfumed herself, put on her best clothes and sat by the road to Timnah waiting for her father in law to pass by. What she expected she was not quite sure; but he was certain to notice her and to be reminded of his obligations. If he would not give her to his son, he could fulfil the law by marrying her himself. So she sat by the road; and when Judah came by he saw her, as she had planned. But when he saw her in her flowing robes, he mistook her for a temple prostitute. Although it was forbidden to Israelites, it was a common custom among Canaanite women to devote oneself to a god by offering oneself as a sacred prostitute at a temple shrine or by the road side, and to give the money to the shrine; married women would take such a vow at least once in their life. So Judah came up to his daughter in law and asked her to sleep with him.

'What will you give me?' Tamar asked, and he offered a young kid from his flock. 'Will you give me a pledge, until you send it?' she said.

'What do you want?' he asked.

Tamar replied, 'The personal seal, which you wear around your neck, and your carved staff'.

Judah gave them to her, and they slept together that night. The next day Judah sent a friend with the kid from his flock to give to her; but she was not anywhere to be found. When they asked where the temple prostitute had gone, the villagers said, 'There has been no prostitute here'. The friend told this to Judah, who said, 'Let her keep the things I gave her as a pledge, or we shall get a bad name. We can always say that we did try to pay her, but she could not be found'.

Tamar had meanwhile returned to her home and resumed her widow's dress. But she had conceived by her father in law the night they lay together; and after three months Judah was told: 'Your daughter in law Tamar has behaved like a common prostitute and, though unmarried, she is pregnant'. Judah was enraged; he could think only that this was the woman who was engaged to his son, and on whom the continuance of his family line depended. Now she had polluted the name of the family of Judah for ever, and brought shame on all his descendants. His anger was uncontrollable; 'Bring her out and let her be burnt', he shouted. Tamar was brought out, but as she was going to the pyre, she went up to Judah, and placed in his hands the seal and staff which she had kept. 'I am with child by the man to whom these things belong'; she said; 'Do you know to whom this seal and this staff belong?' Judah recognized them at once, and for a long while he was silent, looking down at the ground. At last he looked up and said, 'She is more in the right than I am, for I did not give her to my son Shelah. Let her be freed'.

So Tamar bore sons for her husband who had died, by her father in law Judah, and thus she continued his name in Israel, a name which was to become the greatest of all the tribes of Israel, the tribe of the great Kings. Where Onan the son of Judah had failed, Tamar the Canaanite, by accepting shame and reproach, continued God's purposes and promise for Israel and Judah, that, through their descendants, all the world would find blessing.

Joseph in Egypt (Gen. 39)

The merchants who had bought Joseph from his brothers took him with them to Egypt, and there they sold him in the slave market to Potiphera, a high ranking officer of the King, and Captain of the Royal Guard. The Lord was with Joseph, and everything he did was successful. From being a minor attendant in the Captain's household, he gradually rose to become his personal servant. Potiphera observed that he excelled at all he undertook, and he acknowledged that Joseph's god was giving him blessing. Joseph was put in charge of the whole household and had oversight of everything except the preparation of food, for there the Egyptians had religious taboos to observe. The blessing of God rested upon all that was his in house and field and he trusted Joseph implicitly.

Joseph had inherited his mother Rachel's looks and his father's strength; he was very handsome and well built. Potiphera's wife desired him, and tried to seduce him. But Joseph said, 'My master has entrusted me with all that he has, and has withheld nothing from me except you, for you are his wife. Moreover, among my people, to take another man's wife deserves only death, for it is a sin against our god. How, then, can I do such a thing, and break the law of the god of my fathers, when he has blessed this household as he has?' Potiphera's wife continued to approach Joseph day after day; but he always refused her. Then, one day when he was alone in the house at his work, she came up to him and took hold of the loose linen tunic that he wore, and said, 'Come and lie with me'. He tore himself free and ran out of the room into the inner courtyard, leaving his tunic behind in her hands. She was overcome with anger and humiliation and called out to the other slaves, 'Come and help me. My husband has brought a gipsy into this house to insult us. He came in here to lie with me, but I gave a loud scream. When he heard me call out, he left his tunic in my hands and ran out of the house, completely naked'. She kept the tunic until the Captain returned home and told him the same story, saying, 'That gipsy slave whom you brought in to make a mockery of me tried to rape me. But he ran off when I screamed, leaving this tunic in my hands'. When Potiphera heard his wife's story he was furious; he knew something of his wife's nature, and something of Joseph too; and he was fairly sure that what she said was not true. But she had the tunic; and he could not publicly call her a liar. So he had Joseph put into the Round Tower, the royal prison, which was under his command. But the Lord was with Joseph even in prison, and showed him steadfast love, so that he won the favour of the chief warder. He put Joseph in charge of all the other prisoners and their work and left the running of the Round Tower to Joseph, because the Lord was with him and gave him success in everything that he did. Because of betrayal by those who had loved him, Joseph became first a slave and then a prisoner. But wherever he went, God was with him and brought blessing even in the midst of his troubles, because he obeyed God's law and worshipped him in his heart.

Joseph in Prison (Gen. 40)

Joseph had been in prison some time when two high court officials, the King's cup bearer and his master chef, displeased the King of Egypt. The King put them in custody in the house of the Captain of the Guard, which was within the Round Tower, where Joseph was a prisoner. The Captain ordered Joseph to serve them and attend to their needs. One morning, when the courtiers had been in prison some months, Joseph came in to serve them as usual, and saw that they were looking troubled. He asked them why they were distressed, and they said, 'Last night we each had a vivid dream, but there is no one here to interpret the meaning for us'. The Egyptians regarded their dreams as omens for the future, and they had many professional interpreters and magicians who, with the aid of ancient texts and magical techniques, could discern what dreams foretold. In the world of dreams the innermost self and its desires is revealed, and as one wanders in sleep free of the body, one may range through space and time to distant lands or times far past or future. In that strange world, for those who are able to decipher its riddles, one may discover the secret of one's own destiny, and what the gods hold in store. But special gifts of interpretation are needed to enter that world with understanding, principles handed down from ancient lore and preserved in the secret traditions of the magi, the wise ones of the land. In prison there was no access to the secret wisdom, and so the courtiers, who clearly remembered these strange dreams of the night, were disconsolate.

Joseph said: 'I am a servant of El Shaddai, the Lord of Time, who holds the future in his hand. Does not interpretation then belong to God? Tell me your dreams'. The cup bearer looked at the young slave from the wandering tribes of Canaan and beyond. What could he know of the ancient wisdom? And yet his eyes were sharp and keen and his voice held a conviction that was strong and assured; perhaps his god could give him the power of divination. Whether it was so or not, no harm could come of it. So he told Joseph his dream. Joseph listened to what he said; he asked him one or two questions; then he closed his eyes and concentrated in silence for a few moments. Then Joseph said:

'In your dream there was a vine with three branches and the branches bore grapes. You took the grapes and crushed them in the King's cup, which you held in your hand; and you gave the cup to the King. This is the interpretation of your dream: the three branches are three days; within three days the King will lift up your head and restore you to your office and you shall again be the King's cup bearer.'

The cup bearer said, 'You have deciphered my dream well, and taken from it a clear meaning. If you should indeed be correct, what can I give you in return?'

Joseph replied, 'I want nothing; the interpretation is God's gift. But when you are restored, remember me, and mention me to the King and so help me to get out of this prison. For I was stolen unjustly from the land of the Hebrews and I have done nothing here to deserve my imprisonment.'

When the chef heard the favourable interpretation of the dream, he also told Joseph his dream. Joseph said to him: 'In your dream the important incidents are these: you bore on your head three baskets of baked food for the King and the birds were eating out of the top basket. The interpretation is this: the three baskets are three days. Within three days the King will lift up your head from off your body and hang you on a tree and the birds will eat your flesh.' When he had spoken, there was silence in the room, and the master chef rose and left them without a word.

Three days later, the King of Egypt gave a birthday feast for all his courtiers. He called his cup bearer and his master chef out of prison and brought them to the Court. He restored the former to his post; but the latter he hanged. Everything happened as Joseph had said, in interpreting their dreams. God, who knows all the thoughts of men, had vindicated his servant Joseph by giving him the gift of discernment and divination. Nevertheless, the King's cup bearer did not remember Joseph, but forgot him.

The Dreams of the King (Gen. 41)

The King of Upper and Lower Egypt, representative on earth of the hawk god Horus, absolute monarch in the fifteenth dynasty of the Kings of the Nile Kingdoms, had a dream. In his dream, he was standing by the Nile, and seven cows, sleek and fat, came up from the river to graze on the reeds. Then seven more cows, gaunt and thin, came up from the river and ate all the first fat cows. At that point the King awoke, with a strange feeling of unease; but he could make no sense of the dream, and shortly fell asleep again. As he slept, another dream came to him, as vivid and baffling as the first. He saw seven ears of corn, full and ripe, growing on one stalk. Then seven more ears of corn began to grow, thin and shrivelled by the east wind from the desert; and they swallowed up the ears that were full and ripe. Again the King awoke, filled with uneasiness and with the conviction that some hidden meaning was locked in the dreams, which had made them so intense and troubling. When morning came, he summoned the magicians and wise men of his court and told them his dreams. But they could find no interpretation which satisfied him. They consulted their dream manuals, in which good and bad dreams were listed, with their meanings, but such a dream was not recorded there. They consulted the oracles of the goddess Hathor, to whom cows were sacred, but they revealed nothing. They consulted the sacred book of death, and among their occult spells they found one concerning seven cows; but the King was not satisfied. The dream was still clear to him in his memory; it was an omen of some sort, he was sure of that; but who could interpret it for him? Then the King's cup bearer, who was attending his Lord, remembered Joseph and said,

'Now I remember my fault and my wrong-doing. Two years ago the King was angry with his servants and he imprisoned me and the head chef in the house of the Captain of the Guard. One night we both had dreams, each requiring its own interpretation. A young gipsy was there, who had been a slave of the Captain of the Guard; and when we told him our dreams, he interpreted them to us. It happened just as he had said; I was restored to my former place, and the chef was hanged. I promised to mention him to you, for he claims to have been stolen unjustly from Canaan and to be innocent of the charges against him. But until now I forgot.'

The King was intrigued. He was himself one of the Hyksos, the Shepherd Kings who had invaded Egypt from Canaan and Syria as the Middle Kingdom began to collapse. He had little use for the ancient wisdom which had come down from the age of the great pyramid tombs, a thousand years before. Its concern with death and with the city gods of the Nile valley was alien to him, though he used it to bolster his own position, won by force of arms, among the people of the crumbling civilization of Egypt. This Joseph was a tribesman from countries he knew and understood; if he was a prophet of eastern gods, perhaps he could interpret the dreams of the King. At once the King sent for Joseph; quickly, he was taken from prison, shaved and dressed in linen and brought before the King. The King said, 'I have had a dream, which I have told to all my magicians, but they cannot explain it. I have heard that you have the power of understanding and interpreting dreams'. Joseph answered: 'The power is not mine; I have no training in the occult arts. But I am the servant of God, who knows the secrets of men's hearts, and whose spirit discerns all that is hidden from men. If it is his will, he will give the King the answer he seeks.' The King told Joseph his dreams; and Joseph prayed in his heart to God, that his Spirit would give him the gifts of discernment and wise counsel. Then Joseph said: 'Both the dreams of the King are one; God has told the King what he is about to do. The seven fat cows and the seven ripe ears of corn are seven years. The seven lean cows and the seven blighted ears of corn are seven more years. First there will be seven years of great abundance throughout the Nile valley. But then will come seven years of great famine, which will ruin the country and cause the years of plenty to be forgotten. Because the King dreamed this thing twice, God is resolved to do this, and it will begin at once.'

The King was impressed by what Joseph told him and said, 'If this is how it will be, what is there to be done?'

Joseph said, 'It is fixed by God and cannot be changed. But there is one thing the King can do. He should find a man who is astute and wise and put him in charge of the land. And he should appoint controllers throughout the country, to take one fifth part of the produce of Egypt during the seven years of abundance. They should collect all this food gathered in the good years, and store the grain in the cities, under the control of the King and under guard. This food and grain will then be a reserve for the seven years of famine which are to come. In this way, the country will not perish but will survive the famine.'

The King and his courtiers were pleased at Joseph's plan; and the King said, 'This man has the spirit of a god in him indeed. He possesses wisdom and the gift of divination and the good fortune of his god. Where else in Egypt can we find such a man as this?' The courtiers were silent, for they saw that the King favoured Joseph, and they knew that he did not trust or respect the Egyptians. Having no reply, the King turned to Joseph, who had been for thirteen years a slave in his country and said: 'Since a god has made all these things known to you, there is no one so astute and wise as you. You say we should find such a man to rule this country, to be answerable only to me. Very well. You shall be the man. If all goes as you say, you shall be Vice-Regent of Egypt and all my people will depend upon your every word. If it does not, then no doubt you can divine what your end will be.' The King took off his signet ring, the sign of his authority, bearing his personal seal, and put it on Joseph's finger, and said, 'I hereby name you Zaphenath-paneah – the god speaks and he lives – and give you authority over the whole land of Egypt'.

Joseph was robed in the pleated linen of a high court official, and around his neck was hung a gold chain of office. He rode in the second chariot, the chariot of the Viceroy of Egypt, second only to the King, and slaves rode before him calling to the people, 'Bow the knee', as he passed. To seal his incorporation into the Egyptian hierarchy, the King gave Asenath the daughter of the High Priest of Ra to be his wife. The marriage was celebrated in the Great Temple at Heliopolis, the City of the Sun. In scenes of rich splendour and ceremony, beneath the great pillars and statues of the ancient gods of the Nile, Joseph Zaphenath-paneah was joined in marriage to the most noble priestly family of the land. For the next seven years, Joseph travelled throughout Egypt, supervising the storage of grain in huge granaries in the cities. The harvests were so abundant that they stopped measuring the grain which was stored; it seemed beyond measure, like the sand of the sea. During those years, Asenath bore Joseph two sons, whom he called Manasseh and Ephraim. At the end of seven years, it happened just as Joseph had foretold; a great famine came over Egypt, and over all the countries of the Eastern Mediterranean. The King issued an edict, making Joseph overseer of the granaries of Upper and Lower Egypt. Joseph opened the Granaries, as the famine became severe and sold grain to the Egyptians. And many people began to flock to Egypt from Canaan and the surrounding countries to buy grain from Joseph, as the famine spread and showed no sign of ending. The dreams of the King had come true.

The Great Famine (Gen. 42)

The great famine spread throughout the land of Canaan; the barren hills bore no crops and the animals began to die of hunger. Israel gathered his sons together and said, 'I have heard that there is food in Egypt. Go down and buy grain for us there, that we may live and not die'. So he sent ten of his sons to Egypt to buy grain. But he did not send Benjamin, his youngest son, with them, for he was afraid that he might come to some harm.

When Israel's sons came to Egypt, they had to appear before the Viceroy and overseer of the Granaries to ask permission to buy grain. The Viceroy was Joseph their brother; and as they came into his presence and bowed low before him, he recognized them at once. But they did not know who he was and said, 'My Lord, we have come from Canaan to buy food, if you will permit it; for otherwise we do not know from what we shall live'. Joseph did not show that he knew them; he spoke roughly to them and treated them like aliens.

'You have come here as spies', he said, 'to discover the weaknesses of our country'.

'No, my Lord', they said, 'We are honest men, all the sons of one man, and we have only come to buy food'.

'If this is so, tell me about yourselves', said Joseph, 'Who is your father? Is he still alive? Have you no other brothers? How can I know you are not spies?'

They said, 'We were twelve brothers, the sons of Israel, who was called Jacob, living by Hebron in the land of Canaan. Our father lives, and with him is our youngest brother. There was one other brother, but he is dead'. Joseph said to them: 'Now I shall test you, to see whether you speak the truth. By the life of the King, you shall not leave this place unless your youngest brother comes here. You shall all remain in prison, except for one of you, who shall go and bring your brother to me. If he does not return, then you are indeed spies, as I thought.' So Joseph threw his brothers into prison, as they had thrown him into the pit; and they remained there for three days.

On the third day Joseph brought them out of prison and said: 'Do this and you will live, for I fear God. If you are honest men, let one of your brothers remain in prison, and the rest can take back grain to your father's people, and then return with your youngest brother. Then I will believe what you say and you shall not die.' Joseph spoke to them through an interpreter, so they did not know that he could understand them. They said to one another, in their own language, 'This misfortune has come upon us because we are guilty for the death of our brother. We saw his distress, when he pleaded with us, but we would not listen'. Reuben said, 'Did I not tell you not to harm the boy? You would not listen to me; now we are guilty of his blood and the Lord requires a reckoning of us'. When Joseph heard what they said, he turned away and wept; his brothers had not forgotten him, and the guilt of their actions haunted them still. Now they were in his power, and it was for him to exact retribution as he willed. He took Simeon from them, and bound him before their eyes, saying, 'As I bind your brother before you, so are you bound to return to prove your words'. Then he gave orders for their sacks to be filled with grain and gave them provisions for their journey and sent them on their way. He also ordered that the money which they had paid for the grain should be replaced in their sacks; so he repaid their old cruelty with gifts of love.

That night, when the brothers stopped to camp, one of them opened his sack to feed his donkey and he found his money lying on top of the grain in the sack. He told his brothers and they were puzzled and afraid. 'What has God done to us?' they said, 'We cannot tell whether this Egyptian means us good or harm. Now surely the God of our fathers is preparing retribution for us, for what we did to our brother'. When they returned to Hebron, they all emptied their sacks and found that every man's money had been returned. They and their father were dismayed and Israel said, 'You have taken my children from me; Joseph is dead, Simeon is imprisoned, and now you wish to take Benjamin too; great sadness has come upon me in my old age'. Reuben said, 'Put Benjamin in my care, and I will bring him back to you; you may kill my own two sons if I do not do so'. But Israel said, 'Benjamin shall not go with you, for Joseph is dead, and only Benjamin is left of the sons of Rachel. If harm should come to him, I would indeed go down to the place of death in sorrow and weeping. God's will must be done, but Benjamin shall not go'. The brothers stayed in Hebron with their father; and the famine continued.

The Viceroy's Feast (Gen. 43)

In the second year of the great famine, the grain which Israel's sons had brought from Egypt began to run out. Israel said, 'You must go down to Egypt again to buy food'. But Judah said, 'Unless we take Benjamin with us, we cannot go; for the Viceroy clearly warned that we could not see him without our youngest brother'.

'Why did you tell him you had another brother?' asked Israel.

Judah said, 'He questioned us about our family. How could we know he would tell us to bring our brother to him? But now you must send the boy with us, if we are to live and not die, both you and us and our children. Let me bear the responsibility for Benjamin; if I do not bring him back, let me be cursed for ever. Our food is almost finished; if we had not delayed, we could by now have been to Egypt twice over and have all we need.'

So Israel reluctantly agreed to let them return with Benjamin. He sent with them gifts for the Viceroy, of honey, spices and fruit; and the money they had found in their sacks of grain, in addition to money for new grain. Israel blessed his sons and said: 'May God Almighty grant you mercy, that you may return to me with Simeon and Benjamin. But if my children are to be lost to me, then it must be so'.

When the brothers came to Egypt again, they were met by the Viceroy's chief steward, who took them to his master's private residence. The brothers were afraid, when they saw the great palace, with its vast colonnades and richly decorated walls, its luxurious gardens and lily ponds. 'We have been brought here because of the money which we found in our sacks', they said, 'The Egyptian will use it as an excuse to have his guards fall upon us, seize our goods and make slaves of us'. They halted nervously at the door of the palace, and said to the steward: 'My lord, when we returned home from buying corn the first time we came here, we found that our money had been put back into our sacks of corn. We do not know how it got there; and we have brought it with us again, in addition to the money we have to buy more corn. If it is because of the money you have brought us here, we have it with us; we do not know who returned it to us.'

The steward replied, 'You need not be afraid; your god and the god of your father must have given you your money again; I received your money and you owe me nothing. When my master saw that you have brought your young brother with you, he commanded me to bring you here and slaughter an animal for a feast, that you might dine with him at midday'. Then he brought Simeon out of the palace to them; and the brothers were both puzzled and overjoyed. They washed and prepared themselves for the feast, fed their animals and made ready their presents for the Viceroy. But they were still anxious and uneasy; they had come fearing judgement and retribution, for old wrongs which only they knew in the secrecy of their hearts. Now the Viceroy himself had brought them to his palace and slaughtered an animal for a feast. They could not understand this, or drive out their secret fear.

At noon, the Viceroy came to the palace; and they took into him the presents which they had and bowed to the ground. He asked, 'Is your father well, the old man of whom you spoke? Is he still alive?'

'Yes, my lord, he is well and alive', they answered, wondering at his interest in their home.

'Is this your youngest brother, of whom you spoke to me?' he asked. But he did not wait for their answer. As he saw his brother Benjamin, the son of his mother Rachel, after so many years, his eyes filled with tears and his voice broke. 'God be gracious to you, my son', he said gruffly; then he turned quickly away, went into an inner room and wept. After a while, he controlled himself and washed his face and came out again: 'Let the food be served', he said. The Viceroy ate by himself and the Egyptians ate separately, for their taboos did not allow them to eat with those of other races, and the eleven sons of Israel sat by themselves, at a table apart. They looked at one another in amazement when they found that they had been seated in order of age, from the eldest to the youngest. Portions of meat were carved at the Viceroy's table and taken to the brothers; and Benjamin's portion was five times as large as the rest. The brothers' anxiety and amazement did not abate until they were well and truly drunk. Then at last they accepted that retribution had not come, and that the mysterious Egyptian who seemed to know so much about them, and who so strangely favoured Benjamin, was receiving them in his home as honoured guests. Perhaps it was in recompense for their previous imprisonment. So they ate together and were merry, not knowing that the final test was yet to come.

The Sacred Cup (Gen. 44, 45)

When the great feast had ended, the Viceroy said to his chief steward: 'Fill the sacks of the sons of Israel with grain and return their money to them. Also, take my sacred cup and put it in the bag of the youngest brother.' The steward did as he was told; and in the morning, as soon as it was light, the brothers were sent on their way. Soon after they had left, the Viceroy said to his steward, 'Now follow those men; and when you come up to them, say: "Why have you repaid good with evil? Why have you stolen the Viceroy's silver cup, with which he divines what is and what is yet to come? It is a grave crime to take the sacred cup of the ancient mysteries, and it bears a grave penalty" '. The steward quickly caught up with the brothers and said what he had been told to say.

They said to him: 'My lord, why do you say such things? And why should we do such a thing? Did we not return to you the money which we found in our sacks last time? Why should we steal silver or gold from your master's house now? You may be sure none of us has your silver cup. Search us, then; if you find it with anyone among us, let him die; and we will become your master's slaves from this time.' The steward said, 'Let it be as you say; but only the one who has the cup will be my master's slave; the rest of you shall be without blame'. Every man quickly lowered his sacks to the ground and they opened them. They all had the money which had been returned to them again; but the steward was not interested in that. He and his men searched all the baggage, beginning with the eldest. Last of all they came to Benjamin; and there in his sack they found the sacred cup. The brothers tore their clothes with grief and they returned to the city with the steward.

When they came to the Viceroy's palace, they went before him and prostrated themselves on the ground. The Viceroy said: 'What is this that you have done? Did you not realize that I have the power to discern men's secret thoughts?' Judah replied, 'My lord, what can we say to you? How can we clear ourselves? We cannot understand how this thing has happened; it seems that by some dark mystery God has exposed in us a secret guilt, a shadow from our past, which we must face and expiate. Now, therefore, we stand ready to become your slaves, all of the sons of Israel; only spare our brother's life, in whose hands the cup was found, and we will be slaves with him.'

But the Viceroy said, 'God forbid that I should do such a thing. Only the man in whose hands the sacred cup was found shall remain here as my slave. The rest of you are free to return in peace to your father.' With that he began to dismiss them; but Judah came forward and addressed him:

'My lord, I beg you to hear what I say and not to be angry with us, for you are like the King himself. When we first came to you, you asked us if we had a father living, or any brothers. We told you that our father was an old man and had with him our youngest brother, the son of his old age. His brother is dead, so he alone is left of his mother's children and his father loves him dearly. Then you asked us to bring our brother to you, that you might show him your favour. We told you that he could not leave his father; for if he were taken away, his father would die. But you commanded us to bring him, binding our brother Simeon before us. So we did, and it is he who stands accused before you. But our father said to us, "My wife Rachel bore me two sons. One has been torn to pieces and is no more. If you take this one also and any harm comes to him, I will go down to the place of the dead in sorrow". Now therefore, my lord, if we return to our father without Benjamin, his favourite son, he will surely die and go to his grave in sorrow. Moreover, I myself took responsibility for my brother's safety, and said, "If I do not bring him back to you, then I shall bear the blame in my father's sight all my life". Therefore, my lord, I ask that you should take me as your slave in place of my brother Benjamin and let him return to my father with his brothers. For how can I return without Benjamin? I could not bear to see my father's sorrow.'

Joseph listened to the words of Judah and he was deeply moved. The brothers could easily have returned to Israel in freedom, leaving Benjamin in slavery as they had left Joseph himself many years before. But Joseph could see that their hearts were truly changed; they were ready to stay as slaves with their brother and even to give up their lives for his freedom. Now their ordeal was over; they had proved themselves; and Joseph could control himself no longer. He called for the audience chamber to be cleared of everyone but the brothers and himself. When they were alone, Joseph said to his brothers, 'Come closer to me'. They approached him, not knowing what might happen next, in this bizarre and dangerous place. Joseph slowly and deliberately took off his elaborate headdress and his gold chain of office. He took from the table beside him a long sleeved gown, of the sort Hebrew princes wore, and put it on over his Egyptian linen robe. Then for the first time he spoke to the brothers in their own language without an interpreter.

'There was a man', he said, 'who was his father's favourite son, his well-beloved. His father sent him to find his brothers in a far country; but because they hated and envied him, his brothers planned to kill him; they sold him for twenty pieces of silver and threw him into a pit. After three days, he was taken out of the pit and they did not know where he had gone.' The brothers were amazed and terror stricken; this magician could divine the darkest secrets of their hearts and bring them clearly to light. What kind of man was he, who knew so much about them and spoke to them in words they clearly understood?

The Viceroy continued: 'This man, a prince in his father's house, became a slave and was treated as a criminal, though innocent of any wrong, and accused unjustly. But the lord was with him and blessed him in his distress; and he was raised by God's will to become a King among his people, filled with the spirit of God. It was God's will that through him the lives of many men should be saved, and that from all the world they should come to him for life.' The brothers stared at him incredulously, as they began to grasp what he was saying. They remembered his insistent questioning about their father; his knowledge of their ages; his interest in Benjamin; and now his dress and speech made the truth clear beyond doubt. They stared at him open mouthed in dismay and they could find no words to say. Joseph said: 'I am your brother Joseph whom you sold into slavery twenty two years ago. Now you should feel neither sorrow nor anger at what you did; for it was God who sent me ahead of you to save men's lives, to keep alive the promise which you bear, to rescue you from death that your people may survive and flourish and bring new life to the world. So it was not you who sent me here but God, who has chosen in this way to save and deliver you and your descendants.'

Then Joseph wept aloud and embraced his brother Benjamin and asked again: 'Is my father still alive? You must all go to him quickly and tell him to come down to the country of Goshen, with his people, his flocks and all that he has. There I will provide for you, all of you, and see that you are not reduced to poverty; for there are five years of famine yet to come. Tell my father of all you have seen, and that I am Viceroy of Egypt, counsellor to the King, lord of his household and ruler of all Egypt. Go, tell him to move without delay, that your lives may be saved.' He embraced all his brothers and they wept and talked together. Joseph took the sacred cup in his hand, which had indeed revealed the thoughts of his brothers, though not by magic; he filled it with wine and the twelve sons of Israel drank together from the cup, giving thanks for their reconciliation and God's preservation of the company of the promise.

Israel Leaves the Land of Promise (Gen. 45, 46)

When the King heard that Joseph's brothers had come seeking food, he ordered that wagons should be sent to Canaan, to bring Israel, his dependents and their families into Egypt for the duration of the famine. Joseph gave his brothers food for the journey and to each one he gave a fine cloak – though to Benjamin his full brother he gave five cloaks and three hundred pieces of silver. To his father he sent ten donkeys laden with presents and ten donkeys laden with food. 'There must be no recriminations or quarrels among you', said Joseph; 'What is done is done. You must tell my father all that has happened and bring him to me in safety'. So his brothers returned to Hebron to their father Israel. There they told him that Joseph was still alive and was Viceroy of Egypt. He could not at first believe it; but when he saw the gifts and wagons which Joseph had sent and heard all that he had said, he slowly came to accept the almost unbelievable truth. 'It is enough', he said; 'Joseph my son is alive; what you have done shall remain between you and God; I will go and see my son before I die'.

So Israel gathered all his dependents and possessions together and travelled to Beer-sheba, the dwelling place of Isaac his father. He was troubled by the journey that lay ahead of him; for was he not leaving the land of the promise for Egypt, as his grandfather Abraham had done? That journey had been made in fear for the future and in doubt of God's promises; and it ended in shame and dissension. Since that time Abraham and Isaac had remained in Canaan, waiting patiently for the dawning of the day of promise; and though famine came again, they remained in the land of God's calling. Only Israel himself had left Canaan, once more in fear; and for twenty years he had remained in exile from the country he loved. When he returned, his favourite son had been taken from him, and for twenty years Joseph was not seen again. Now famine had returned to the land, a greater famine than any yet seen; and his son called to him from Egypt to go to him there. Could it be the purposes of his god to take him from the land of promise, where he had vowed to stay and die by the grave of his fathers in Hebron? Or was this a further test, more subtle than any other, to deflect him from the way of his god?

Israel went to the place where his father Isaac had worshipped, Isaac who had remained in the land all his life, from birth to dying. He went to the altar his father had used; the thick stones stood where they had been in his father's time at the centre of a sacred grove of terebinths. He washed himself in the stream that ran nearby and put on a white robe, that had never been worn. For two days he sat in the grove without food, an old man seeking the blessing and guidance of his father and his god. On the third day, he took his two finest rams from the flock and brought them before the altar. He stood between them and laid his hands on their heads; now his spirit and theirs were one; in offering them, he offered himself in obedience and supplication. Solemnly, he lit the flame and prayed that God would accept his sacrifice. Then he took the long curved knife and slit the throat of each animal, quickly and silently, letting the blood flow into a large silver bowl. Thus he gave his god the ultimate gift, the gift of life itself, offered up to the giver of all life. He took the blood and threw it against the altar; here was the very force of life, thrusting through veins and sinews, power of renewal and vitality, consecrated to the god who gave it, offered out of destruction and death, that death might be defeated by being accepted and freely offered to the unknown giver of all. So the enemy is overcome in the moment of its triumph; the blood which stains the altar is the crimson of a savage death and of the ultimate obedience. Israel took the carcasses and cut them up in ways which had been handed down from ancient time and burned them on the flame before the altar. He watched the smoke rise towards the open sky; and in the flames he saw destruction, terror, cleansing and power. All was burned away, and the burning was a sort of purifying, leaving only the smoke as an offering to the gods, the transfiguration of gross flesh into the freedom of the boundless sky; the last elements of flesh, passed through fire, rising to become one with the wind of the spirit which blows where it will, until flesh and spirit merge and become indistinguishable; the smoke disappears and only the limitless air blows free over the world of death. Finally, in accordance with the ancient rites, he took the parts of the flesh which he had left whole in the flame and ate them. So he shared with the god in the sacred feast; and as he had given the god life as a sign of obedience, so he was given back life again by the one who accepted his offering and by it bound the giver to himself in unity.

When he had offered the sacrifice at the altar of his father, Israel walked to the edge of the sacred grove and looked Northwards over the land of Canaan. On one hand, the mountains stretched as far as the eye could see, brown and bare in the hot sun. On the other hand, the wide plains where the Canaanites had their cities ran towards the west and the setting sun hovered in the air over the unseen sea. The sun, the life giver, unveiling the glory of the many coloured world, now burned the earth dry, cracking the scorched soil, withering the leaves and draining life from the rivers. Under its inescapable glare, the cattle died where they stood, gaunt and listless without food or drink, and the fields stood empty, returning nothing for the year's toil. This land of beauty and promise had become the bringer of barrenness and death; where once birds had sung in the olive groves, an empty silence lay on the withered branches.

Israel felt a great sadness flood over him. This land he had desired so much had not been given to him; even the land itself had rejected him at last. As he looked, he knew that he would not see it again; he was going to his last exile. He sat alone as dusk fell, and his eyes were wet with tears. For long hours he sat, scarcely moving, and he tried to understand the strange pattern of his life. Surely he had been given the promise and the blessing; surely he had paid for his deceit; why had it come to nothing? His thoughts circled around the nagging questions, drifting into vague nostalgia, always sharpening again to the unanswered questions. Then, in the dark hours of the night, there came a moment between sleep and waking, a moment of vision, perhaps, or a dream, when he could not clearly tell whether he thought, or whether there was a voice other than his own, heard like a thought. But it was definite and unambiguous: 'Do not be afraid. You must go down to Egypt. The god of your father will go with you, and in time your people shall return; you shall see Joseph before you die'.

Israel's questions were not answered, but now his mind was at rest. He knew nothing that he had not known before; he had no answers which he had not had before; yet he had learned something profoundly important, something about himself and his own grasp of life; he had learned the way of living with questions which lies between agony and complacency. Now he could cease to ask, not because of despair nor from lack of interest, but because he had found within himself the truth higher than thought wherein all questions are transcended. He had learned something, too, of the promise; it was a promise of the land of Canaan, a homeland for the tribes of Israel; but it was mysteriously and immensely more, something that involved the whole world; something to be fought and suffered for; to be won and lost more than once; to be given in God's own way, not by the will of men; to escape men as they grasp for it and be given at the time of greatest loss. He was the guardian of this gift; and he knew without understanding that this moment of his sorrow was an essential moment in the unfathomable purposes of God for the people he had chosen.

In the morning Israel and his sons, their wives and their dependents turned from the land of Canaan, the land of the promise, for the last time. The small band of survivors, sixty seven members of Israel's immediate family, entered Egypt in the third year of the great famine. None of them would ever return.

Israel in Egypt (Gen. 46, 47)

When Israel came to the borders of Egypt, he sent Judah before him to tell Joseph of his coming. At once, Joseph prepared his chariot and set out for the eastern delta of the Nile with his retinue to meet his father. They met by the wide mud flats at the mouth of the estuary, the straggling horde of nomadic hill warriors with their herds and flocks and families, and the disciplined and courtly retinue of the Viceroy of Egypt. Joseph urged his chariot forward into the camp, until he came to Israel's tent. He jumped to the ground and walked eagerly to the tent. There his father stood waiting for him; and for the first time in twenty two years father and son saw each other. Joseph ran to embrace his father and wept with joy. Israel, holding in his arms the son in whom he had delighted, by whom he and his people were now saved from death, wept with him and said, 'Now God may let me die in peace, for I have seen your face and know that you live'.

After Israel and Joseph had talked together for some time, Joseph took his father and five of his brothers to the court of the King to obtain his permission to settle in Egypt. 'The Egyptians will not live with shepherds', he told them, 'But do not disguise from the King the fact that you are shepherds; for then he will let you settle in the Nile delta, in the border provinces and near my residence'. Joseph went into the King and said: 'My father and my brothers, with their flocks and herds, have come from Canaan, in accordance with your command; and they are now in the province of Goshen'.

He presented his five brothers to the King, who said, 'What is your occupation?'

They replied: 'We are shepherds, as our forefathers were; but there is no pasture in Canaan because of the famine. Therefore we ask your permission to let your servants stay in Goshen, where we now are'.

The King said to Joseph: 'You have saved the land of Egypt by your god-given wisdom. Your father and brothers may follow the way of their god in the best land we have. By all means they may remain in Goshen; and if there are able men among them, let them be put in charge of the royal flocks, if you so wish'.

Then Joseph brought Israel his father before the King. The King, seeing before him the aged Patriarch, said, 'How old are you?'

Israel replied: 'The days of my pilgrim journey have been few and evil; they do not compare with the days of the pilgrimage of my fathers. I have walked in sorrow and disappointment, and the promise of my youth is further from me now than it was at the beginning. I follow the way of my god and the god of my fathers; but I cannot see where it leads'.

The King said: 'Your god has saved my country, and now you may find life in it with your sons. Your god is indeed powerful, and his way surely leads to safety. Give me now the blessing of this god before you go'. So Israel blessed the King of Egypt and returned to his tents in Goshen.

Over the years of the famine, Joseph carefully conserved the stores of grain and sold them to the people, so that they survived, and they regarded Joseph as their saviour and preserver of the nation. It was in his time that the power of the King of Egypt over his subjects began to increase. For when the people's money was spent, they bought grain by selling their herds to the King; and when they, too, were gone, they sold themselves and their land to the King for grain. Thus eventually all the land and the people of Egypt belonged to the King, and he took a fifth of their harvest each year, when the famine ended. Only the temple lands were not owned by the King, because of Joseph's policy of selling grain.

The tribes of Israel remained in the border province of Goshen, and they were highly regarded by the Egyptians because of Joseph. In time they became rich and powerful and they began to gather possessions and wait until the time was ready for their return. They eagerly looked forward to the day when they would be strong and wealthy enough to journey to Canaan in triumph and take possession of the land of promise in honour and acclamation. What God was going to do for them and through them was in fact something more terrible, more wonderful, vaster and greater by far than anything they could ever have dreamed, or have foreseen.

The Adoption of Joseph's Sons (Gen. 48)

It was said that Israel was ill and about to die; Joseph went to him, taking his sons Manasseh and Ephraim, born in Egypt of Asenath, daughter of the High Priest of the Sun. When Israel heard that Joseph had come, he sat up on his bed, leaning on his staff, and said:

'El Shaddai, the almighty god, appeared to me at Beth-El in Canaan and blessed me. His promise to me was that my descendants would be as many and great as a host of nations and that the land of Canaan would be the possession of my descendants for ever. Now your two sons, who were born in Egypt before I came here, shall be counted among my descendants; Ephraim and Manasseh shall be my sons, just as Reuben and Simeon are. Any other children you have shall share in their brothers' tribal territory; but they shall be full tribal chiefs, with a share in the possession of Canaan. I know that I am dying. God will be with you and will bring you back to the land of your fathers. Now I give you, for your two sons, one mountain ridge more than your brothers, of the land which we captured from the Canaanites. For you have always been dear to me, because of your mother Rachel, whom I lost even as I returned from exile, on the road to Bethlehem.' Israel's voice faltered and his eyes moistened as he felt that loss of his first love through all the years. For all his longed-for return to the land of promise, for all his pleasure in Joseph and Benjamin, for all his joyful reunion with his son; for all this, Rachel's beauty haunted his memory without ever fading, and her absence brought sadness often unawares upon him as he sat alone at evening.

There was silence in the tent for some moments and then Israel sensed that there was someone with Joseph, though he was blind and could not see who it was. 'Who is with you?' he said.

Joseph replied, 'These are my sons whom God has given me here'.

'Bring them to me', said Israel, 'and let me take them on my knee'. Joseph brought the boys near, and Israel took them on his knee, and so, by the custom of the tribes, formally adopted them as his sons. He kissed and embraced them and said to Joseph, 'I had never expected to see your face again, and now God has granted me to know your sons also. May God be thanked'. Joseph took the boys from his father's knee and bowed to the ground, thus ratifying the adoption of his children into the tribal company. Then he placed the two boys before Israel for his blessing, placing Manasseh by Israel's right hand and Ephraim by his left. First of all Israel blessed Joseph and said:

'The God in whose presence my forefathers Abraham and Isaac lived; who has been my shepherd and led me and protected me all my life until this day; who has redeemed me from all evil, freeing me from harm and misfortune; may he bless these boys. They shall be called by my name and belong to the family of my forefathers Abraham and Isaac; may they grow to be a great people on earth.' Then he began to bless Joseph's sons; but as he did so, he crossed his hands over so that his right hand lay on Ephraim's head and his left on Manasseh's. Joseph took hold of his father's hand to move it and said, 'Manasseh is the elder son;

lay your right hand upon his head, my father'.

But Israel said, 'I know, my son, I know. Manasseh shall become a great people. Yet God's blessing is not bound by human law. The blessing which he gives is the blessing of his presence, his care and redemption from evil; and he gives this blessing, not to the rich and powerful, but to the poor and the oppressed, to those whom men value little and to those who serve. Now therefore, I bequeath to you in faith the promise of the Almighty God of Beth-El, given to me as I fled in fear from Canaan, passed on by me as I die in exile from my homeland. You shall be a great people and your children shall return to build the city of the vision of light, and all the world will find blessing because of the sons, the nation, of Israel. These things I see; and I also see that it is the will of God that the one whom he favours is the one who serves, the poor, the humble and the young. Therefore I put Ephraim before Manasseh, the younger before the elder; the second child before the first born son. This is God's way with the people he has chosen.' So Israel blessed the sons of Joseph, and in his action he declared God's will to give his blessing to the poor, the gentle, merciful and kind, throughout all ages to the end of time.

The Blessing of the Tribes (Gen. 49)

Israel called all his sons together and said, 'Assemble and hear me, sons of Israel; listen, that I may tell you what shall befall you in times to come'. Then he was filled with the Spirit, and spoke to his sons of the destiny of the tribes which would spring from them. This is what he said:

'Reuben, you are my first born, my might and the first fruits of my strength, pre-eminent in pride and power. Yet you are as turbulent as water and you shall not excel, because you slept with Bilhah my concubine and usurped my place. No king or prophet, priest or judge shall spring from you; your line shall disappear from Israel and your pride shall be brought low.

Simeon and Levi are brothers in violence; in their anger at Shechem they slew men and women and hamstrung the cattle of the city. I curse your anger, for it is fierce; your vengeance, for it is cruel. I will not join myself with your purposes; but you will be divided and scattered throughout the land.

Zebulun shall dwell by the sea, bordering on Phoenicia, and shall live by coastal trade.

Issachar shall be like a gelded ass lying amongst the cattle; he shall seek a pleasant home in the plains of Canaan and shall become a vassal to the Canaanites, submitting to their domination.

Dan shall achieve justice among his people as one of the tribes of Israel; a small tribe, surrounded by powerful enemies, he shall strike as a snake who bites the horse's foot and unseats its rider; thus he shall survive and overcome.

Lord God, we are a small and insignificant people; the great nations of the world surround us; help us to survive, deliver us from evil that we may praise your name in the land you have given us. We wait in hope for your salvation, Lord.

Gad shall be raided constantly by Bedouin tribes; but he shall raid them in return from the borders of the land.

Asher shall prosper; he shall have rich food as daily fare, and provide fine produce for the royal courts.

Naphtali shall be a spreading terebinth putting forth lovely boughs, fertile and free from restraint.

Joseph is a fruitful tree by a spring, its boughs spreading over the wall. The Canaanites will attack him savagely and press him hard. But they will be scattered by the Eternal; and his arms will be strengthened by the power of the mighty one of Jacob, by the name of the Shepherd, the Rock of Israel. Then the god of your father will help you; the almighty will bless you with all the blessings of fertility, the blessings of heaven above, the blessings of the waters below the earth, and the blessings of breast and womb. The blessings of your father, given in the power of God's spirit, are greater than the blessings of Egypt or Canaan, the blessing of Ra, god of the sun, or of the eternal mountains and everlasting hills. My blessings shall be upon the head of Joseph, on the brow of the Prince who was cursed by his brothers.

Benjamin shall be great in courage and might; like a ravenous wolf, he shall devour his prey in the morning and divide the spoils at night.

Judah, your brothers shall praise you and bow down before

you; your hand shall bring your enemies to submission; for, like a lion, you return from the kill and take your rest and no man dares to disturb you. The royal sceptre shall not depart from Judah, nor the ruler's staff from his descendants, until at last he comes to whom they rightfully belong, the Prince of Peace, to whom all nations shall come in obedience. He shall tie his foal to the vine tree and wash his clothes in wine, the blood of grapes. For he shall found a Kingdom of plenty and peace, where all things exist in abundance; his eyes shall sparkle like wine and his teeth will be whiter than milk; for with him the destiny of Israel will be brought to its fulfilment, and men will walk again in the lost garden of delight. This is what I foresee for the tribe of Judah, tribe of Kings.'

Thus their father spoke to the twelve tribes of Israel and blessed them each in turn, for good or ill, as the Spirit of God revealed to him, as in a misted mirror, the things that were to be.

The Death of Israel (Gen. 47, 49)

When Israel had blessed all his sons, he knew that he was about to die. His life was over, with all its interweaving of sorrow and of joy, of evil and of good. His had not been the firm and faithful following of Abraham, who walked unswervingly in God's way. Nor had it shown the hidden loyalty of Isaac his father, who remained quietly in the land of the promise, waiting for God's word. Out of the intensity of his passion, the man who had been Jacob had grasped at the promise of his god and defrauded his own brother of the divine birthright and blessing. The blessing became his; but in his hands it brought upon its bearer a sorrow and a destiny he could not have foreseen. The first sorrow it brought at once; it drove him from the one land he loved above all others, the homeland upon which all his dreams were set, to wander in a far country, an exile and a stranger. The second sorrow came on his return; Rachel, the one woman he loved with all the passion of his being, died on the road to Bethlehem. Nothing had ever consoled him for that loss, and even the land he had long dreamed of became mute and empty, a land of silent beauty that no longer moved his heart. Only in Joseph, so like his mother in character and grace, had he found some consolation;

and Joseph, too, had been taken from him by the envy of his brothers. Now, at the end of his life he had found Joseph again; but not without the last piercing sorrow of a death in exile, the fulfilment of the promise as remote as when he had begun.

He called Joseph to him: 'Place your hand upon my thigh', he said, 'and swear by the Lord that when I die you shall take me and bury me with my forefathers in the sepulchre in Hebron, with Abraham and Sarah, with Isaac and Rebecca and beside Leah my wife'. Joseph did as he asked and said, 'I swear'. Israel lay back upon his bed; now all was done that had to be done. He had been deceitful, cowardly, obstinate and foolish; that he could not undo. But he had held to the promise and bequeathed it to his sons. And as he gave his blessing to his sons, the patriarchs of Israel, he had been taken up into the Spirit and he had seen the future. He had seen his people spread throughout all the world, carrying the covenant and blessing of their god. He had seen the land of Canaan flourish and grow fertile under his people's care. He had seen the city of Abraham's dream stand like a citadel on a hill, its walls and towers strong and secure, with men from every nation making their way in pilgrimage, an endless throng of men of every race and speech. And in the city he had seen the throne of the King to come, born of the tribe of Judah, the King of righteousness and peace, the Lord of Israel. These things he saw; and worshipped God. Now there was one more thing he saw, a thing he could not understand, a thing he tried to turn from in dismay. Yet there was no turning away; his vision held him fast, even as he shrank from it. It was a thing more felt than seen, and the feeling penetrated all that he had seen, running through it like a cold wind in summer, searing all it touched. The feeling was the familiar sorrow that he had known all his life; but it was immeasurably more intense and deep; it was the sorrow of Israel and his children's children to the end of time; as if all the pain and sorrow in the world had been gathered into one, all griefs and agonies, all anger and despair, and placed upon the people of his vision. Theirs was the promise; and theirs the price of bearing it, until the time beyond this world's time when promise and reality are one and sorrow is finally transfigured into joy. That he could not see. The old man lay in the presence of his sons; they heard him cry three times, as if in grief,

'Israel, Israel, Israel'. Then vision passed into sight; he held out his hand for Joseph to take; softly he began to smile; and so he died.

Waiting (Gen. 50)

When his father had died, Joseph threw his arms around his father's neck and wept and kissed him. Then he ordered the court physicians to embalm him, and all the family of Israel and the Egyptian court mourned him for seventy days, only two days less than was ordained for the King himself. Joseph had to avoid the royal Court during the time of mourning, so he sent messengers to ask the King for permission to leave Egypt to bury his father. The King granted Joseph's request and sent with him many high Egyptian officials, his servants and the elders of his household, and a military escort of chariots and horsemen.

All the household of Joseph and his brothers went up to Canaan also; only their children and flocks were left in Goshen. So the great funeral procession left Egypt to make for Canaan. When they came to the threshing floor of Atad, they halted for seven days and mourned Israel with such great ceremony that the Canaanites were astonished, and named the place Abel-mizraim, the river of the mourning of Egypt. Then the twelve sons of Israel buried their father in the cave of Mach-pelah with his forefathers, as he had wished; and they returned to Egypt.

Now that their father was dead, Joseph's brothers were afraid that Joseph would punish them for the harm they had done him. So they sent a messenger to him, saying: 'Before he died, our father said to us, "Ask your brother Joseph to forgive you your crime and wickedness; for I know you did him harm". So now we ask you to forgive our crime; for we are servants of your father's god'. His brothers then came before him and bowed to the ground, saying, 'See, we are your slaves'. When Joseph heard his father's request and saw his brothers bow before him, he remembered his youthful dreams of the sheaves and the stars, and the long years of happiness in Hebron by his father's side, and he wept. After many years, and by unforeseen ways, the dreams had been fulfilled; now his brothers bowed down like the sheaves in the field and the stars in the sky; the end had returned to the beginning.

He said to them: 'Do not fear. Am I in the place of God? You meant to do me harm; but God meant it for good, to save the lives of many, as we see now. When you meant evil, God used it for good; your evil will has become part of the saving act of God. You are forgiven already, and it is not in my power to set that forgiveness aside.' So Joseph reassured his brothers; and he provided for them and their dependents during his lifetime.

The children of Israel remained in Egypt; and after many years, Joseph called his brothers to him and said:

'I am about to die; but God will not fail to come to you and take you from this land to the land which he promised to Abraham, Isaac and Jacob. Long ago he called our father Abraham out of his own country, on a journey towards an unknown place. He showed to him a land which he promised to his descendants, and bound himself by covenant on the night of the vision of fire. Twice at Beth-El, at the meeting of earth and heaven, the promise was renewed to Jacob, who became Israel and carried ever after in his body the visible memorial of his meeting with the nameless adversary at the river of the long night striving. Now, by God's unfathomable will, our people has been brought to Egypt; and here we must wait for the time of God's coming. For a while we must rest on our journey. We have obeyed the call of our god; we have seen the promise from afar; in faith we look forward to the founding of the Kingdom that our God will give in the way he wills. Now is perhaps the hardest time of all, the time of patient waiting. But God will surely come; and you must swear that you will bear my body with you, when God comes to you and calls you to begin again the journey to the Kingdom of the promise.'

Then Joseph, Viceroy of Egypt and son of Israel, died; his body was embalmed and laid in a coffin, made of wood and richly painted and inlaid, where it lay in state, for the people to see and honour the memory of their saviour. Time passed, and all his brothers and that whole generation died. Year by year, their children and their children's children visited the place where Joseph lay, to bow before his coffin and to remember the stories of the promise that their fathers told. Year by year they remembered Abraham, Isaac and Jacob and the desert god who bound them to himself; they remembered, and waited for their god to come again.

The Mountain

The Bondage of Israel (Exod. 1)

When the tribes of Israel had come into Egypt, they had come with the blessing of their god, who had promised to be with them, to make them into a great nation, and to bring them back again to the land of the promise. At first they had flourished, under the patronage of Joseph and the semitic Hyksos Kings, living and growing strong in the Nile delta. But then the princes of Thebes had broken the power of the Hyksos and driven them back to the Syrian border. They established the eighteenth dynasty of the Kings of Upper and Lower Egypt, and the country entered the age of its greatest prosperity and military success, the age of the New Kingdom. Egyptian armies, strengthened with the horses and swift chariots which the invading Hyksos had introduced, subdued all the territories surrounding Egypt from the Euphrates to the upper reaches of the Nile. Colossal temples, cities and monuments were built, rivalling and surpassing the grandeur and beauty of the ancient pyramids of the Old Kingdom. Trade and culture flourished, and Egypt, the old and indestructible, became again the dominant power in all the known world, the envy of all who saw her.

In all this revival of national pride and power, the name of Joseph, saviour of the people in the great famine, High Steward of the alien Hyksos Kings, was soon forgotten. The people of Israel, a band of nomadic foreigners living in privilege on fertile farming land near the border of Egypt, began to be feared and hated. As yet another dynasty came to power, and the Egyptians began to be troubled by military risings and attacks from the sea peoples, and from countries at the borders of their distant provinces, the King looked on the Israelites as a potential threat. They were very numerous, and could well join with a semitic invader to overrun Egypt, and become masters of the country, as the Hyksos had before them. So the King decreed that all the Israelites should be put to work in building the great cities and temples of the New Kingdom. They were organized into labour gangs, under foremen, and ordered to build the city of Pithom and the royal residence of Ramasses, in the delta. Gradually, their situation grew worse, as they were forced to work in the brick-yards and in the fields, and the Egyptian foremen began to treat them with callous brutality. Within one generation, the people of Israel became slaves, put to any sort of hard labour, as their Egyptian masters sought to break their spirit with cruel severity.

Although the Egyptians had forgotten Joseph, the Israelites had not. His embalmed body lay undisturbed in its coffin, and the people came to walk past it and revere it each year, remembering his dying words: 'God will surely come to you again; then you shall take my bones from this place'. As the years passed, their calm assured hope became more anguished and bewildered; but it never entirely disappeared. As the Israelite slaves of the nineteenth dynasty filed past the body of their lost leader, they repeated his words, each in his own way, silently in his own heart. Some were cynical, and the words were almost like a curse of bitterness; yet something made them come and return each year; perhaps the unthought wish that their anger would arouse God to act, if there were any god. Some were wistful, thinking of the freedom of the tents under the open sky in Canaan, and of their back-breaking slavery in the flat and featureless Egyptian delta; the words became a wish, a hope, a dream, a moment of illusion in the long sadness of daylight. Some, a few, were pious, clinging to God's promise to give them their own land and the greatness of their own people; but they were puzzled and more deeply shaken than they knew. They should have returned in glory to Canaan, laden with honours and riches; they had come in obedience to God's command, with his blessing, with his promise; they bore the marks of his covenant on their bodies; they were ready to rule the land he offered, to be a people wholly devoted to him, in their power and splendour showing his absolute sovereignty. Yet he had sent them to a strange land, and there they had become slaves; his people, his own chosen, were daily beaten and insulted, brutalized by mindless labour and ceaseless hardship. Their cry of hope and assurance became a cry of distress and sorrow, of tortured questioning, a cry from helplessness, from the deepest need of the oppressed and suffering. Where was their deliverance?

And more piercing still, why had they come to this state in which deliverance was so desperately pleaded for? Why had their god deserted them? Some continued to voice the old hopes, as though nothing had happened in Egypt. Some kept to the promises, but in their eyes was a new sadness and in their hearts a new anguish. Some said the words, without knowing what they meant; but hoping that there was hidden in their experience, for one who might some day see, the secret of the world's salvation from its own long slavery.

The Birth of Moses (Exod. 1, 2)

Though the Hebrews were oppressed in Egypt, they continued to grow in numbers, and the Egyptians began to blame them for the continued unrest and disorder in the conquered territories, and for the alleged decline in national prosperity; the King decided to enforce more drastic measures. He ordered the Hebrew midwives, whose names were Beauty and Splendour, to kill all male children born to their people, and to let only the daughters live. But the midwives feared God and kept his laws, and they refused to kill the male children. When the King demanded an explanation, they said, 'Hebrew women are not like Egyptian women; they are vigorous and quick in child birth, and the child is usually delivered before we arrive'. Because the midwives feared God, he gave them good fortune, and gave them healthy families of their own. The King saw that Hebrew women would not carry out his command, and so he issued an order to his own soldiers, that every Hebrew male child should be thrown into the Nile. A whole generation of the male descendants of Israel was slaughtered in infancy; the first of the host of innocent martyrs who died because of the unreasoning fear that the people of the covenant have aroused throughout their history. Weak, powerless, divided and oppressed, they indefectibly bear the hidden power of the promise, a power which arouses envy and fear and hatred, which all the powers of darkness have united to destroy, yet which can never be grasped by any enemy, which endures in the utmost extremes of weakness and sorrow.

So, at that first massacre of the children of Israel, the promise endured; for one child did not die. Jochabed, a descendant of Levi, bore a son by a husband of the same tribal lineage. He was a handsome child, and she hid him for three months, until his crying made it impossible to conceal him any longer. Then she made a small boat out of reeds and bulrushes, sealed it with tar and pitch, placed her baby in it, and floated it among the reeds by the edge of the Nile. The child floated on the wide waters, as Noah's great ship had floated over the flooded earth, and he bore with him, hidden and unseen, the hope of Israel's freedom and of the world's redemption.

By chance, or so it might have seemed, one of the daughters of the King came to bathe in the river, and saw the little basket floating among the reeds. She sent one of her maidservants to bring it to her; and when she opened it, she saw the baby inside, crying. She knew at once that this was a Hebrew child, and she knew her father's edict. But as she looked at the baby, she could not bear to think of him being thrown into the river to drown; yet he could not be returned to the Hebrews either. With sudden impulsiveness she said, 'I shall take this child as my own; he shall be my son'. Miriam, the child's sister, who had been standing by to see what happened to the basket, came to her and said, 'My lady, if your heart is moved to take this child and save him from death, shall I go to find a nurse for him from my own people, until he is weaned?' 'Do so', said the princess. So Miriam went and called her mother, who nursed her own child in safety for three years, until he was weaned. All that while, the princess paid her as a nurse; and then she took the child as her own son. She called him Moshe, Moses, because she said, 'I drew him out of the water'. That little child, born by water, cast adrift on the care of God, was already marked out to be the liberator of his people, the one who would herald the great deliverance of God.

The Death of an Egyptian (Exod. 2)

Moses was brought up in the harem of the palace of the King of Egypt, and taught all the wisdom of the Egyptians. He lived in luxury, was given everything that he wanted, and was treated as the princess' own son. One day, when he was a young man, he walked out of the palace on his own, and wandered into parts of the city which were strange to him. There he saw three things which were to change his life irrevocably. He saw hunger; people living in bare mud dwellings among open drains and rotting refuse. He saw sickness; people covered with running sores and flies, lying unattended in the streets. He saw old age; people wrinkled and bent, vacant eyes staring listlessly at the squalor around them. The Egyptians walked amongst the poverty and degradation of the Hebrews with contempt, striking and pushing them aside, urging the labour gangs to work with whips and coarse shouts. At first he was filled with distaste, that human beings should live like animals in the dirt. He was tempted to turn and leave the area as quickly as possible, to return to the civilized pleasures of the palace. But even as that thought crossed his mind, he was grasped by another. For these were his people; he was one of them; and only by chance was he other than they. All the years of ease he had lived were taken at the expense of these slaves; his riches were taken from their poverty. Worst of all, he should have stood where they now suffered and served; his fine court robes were a form of treachery, a betrayal of his blood.

He was walking out of the town into the desert, trying to cope with the violent emotions which flooded over him, when he saw a fourth thing, the most final and decisive of all; he saw death. What the Hebrew slave had done Moses did not know; probably some trivial offence or imagined insult; whatever it was hardly mattered. The slave screamed twice as the heavy staff of his Egyptian overseer smashed into his skull, and then he lay still. Moses looked around him; there was no one in sight; no one had seen the death but him; no one but he would ever know what had occurred. With sudden resolute fury he strode over to the Egyptian, who regarded him with mild perplexity, tore the staff from him and beat him savagely about the head. The Egyptian still looked surprised as he hit the ground, eyes staring, his lifeless body twisted awkwardly. Moses stood, trembling violently. He had killed an Egyptian, and even he would have to die for that, if he was discovered. But no one had seen him; he looked around; the desert was silent, the few scattered mud houses at the outskirts of the city were shuttered against the heat and flies; no one moved.

Quickly Moses scraped a shallow depression in the sand, pulled the body into it, and piled sand over it, scraping desperately with his bare hands. Then he turned and made his way quickly back to the palace.

The next day he determined to find out more about the Hebrews and the conditions under which they lived. He walked into the slave quarter, and observed all that he saw carefully. As he walked through a narrow street, he saw two Hebrews fighting together, watched by a listless group of people who did nothing to intervene. He walked over to them, and called out, 'Why do you fight each other? There are greater things to be done, if you would first unite together'. The two men pulled apart and looked at him with barely concealed dislike; then the one who had begun the quarrel said: 'We know who you are; you live in luxury in the King's palace, and think you can right our wrongs with a word. But who made you a prince and a judge over us? Perhaps you mean to kill me as you killed the Egyptian?' Moses looked at him for a moment in dismay; then he hurried on without a word. What he had done had been observed, after all, and now it was public knowledge. With the King's network of informers, it would not be long before Moses was apprehended and brought to account. There was no going back on what he had done. He stayed at the palace only long enough to collect a few things necessary for survival. His impetuous attempt to help the Hebrew slaves had ended quickly, in violence and failure. Now he rode out of the city of the King into the wilderness of the desert alone, himself a fugitive, seeking perhaps to find the hidden savage god of his own forefathers among the bare rocks and the burning sun, where the long search for the promise had begun.

The Years in the Wilderness (Exod. 2)

For many years, Moses lived in the wilderness of the Arabian desert, moving from oasis to oasis, a solitary figure in an empty landscape, living on what he could find or take by force. At such an oasis, as he was resting in the shade, he saw seven women bringing a flock of sheep to the well. They drew water and poured it into troughs for the sheep. But before the sheep could drink, a group of shepherds, laughing and cursing, thrust the women aside and led their own sheep to the troughs. The women protested, but it was clear that this was a common occurrence; the women had to wait at one side until the others had taken what they wanted, and be content with anything that was left. Perhaps because he was bored, or perhaps because such discourtesy still offended his courtly upbringing, Moses decided to intervene. He rose from the shadows and walked slowly over to the well. 'Let the women be', he said softly but deliberately. The shepherds looked at the stranger in some surprise, and then dismissed him with a threatening gesture. With a swift movement, Moses unsheathed his long curved knife; it flashed in the sun as he swept it in a wide arc through the air, barely flicking the throat of the nearest shepherd; then rested, poised, at his waist. The shepherd fingered his throat with alarm, then with relief, as he felt no blood flow. Moses did not need to say anything further; the shepherds returned with their flock to the shaded palms, and Moses signalled to the women to continue watering their sheep.

When they returned to their father, he was surprised that they came so much more quickly than usual. They explained that an Egyptian had driven off the shepherds and helped them to draw water and fill the troughs. 'What is the man?', he said, 'Why have you left him? Go and invite him to share a meal with us'. So Moses met Jethro, the priest of the tribe of Midian, which was descended from Abram by his second wife Keturah, but which was not covenanted to El-Shaddai, as the descendants of Isaac and Jacob had been. Thereafter he agreed to stay with him and look after his sheep. Moses married one of the priest's daughters, Zipporah; in time they had a son, and he lived for some years in the desert with the Midianites.

But all the time Moses was seeking to know more of the god of his forefathers, and of the covenant and the promise which he had made before the days of slavery. He had learned in his youth the mysteries of the great gods of Egypt — Amun, the hidden one; Ra, god of the sun; Isis and Osiris, gods of death and the renewal of life; Horus the hawk-god of the dynastic Kings. These and a host of other gods he had learned of, and participated in their rites. He had come to share in the long spiritual tradition of the great and ancient culture of Egypt, to feel its brooding concern with death, the rhythm of a life measured by the rise and fall of the Nile, the treasured memory of long dead heroes, the short and brilliant splendour of a civilization hewn out of a hostile desert, borne by the sun, the life giver and burning enemy. As he worshipped the gods of the cities and the elements, he entered inwardly into the heart of the people, their values and ideals, their vision of the encircling reality which bore them, their inexpressible relation to the powers of fulfilment and destruction, their understanding of human life, its limits and capacities, their grasp of existence, its beginning and its end.

Yet even as he understood, he felt a sense of alienation and emptiness. The ancient gods had lost their power to unfold the startling vision, to challenge, to set the pattern of life, to give new life. Their vitality and mystery had flourished long ago, in the Old Kingdom, and was etched in the brutal simplicity of the early pyramids, stating with stark clarity man's meeting with the elemental forces of his being. Now they were lifeless; their stories stereotyped and well-defined, their rites preserved by a wealthy priesthood in monumental temples which grew more featureless and blank the larger and more magnificent they appeared. The one ill-fated attempt of Akhenaton to renew religion had failed and been obliterated completely by the re-instating of a State religion with pomp but without life and force. The old gods of Egypt were already dead at the height of the nation's military power; only the empty rituals, the gaudy idols, the tombs glorifying men more than gods, remained.

In the desert wilderness, Moses was nearer to the god of his own people, a god who lived though he seemed lost, silent and unmoving. From escaping slaves and from the warrior nomads of the desert he learned of El-Shaddai, the all-powerful god of the mountains, the god who had appeared to Abraham in fire, who had showed Jacob the gateway to heaven, who had made the children of Israel his own. That was the god he sought, sometimes talking with Jethro, the priest of the Midianites, who knew of the mountain god and the tribes who followed him; more often alone among the mountains, pondering the mystery of the silence of the god of power, seeking to understand the meaning of his choosing and of his will for his people, seemingly abandoned and enslaved. For all that one could tell, Moses was a shepherd, living simply with his family among the warrior nomads of Midian. Inwardly, his mind and will was concentrated with intense simplicity of purpose. As an arrow speeds towards its target, so Moses aimed for God. Although he could not know it, the end of his search was to be a sequence of actions which would change the history of the entire world.

The Sacred Mountain (Exod. 3)

As he led the flock of Jethro, his father in law, through the desert lands, seeking for sparse scrub and yellowed grass among the cracked rocks and gullies, Moses would often journey to the sacred mountain, at the western side of the great wilderness. The mountain rose sheer from the plain, a solitary, brutal pyramid of sheer rock, higher than any peak in the distant ranges of hills and yet completely alone, as if thrust out of the earth by some gigantic force below. Indeed, that force was not yet dead; deep rumblings, heavy with menace, were often heard by those who ventured on the mountain slopes; and often the ground would move and quiver, dislodging great boulders or cascades of stones and dirt into vast cravasses far below. Those who walked in the wilderness regarded the mountain with awe and dread; somehow the massive solidity of its towering precipices came to stand for ageless strength and unchanging security; more than that, in a way that no words could explain, it was itself, in its inner being, the ageless and immoveable, standing impassive before a thousand births and deaths beneath its long shadow. In its fearful tremors and its deep hidden thundering, it was like the capricious, unpredictable power of fate, which caught man at his least prepared moment and threw him into a world out of his wish or will. In the heat of the day as it brooded over the wide plain, stunted trees and desert scrub grew in its shade; and in the evening, as the high rocks glowed red before the descending sun, it was a burning beacon, closing each day with a last prayer to the encircling sky. Many were the stories that were told of the magic mountain, whose summit was the last meeting of earth and sky, on whose slopes even the birds and quick creeping animals were omens of fortune, good or bad, from whose topmost peak one could see the whole earth, and perhaps more beyond, which no man could tell.

Moses felt the power of the great mountain; he sensed the presence of a spirit there, harsh and austere like the desert itself, remote and yet not wholly indifferent to the living things that crawled around its boundaries. For generations, the Midianites had offered sacrifices to Horeb, the Great Mountain. It was their most sacred sanctuary, where innumerable prayers had been heard and the lives and desires of men had been offered and consecrated. When he was alone, and the sheep safely gathered, Moses liked to climb to a special place he had made his own, a high outcrop of rock on the westward face of the mountain, looking out from the wilderness towards the green borders of the sea in the far distance, where the sun set in a flame of orange and red. There he would sit while the world turned to black, and the moon etched the mountain into a pale and spectral sail against the sky. There he would seek to enter into the heart of the mountain's being, to merge himself with it, to penetrate beyond it to the hidden centre of its life and power, where he and the mountain were one and yet each impenetrably alone. At dawn he would return, and become again the shepherd leading his small flock, having sometimes touched the mystery of the mountain's being but never having broken through to the union that he desired beyond the boundaries of self.

Until one cold spring morning, when the scrub under his feet was wet with mountain dew and the early sun sent shadows leaping across the rocks and shafts of white light driving over the lower rifts. As he came down the rocky slope towards the gully where he had left the sheep, penned in with a screen of brushwood, he saw something which made him stand suddenly still and look closely with surprised delight. Above and to his right, on a small levelled plateau, was a single thorn bush, its jagged branches outlined starkly against the dawn sky. With the rising sun behind it, it seemed to be on fire, burning in a bright flame of light, yet without being burned away. As he looked, admiring its unique beauty, he realized that the flame was not just the light of the sun;

it was a fire which seemed to spring from the bush itself, which throbbed and scintillated, formed into a shape he could not quite catch and then dissolved again into the purity of flame. Amazed, he began to scramble towards the bush, to try to make out more clearly what it was. As he did so, he suddenly heard his name called quietly and clearly: 'Moses, Moses'. It was not really called; for he knew perfectly well that voice had not come from anywhere in the rocks around him. Yet he had been called by name, by a voice that was not a voice, and he heard it without hearing anything. 'Yes; here I am', he said fearfully in his heart, without knowing what to expect, or whether he was perhaps going mad – though it was not the heat of the day, the time of hallucination, and he felt healthy and in possession of his senses. For a while there were no words; instead, his whole being was flooded with powerful and intense feelings unlike any he had experienced before. Terror and desire, absolute incomprehensibility and the clear illumination of perfect rationality, the inflexible demand for obedience and the total acceptance of his human weakness – all these interwove together and left him humbled and bewildered before the felt presence of a reality infinitely and ineffably greater than himself. Instinctively, he bent to remove his sandals and covered his face with his hands, kneeling on the ground. This was sacred ground, a place of danger and disclosure; here the god of the sacred mountain had recognized by name the one who sought it. In fear before its terrifying menace, Moses waited for what now must come for good or ill, from this morning meeting by the burning bush of thorns, the tree of life and death, and the undying fire which enclosed its heart in impenetrable mystery.

The Name of God (Exod. 3; cf. 6)

As Moses knelt before the tree of fire on the mountain of God at the west side of the wilderness, the almighty god touched his mind with creative power, and thoughts formed themselves without effort or concentration; words that he could never afterwards forget, that remained indelible in his consciousness; words that possessed a beauty and power which he could not have imagined; which moved strong men who heard them in later years to tears; which carried within themselves a meaning for those who could understand, which was uniquely personal and totally beyond all possibility of expression. These were the words of the creator god, hidden in the words of men, confronting each human soul with the final mystery of its being and the challenge of its eternal destiny. This is the remembrance of the words of God to Moses, though written imperfectly and in another tongue:

'I am the Lord, the god of your father, of Abraham, of Isaac and of Jacob. With them I established my covenant, to give them the land of Canaan, the land in which they lived as strangers and travellers in their own time. Now I have seen my people who are in Egypt, and their affliction; now I have heard their cry for help in their distress; their cries under their bondage have come before me, and I know their condition; I myself have shared in their sufferings. I have not put my covenant out of mind, but I have remembered it, as I always will remember. I am the Lord; and I will come down to deliver my people out of the hand of the Egyptians, to free them from their bondage, and to bring them up out of that land to a good and broad land, a land flowing with milk and honey, which I will give to them to possess as their own, as I swore to Abraham, to Isaac and to Jacob. I am the Lord; I will redeem my people with an outstretched arm and place them beneath the shadow of my wings; I will come in mercy and in judgement, mercy to those who hear and judgement for those whose hearts refuse my call. I will take them for my own people, and I will be their god; and they shall know that I am the Lord their god for ever, who has brought them out by judgement from the power and rule of Egypt. I am the Lord.'

As the words imprinted themselves in Moses' mind, he heard them with silent wonder. At last the god whom he had long sought had spoken, and spoken unmistakeably about the liberation of the Hebrews, a task which had always seemed so hopeless and impossible to Moses when he had thought about it since his flight from Egypt. Yet now God himself had said that he would do it; surely all things were possible for God. But Moses could not stop the question from arising in his mind, however impious it might seem — how would it be accomplished, and by whom?

As the question arose, so it was answered, as clearly as anything that had yet been said: 'I will send you to the King, that you may bring out my people, the sons of Israel, from Egypt'.

'Who am I, that I should go to the King and bring the sons of Israel out of Egypt?' asked Moses, in astonishment.

God said, 'I will be with you; and this shall be the sign for you, that I have sent you: the elders of Israel will listen to your words, and the King will let my people go, and you shall bring them here and worship me on this mountain'.

Then Moses said, 'If I go to the people of Israel and say to them, "The god of your fathers has sent me to you", and they ask me, "What is his name?", what shall I say to them?' Moses knew now that the god who had made himself so clearly known to him was not the mountain god of the Midianites; he was the god of the fathers of Israel, who had declared his will to redeem this people from their captivity. But what was the nature of his inmost being? What was the secret and centre of his nature, that would be captured and expressed by the disclosure of his unique name? Would the god of the tree of fire reveal to man the final mystery of his inwardness? Moses waited, fearing the audacity of his own question, and yet driven to ask by the intensity of his desire to know this god as fully as possible, even if the knowledge destroyed him.

Then God said, '*Ehyeh aser ehyeh*; I am that which I am; I will be what I will be. That which I am, I will be; and that which I will be, I am. I was known to Abraham, Isaac and Jacob as El-Shaddai, the almighty god; now I give you my true name. You must go to the elders of Israel and say, "I am" has sent me. This is my name for ever; by this name, Jahweh, He Who Is and Will Be, I am to be remembered in every generation.'

It could not be said that Moses understood the words he heard, though he remembered them exactly to the day of his death. To comprehend fully the name of God would be to comprehend God himself, the one who absolutely is. He alone, of all things, exists by his own power, dependent on no other, without beginning or end, ingenerable and incorruptible. He alone determines solely all that he will be, and remains unchangeably the same in all that he becomes by his own will. He alone is ceaselessly and wholly active, upholding all things by his creative presence at every place and at all times. He is the god who disclosed himself before the tree of fire, in his most inward name, to the shepherd prince who knelt before him, silent before the mystery he knew but could not comprehend.

The Reluctant Prophet (Exod. 4)

Moses heard the name of God; a name infinitely far from any god of mountain or storm; infinitely beyond the god of any tribe or city; infinitely above any possibility of imagination or representation in human terms. He heard and was afraid. 'They will never believe me or listen to me', he said; 'They will say, "Who could know such a god and live? The god whom you name, 'The One Who Is'; such a god has not spoken to you or shown himself to you".

God said, 'What do you hold in your hand?'.

'My shepherd's staff', said Moses.

God said, 'Throw it on the ground'. Moses threw it down; and as it touched the ground there lay, not a shepherd's staff, but a snake, hissing and writhing among the rocks of the sacred mountain. Moses jumped to his feet in alarm; the twisting shape raised in his mind all the ancient fears of man for his age-long enemy. Confused and forgotten images ran darkly in his thoughts; the image of the great dragon of the deep, from whose torn agony the world was formed and ordered in the primeval times; the image of the serpent in the garden of bliss, symbol of the world's wisdom and cunning, denying death, urging towards the knowledge which is power, the desire for mastery of one's destiny; the image of the crippled beast, condemned to crawl in the dust, locked in conflict with men for ever, cunning and venomous still, in its heart dark hatred for all the children of Eve. But the voice of God said, 'Put out your hand and seize it by the tail'. Fearfully, Moses stretched out towards the slow-moving coils and took hold of the tail. At once, as he gripped it, it became again his firm familiar staff, symbol of his shepherd's care, the care of one who leads and protects his flock, keeps them from harm, watching by day and night for their well-being.

'This is a sign', said God, 'for the elders of Israel, that the god of their fathers, of Abraham, Isaac and Jacob has appeared to you and that my name is Jahweh, as I have declared. I will give you two other signs and they will understand and believe you. Put your hand inside the fold of your cloak.' Moses did so; and when he withdrew it, the skin was scarred and diseased, white like snow. God said, 'Put it back again', and he did so. When he took it out, it was completely healed, as healthy as the rest of his body. 'The third sign is this', said the Lord, 'If you take water from the Nile and pour it out on the dry earth, that water will turn to blood on the ground'.

Moses understood that these three signs were not simply magic tricks, but that they were signs of the nature and being of God himself, and of his purpose for his people. The mysteriously ambivalent sign of the serpent enemy which was also the staff of leadership and love, expressed the nature of the One who forms the light and creates darkness, who makes peace and creates evil; and of the world where good and evil, the pride of cunning and the humility of wisdom, intertwine and create out of their conflict the life beyond harm which is only won through death. The sign of the healed hand expressed the divine will to make whole all that is hurt or harmed in all creation; even the leper, the one who is beyond human contact, the unclean and untouchable, is renewed by God's power. The sign of the water turned to blood expressed God's purpose to liberate his people through the shedding of blood, through a destruction and judgement which is also the offering of love and the washing of the soul with the water of life and the blood of sacrifice. Yet Moses, knowing all this, said: 'Lord, I have never been an eloquent man, never in my life, and not even now that you have spoken to me; I am slow and hesitant of speech; how will the people listen to me?'

God said to him: 'Who is it that gives man speech? Who makes him dumb or deaf, seeing or blind? Is it not I, Jahweh? Now therefore go, and I will be with your words and tell you what you are to say'.

But Moses still hesitated. 'Lord', he said, 'send someone else to do your will'. The fire flared in the bush, until Moses felt that its heat would overcome him; a spasm of fear ran through his body, as if he were faced by an angry and implacable enemy. He flung himself to the ground in submission, and accepted at last that it was the will of God to send him and no other, to liberate his people. The voice returned, a final time: 'I will send to you Aaron the Levite, your brother; he is an orator, and he will speak for you. You shall tell him what to say, as I command you; and he shall speak to the people and do as you tell him. Now go, return to Egypt and to your own people; for the King who sought to kill you is dead.' For a long while there was silence; then Moses looked up. The fire was gone; the tree of thorns stood, dark and alone; night had fallen; a whole day had passed, while Moses had been found by the god he had so long sought. He picked up his staff, wrapped his cloak tightly against the evening chill, and walked down the mountain slope to the place where his little flock waited.

The Circumcision (Exod. 4)

Moses waited by the mountain of God until Aaron the Levite his elder brother, came to him, as God had promised. It was the first time the brothers had met, though each had known of the other by frequent report. Aaron was led into the wilderness by God; hearing the command to evade the ever vigilant overseers, to go alone into the empty wilderness and to meet the brother he had never seen, he did not hesitate, but obeyed at once. He travelled to the sacred mountain, directed by Midianite tribesmen along the way; there he found his brother and embraced him gladly. Moses told him all the words of God and showed the three signs. Aaron understood at once that this was the god of his fathers, who had revealed himself by his true name to Moses. He knelt and kissed his brother's hand; and Moses laid his hands on Aaron's head and commissioned him to speak the words and perform the signs of Jahweh before the elders of Israel. Moses obtained the blessing of Jethro his father in law for his return to Egypt, and they took his wife and his sons and set out for Egypt.

While they were on the way, at a desolate place where they camped for the night, Moses was overwhelmed by a delirious fever as he slept. He thought of the splendour of the Egyptian Court where he had been reared, and of the power of the imperial Egyptian army; he thought of his solitary vision on the mountain, and of the impossible task that God had given him to conquer all the might of Egypt and deliver the children of Israel from slavery virtually single handed. He thought of the first man he had killed and his flight into the desert. He thought of his weakness and the absurdity of what he had to say to the King. Yet the burning bush flamed in his mind and bound him to do the absurd and impossible, in the name of his god. Perspiration soaked his body and he cried out and groaned as he tried to come to terms with the task laid upon him.

Zipporah his wife heard him cry out and thought that he was on the point of death. As she heard him cry out, 'Yahweh', she discerned that he was locked in inner struggle with his god and thought that Jahweh meant to kill her husband. She remembered that Gershom, their first son, was uncircumcised, for the Midianites did not circumcise their children in infancy; and she knew that circumcision was the sign of God's covenant with the sons of Abraham. She took a sharp flint, cut off her son's foreskin and touched Moses with it. 'As I was a bride of blood on our wedding night, so now you are a husband of blood to me, by the circumcision of our son', she said; 'Now the law of God is kept, and we are bound to him forever'. This is how the ritual expression, 'You are a husband of blood' arose, once used at the time of circumcision among some tribal groups. By morning the fever had left Moses; he was prepared for what lay before him in Egypt and beyond; and he and Zipporah bound themselves to obey the voice of God and follow his way forever. With Aaron and their children, they crossed the wilderness to seek the deliverance of Israel.

The First Encounter with the King (Exod. 5)

When Moses and Aaron came to Egypt, Aaron gathered together the elders of the people, the tribal chiefs. He repeated to them the words of Jahweh and showed them the sacred signs. When they heard and saw him, the people believed that Jahweh the god of their fathers had seen their affliction and that he had come among them to deliver them; and they bowed their heads and worshipped. Then Moses and Aaron and the elders of Israel sought an audience with the King. They said to him: 'Jahweh, the god of the Hebrews, has appeared to us, and commanded us to go towards a mountain which is sacred to him, three days' journey into the wilderness; and offer sacrifice to him there, your servants and all the children of Israel.'

But the King said, 'Who is this Jahweh, that I should listen to him and let Israel go? Amun I know, and Horus and Set, and all the gods of Egypt, ancient and powerful. But I do not know of Jahweh, and I will not let Israel go at his command.' When the Israelites persisted, he became angry and said, 'You Hebrews are a lazy people, and you are only seeking an excuse to escape from your work; you may be sure that I will not let you go'. He called the overseers of the people to him and said, 'These Hebrews are idle and growing arrogant; they even want to disappear into the wilderness and offer a sacrifice to their barbarian god. You shall ensure that they work harder, so that they have no time to listen to the fairy tales of this Moses and Aaron. You shall no longer provide them with straw to make bricks; they must gather their own straw. But you shall ensure that they produce the same number of bricks as before; that will cure their idleness'.

The King dismissed Moses and Aaron and the elders of Israel, and the people were compelled to gather stubble and straw, in addition to their normal work. When they failed, the Hebrew foremen were beaten and asked, 'Why have you not completed your daily quota of bricks, as usual?' After some weeks, they sought audience with the King and said, 'Why do you treat us like this? You command us to produce the same number of bricks as before, yet you give us no straw; your servants are beaten, yet the fault is in your own people'. But the King said, 'You are idle; you are idle; that is why you say, "Let us go and sacrifice to our god". Return to your work. No straw shall be given to you, yet you shall make bricks as before'. As they left the presence of the King, the foremen of the people of Israel met Moses and Aaron, who were waiting for them, and they said, 'May God look upon you and judge, because you have made us offensive to the King and his servants, and have put a weapon into his hands with which he means to kill us. Because of you, we are in greater distress than ever; it does not seem that we can survive'.

Moses turned again to God and said, 'Lord Jahweh, why have

you brought evil upon this people? Why did you ever send me to them? For since I came to the King to speak in your name, he has brought misfortune on your people, and you have done nothing to rescue them; now their condition is worse than it was'.

Then God spoke to Moses and said, 'I am Jahweh; I will release you from slavery in Egypt and lead you to the land of promise; you will be my people, my first born son and I will be your god. Return to the King and tell him to set the Israelites free. But I know the heart of the King; he has refused you and he will refuse again. Yet do not lose faith. For now you shall see what I will do to the King. I will harden his heart, which is turned against my people, so that he will not let my people go, whatever happens. Then I will show my power in Egypt, sign after sign and portent after portent. At last I will release the King from my power, and leave him to his fear. And in the end, he will let my people go; he will drive them from Egypt in his terror and anger. So I will bring the tribal host of Israel out of Egypt, by mighty acts of judgement; and Egypt shall know that I am the Lord.' Moses bowed before the words of God and worshipped; he went to the Israelites and told them what God had said; but this time they did not listen to him, for they were broken and discouraged by the King's decrees. Moses and Aaron were left alone, to take the commands of their god to the King.

The Ten Plagues Begin (Exod. 7)

Moses and Aaron came before the King a second time, and said, 'You must let my people, the children of Israel, go out of Egypt; it is the command of God; we have a sign to assure you that it is so'.

'Moses, you are an obstinate man' said the King; 'It is only because you are a child of the royal harem that I hear you at all. You can only make things worse for these slaves, whom you call your people. As for this fairy tale about a god whose name I cannot even pronounce, you should know better than to invent it. But let me see this sign you speak of.' Aaron threw Moses' staff on the ground, and there was the dark serpent, hissing and writhing before the throne. The watching courtiers drew back in alarm; Aaron bent down and put out his hand and held up the harmless shepherd's staff.

But the King merely said, 'This is a trick I have seen before; I am disappointed in your god, Moses, if he can do no better than that'. With that, he summoned the magicians and sorcerers of the Egyptian Court, and told them what Aaron had done. They consulted among themselves and arranged a time when they would confront Moses and Aaron before the King.

The time came; Moses and Aaron stood on the left of the throne, and the magicians on the right. The throne room was filled with braziers of incense and rows of candles, the noise of chanting and the beating of drums. The King and his courtiers drank wine and watched the tumbling of acrobats and dancers until the magicians were ready to begin. Then a great gong sounded; the chief magician solemnly stepped forward and called out, 'Moses and Aaron, throw down your magic staff'. They did so; and the serpent lay, as before, on the floor between them.

'Now', said the magician, 'By the power of the gods of Egypt, we shall show a greater sign'. He flourished his arm dramatically, and Moses saw that he held a wooden rod. He gestured again, and a second magician stepped forward, also holding an outstretched rod in his hand. As the gong sounded again, they threw them to the ground and immediately the rods were transformed into snakes. The courtiers applauded loudly. Moses guessed that this must have been a trick, that the rods had been snakes all the time, somehow made rigid in the magicians' hands; but it had worked and the courtiers were impressed. The King laughed, and the magicians smiled arrogantly at Moses and Aaron. Suddenly, the laughter stopped. To the amazement of all who saw, the serpent of Aaron attacked and ate the other two snakes, before Aaron could take it into his hand. Then the King laughed again, 'Moses, your snake has not been well enough fed', he said, 'This is enough of these petty tricks; you have seen that our magicians have all your powers. Go and tell the Hebrews that they will never be free. Go; you are dismissed.'

That night, as Moses prayed, God told him what he must do. The next morning, the King went to the river to make a libation to the great god of the Nile; for it was the time of the inundation, when the rains came to the far mountains of the South, where the Nile began, and flooded the river, so that it brought life and fertility to the lower valleys. Moses and Aaron met him on his way to the river; and Aaron said,

'Jahweh the god of the Hebrews sent me to tell you to let his people go to worship him in the wilderness. Twice you have refused; so now Jahweh says, "By this you shall know the power of Jahweh. I will change the waters of the Nile into blood. The fish will die and the river will be polluted, and you will be unable to drink water from the Nile. The river which brings you life will bring you death".' He stretched out Moses' staff over the water, and even as he spoke, the waters began to turn first muddy brown and then red, the colour of blood. The King gestured to his magicians, who were with him to celebrate the festival of the river flood, and they said: 'This is nothing new, my lord King. Each year the great Nile turns to red at this time; it is the work of the ancient gods who watch over Egypt, and it brings life, not death. We, too, have the power of turning water to blood by our occult arts, and this we can show you.'

So the King did not listen to Aaron and Moses, but turned away and went into the palace, dismissing the whole matter from his mind. But the floods that year were greater than they had ever been; the red earth which was brought down from the far mountains was coarse and acid; all the fish died and rotted; the river stank and the people had to dig for drinking water around the river banks. The King's magicians were able to turn water to blood, with chemical potions they possessed; but they could not purify the waters of the Nile, and what God had foretold through Aaron came about. This was the first sign of God's power in Egypt, with which he began to bring his people out of their long bondage.

Plagues by Water and Earth (Exod. 8)

For seven days, the river Nile ran red; the waters of life and prosperity brought death and ruin to Egypt. Then Moses and Aaron went before the King again and Aaron said to him:

'These are the words of Jahweh: "Let my people go, so that they may worship me. If you refuse, I will plague your country with frogs. The Nile shall swarm with them and they shall come into your houses, your kitchens and your bedrooms, until the whole country is infested with them; this I, Jahweh, shall do".' But the King would not listen to them; so on the eighth day, Aaron held out the staff over the Nile; and on that day, the plague of frogs began. Driven from the river by the rotten and decaying fish, millions of frogs flooded over the countryside, into houses and market places, covering everything with squashy slimy bodies, uncountable hordes of obscenely flopping reptiles, more than had ever been known. In alarm, the King called his magicians, and they said, 'O Lord King, the frog is a symbol of fruitfulness, and of the renewal of life; it is not to be feared. We too can conjure frogs from the water by our occult arts'. The magicians showed the King how they could draw frogs up from the water, by skills which had been handed down from time immemorial. But they could not conjure the horde of frogs back to the Nile; the frogs continued to overrun the land. The King called Moses and Aaron and said,

'These reptiles are a continual irritation; if your god called them from the river, pray to him and ask him to send them away, and I will let the people go to sacrifice to him'.

Moses knew that the King did not mean what he said, but he took him at his word: 'Tell me when I am to pray for the frogs to be destroyed, that you may know there is no one like Jahweh our God'.

The King said, 'Tomorrow'. So Moses and Aaron prayed to God the next day; and on that day the frogs began to die in their thousands, until there was not one of them left. There were so many that they had to be gathered into heaps, and the countryside stank with the smell of them. This was the second sign of God's power in the land of Egypt. When the King saw that the frogs were all gone, he said, 'This was no more than an inconvenience; now it is over.' So he hardened his heart, and ignored his lightly given promise to Moses and Aaron.

As Moses prayed that night, God told him what he must do. Moses told Aaron to take his staff and strike the dust of the ground; and as Aaron did so, maggots began to reproduce in the corpses of the fish and the frogs and to spread throughout the country, until they were everywhere, both on man and beast. The King's magicians tried to produce maggots by their spells, but this time they failed. 'It is the finger of their god', they said to the King, 'He brought plagues by water, and now he brings plagues from the dust of the ground; only the greatest of gods can bring life from dust; this is his work'. This was the third sign of God's power, shown in Egypt. But the King ignored the words of his magicians and dismissed them from his presence.

God told Moses to meet the King once again by the river, and say to him: 'These are the words of Jahweh: "Let my people go, so that they may worship me. If you will not, I will plague your country with swarms of flies. But I will set apart the land of Goshen, where my people live, and there shall be no swarms of flies there. So you will know that I, Jahweh, am here in Egypt, and that I distinguish between my people and yours".' When the King refused Moses, swarms of flies rose from the ground, from the stagnant waters left by the Nile floods, and infested the whole country of Egypt, threatening the land with ruin and disease; but Goshen remained free of the plague.

The King sent for Moses and Aaron and said, 'You may sacrifice to your god; but it must be in this country'.

'We cannot do that', said Moses, 'Because we must sacrifice cows and bullocks to Jahweh, and such a sacrifice is offensive to the Egyptians, who offer only fruit to the gods. If they see us sacrificing a cow, after the manner of our fathers, they will surely rise up in anger and stone us to death. So we must go a three days' journey into the wilderness to sacrifice to Jahweh, as he commands us'.

'I will let you go', said the King, 'And you shall sacrifice to your god in the wilderness; but do not go far, for I fear that you may not return. Now pray for me, to end this plague.'

Moses said, 'I will pray to Jahweh this very day and tomorrow the swarms of flies will depart. But', he said, and a new note of warning came into his voice, 'do not trifle any more with the people by preventing them from going to sacrifice to Jahweh.' So he left the King and prayed to Jahweh; by the next evening not one swarm was left. This was the fourth sign that God showed in Egypt. But the King's heart was hardened; 'These are just extraordinary coincidences', he said; and he did not let the people go. However, the mighty acts of God had hardly begun; the time was soon to come when the King would drive out the Israelites in desperate fear.

Plagues by Air and Fire (Exod. 9)

Moses and Aaron went to the King and said, 'These are the words of Jahweh, the god of the Hebrews: "Let my people go, so that they may worship me". If you refuse to let them go, disease will strike all the horses and asses, cattle and sheep that are in your fields. But Jahweh will make a distinction between his people and your people; not a single animal which belongs to the children of Israel will die. Tomorrow is the time he appoints, if you do not hear his command.' But the King sent Moses and Aaron away; and the next day disease struck the herds of Egypt. Where the maggots and flies had infested the food stocks and the animals' quarters, animals began to fall sick and die. Only in Goshen, away from the river, where the flies had not swarmed, covering everything with dirt and filth, the disease did not strike at all. The King sent to enquire, and was told that not one animal belonging to Israelites had died; yet he brushed this aside, and hardened his heart, and did not let the people go. This was the fifth sign of God in Egypt.

Again Moses and Aaron went to the King; Moses took handfuls of ashes from the brick furnaces, where the Israelites worked to make bricks, and threw them into the air in front of the King. 'Jahweh, the god of slaves, has brought disease and death to your cattle. Be warned, therefore, when he brings disease to you also, and obey his command before it is too late. By this dust of our labour, scattered into the air, he will show his judgement upon your injustice and oppression.'

They turned and strode from the court; and throughout the land of Egypt men as well as animals began to be covered in sores, boils and festering irruptions of the skin. Even the magicians of the royal court were attacked with sores, and there was nothing they could do to prevent the spread of the plague. But the King still did not listen to Moses and Aaron. This was the sixth sign God showed in Egypt.

So they went to the King yet again, early in the morning, and said: 'Jahweh, the god of the oppressed, has shown you mercy up to now. The signs he has shown have left you alive, when he could have wiped you from the face of the earth with disease or disaster, many times. He has brought plagues upon you by water, by the dust of the earth, and by air; and you have remained unmoved and will not let Israel go. Now he will bring upon you the sign of fire, flashing from the sky to bring death to all who are in the fields, both men and animals. Now you will know that there is no god in all the world like Jahweh; he will openly show his power in Egypt, so that his name will live and be known throughout the whole earth. Tomorrow, at about this time, a storm shall strike Egypt such as there has never been from the foundation of the first Kingdom until now; with lightning, thunder and hail. Send now and get all your surviving herds under cover; for if anything, man or beast, is not under cover when the storm of Jahweh strikes, that thing will die.' There were those in the court of the King who now believed Moses and feared the words of Jahweh that he brought; they hurried to get their cattle and slaves into their houses. But those who did not take to heart these words left their slaves and cattle out in the fields.

The next day the storms from the high mountain regions of the south, which had caused the Nile to flood and brought the long chain of disasters upon Egypt, moved northwards into the Kingdoms of Upper and Lower Egypt. They were of a savage ferocity never seen before in that country. Great hail stones, the size of a man's hand, beat down on everything in the fields; slaves, cattle, plants and trees. Lightning flashed continually across the sky, the thunder roared and exploded so that all who heard it cowered in fear. Streets and homes were flooded as water cascaded from the sky; no man could go out in it and survive. The flax and barley crops, just coming to maturity, were flattened and destroyed; the trees were shattered by lightning and stripped of leaves by the hail. All living things caught in that storm were ruthlessly struck down and left crushed and lifeless. In Goshen, the Israelites saw the great storm with fear and wonder; but it did not touch the land where they lived.

At last the King sent for Moses and Aaron; 'This time I have sinned', he said; 'Your god is in the right; I and my people are in the wrong. Pray to your god, the god of storms, for we cannot bear the fire from heaven, the thunder and hail any longer. I will let you go; you need wait no longer.'

Moses said, 'As soon as I leave you, I will raise my hands in prayer to Jahweh, and the storm shall cease. Thus you will know that the earth is under the control of Jahweh. But I know that you do not yet mean what you say; you and your servants do not truly fear Jahweh.'

Moses went out and prayed to God, and the storm ceased. But the King said, 'Surely this series of disasters has at last ended'. So he sinned yet again and hardened his heart, and did not let the people of Israel go – just as Jahweh had foretold. This was the seventh sign by which God openly showed his power in Egypt; yet his people still remained in slavery.

The Coming of Darkness (Exod. 10)

Once again, Moses and Aaron went before the King and said: 'These are the words of Jahweh, god of the enslaved people: "How long will you refuse to obey me? Let my people go, so that they may worship me". If you refuse to let them go, he will bring locusts over your land; they will cover the ground, until it cannot be seen. They will eat every green thing that the storm has left. They will strip every tree that is still standing. They will fill your fields and houses. They will consume Egypt with a devastation such as your ancestors have never seen, from the time they first lived until now.' They turned and strode out of the court.

By now, many of the courtiers feared Moses, and they said to the King, 'How long must we continue suffering, because of this man? Let the men go and worship their god. Do you not yet understand that Egypt will be ruined?' So the King summoned Moses and Aaron and said, 'We decree that you may go and worship your god. But who is to go with you?'

Moses said, 'We shall take young and old, men and women, sheep and cattle with us; for all the people are commanded to hold a feast to Jahweh'.

The King felt anger rise uncontrollably within him. Despite the seven plagues his people had so far suffered, and his knowledge that what Moses forewarned would yet again come true, he was irritated beyond endurance at the sight of this harem-reared gipsy slave boy giving him, the King of Upper and Lower Egypt, orders and laying down conditions to be met. He stood and shouted at Moses, 'May your god be with you indeed, if I ever let you go with your families and cattle. Would you then ever return? Do you not have some evil purpose in mind? No — the men among you may go to worship your god — that is all you asked for — your families and cattle must remain here.' Then he had Moses and Aaron driven out of the palace and sat, trembling with rage and frustration. He was no longer master of his emotions, and the more reasonable it became to let Moses have his way, the more he was driven into an obstinate fury by the man's increasingly arrogant demands. So he was driven along by the course of events into an ever intensifying conflict; his early hatred had now driven him far beyond reason, and he had no power to avert the tragedy that his every impassioned action brought nearer to himself. 'How can a desert storm god bring locusts upon us?' he said; 'This time Moses has over reached himself. It will not happen; you will see'; so he rationalized his obstinate refusal.

Jahweh said to Moses: 'I have hardened the heart of the King, so that he is caught in the grip of his own hatred and fear, and cannot escape. Now you can tell your children and your grandchildren the story of how I showed the signs of my judgement in Egypt, and of how I made sport with those who enslave and oppress their fellow men, to make them fear my judgement and to free my people. Thus you will know that I am Jahweh. Now, therefore, stretch out your hand over Egypt, and the locusts will come.' Moses stretched out his staff, and all that day and all that night a great wind arose and roared over the desert from the east. When morning came, the east wind had carried into Egypt the most feared and terrible plague known to men, darkening the sky, covering the ground, a screeching, scraping, fluttering, jumping mass of insatiable insects, obliterating every scrap of greenery, stripping every piece of bark from the trees, completely unstoppable, leaving no crevice unscoured. They moved on systematically, slowly, in their millions; and where they had been, not one leaf or blade of grass or growing thing remained; just bare, dead, barren land, cleared of all vegetation. The locusts had come; dense black clouds over the wheat fields, which turned to dust as they passed by. Urgently, the King called Moses and Aaron to him. 'I have sinned against your god and against you', he said, 'Forgive me, just this once; pray to your god and ask him to remove this plague, for it is death for my country'. So Moses left the King and prayed to God. That very day the wind changed; a strong westerly gale blew up, which carried the locusts away and swept them into the sea; not one locust was left alive in Egypt. This was the eighth sign of God's judgement on Egypt; but the King hated Moses more than ever, and hated himself for giving in to him; and he could not bring himself to let the Israelites go.

Then Jahweh said to Moses: 'Stretch out your hand to the sky, and darkness will come over the land of Egypt, blotting out the light of the sun, a darkness so intense that it will be felt, like the darkness of an enclosed room without light, like the darkness of the grave.' Moses did so; and the wind blew out of the desert a khamsin dust storm, obliterating the sun and filling the air with coarse particles of dust which were unpleasant to the touch and choked the nose and throat. For three days no one could move from his house; for three days it was pitch dark and nothing could be seen. Some prayed to the gods to deliver them from the power of darkness; but Ra himself, god of the sun, remained hidden and unmoving. Some thought the gods themselves had perished, and that this strange silent oppressive dark was the beginning of the long eternal night into which the whole world would descend at its ending. Only in Goshen was there light; the Israelites saw the tangible cloud of darkness lying over the land and they knew that the time of their deliverance was near. This was the ninth sign of the power of God, dark with menace in its silent waiting.

The Last Warning (Exod. 10, 11)

On the third day of darkness, the King summoned Moses and Aaron into his presence for what was to be the last time. 'Go', he said, 'and worship your god. Your families may go with you; but you must leave your flocks and herds here, to ensure your return'.

Moses said, 'Our flocks and herds must go with us; not a hoof may be left behind. Not only that; but you must provide us with animals for sacrifices and fire offerings to Jahweh our god. We must take them all to worship Jahweh; for we do not know what our god will require of us until we come to the place to which he calls us'.

The King was enraged at the sheer arrogance of the man; he leaped up and shouted at Moses, 'I shall never let you go free. Get out of my presence, and trouble me no more. There is no end to your absurd demands'. But Moses did not go. He stood impassive as the King ranted and raved before him. Then he held up his hand and the King stopped in sheer astonishment at such effrontery. Moses spoke, softly and distinctly but with great anger; in his voice there was a chill which caused all who heard it to feel a sharp premonition of fear.

'There is one last plague that will come upon the King and upon his country', he said; 'After that you will let my people go; indeed, you will drive us out in haste, laden with jewellery of silver and gold, like a man dismissing a rejected bride'. He paused, and looked slowly around the throne room; but no one moved; they were all watching Moses with fascinated dread. Even the King was silent, waiting for what was to come.

'These are the very words of Jahweh, god of the Hebrews', said Moses: "Israel is my first born son. I have told you to let my son go, so that he may worship me in the wilderness. You have refused time and again to let him go; you have tried to destroy him by drowning every male child; you have cowed him into submission by contempt and cruelty. I have warned you time and again; and all that has come upon you has been only the outward sign of the corrupting evil within your own hearts. Now, therefore, I shall let that evil which is within you be revealed in all its power, and you shall see it for what it is. At midnight I shall pass through the land of Egypt and execute my judgement upon all your gods, upon all the injustice and blindness and corruption of your land, upon all your idols of ambition and vanity. At midnight I shall walk among you, and every first born creature in the land of Egypt shall die. None shall be spared, from the highest to the lowest; not even the cattle in the sheds. There shall be a great cry of anguish throughout the whole land of Egypt, a cry such as has never before been heard, nor ever will be again. Only among my people Israel will no creature die, neither man nor beast. Thus you shall know that Jahweh has judged between Israel and Egypt". After that, my Lord King, your courtiers shall come to me and bow before me and beg me to leave, me and all my people. After that I will go.'

When Moses had finished speaking, the King sat, gripping the arms of his throne with whitened fingers, and shaking his head in disbelief. At last, through clenched teeth, with a high unnatural voice, he said, 'Go, and take care never to see my face again. For on the day you do so, you shall die'. Moses looked straight at the King and said, 'You speak the truth; I shall never see your face again'. He left the throne room in great anger; in the darkness, the King was alone with the soft whispering voices of his people's fear.

The Night of the Destroyer (Exod. 12)

That night Moses summoned the elders of the people of Israel and said: 'This is the night when Jahweh will watch over Egypt, to bring his people out of captivity and set them free. This is the night our descendants shall remember for ever; it is the night of Jahweh, when he shall free this people from darkness and enslavement and claim them for his own. You must go and tell each family to take a lamb, perfect and without any flaw, and slaughter it in their homes, as a sacrifice to Jahweh. Then they must take a bunch of marjoram, dip it in the blood of the lamb, which shall be poured into a basin, and smear the blood on the doorposts and the lintels of their houses. No one is to pass through the door of his house until morning comes; for in the middle of the night Jahweh shall allow the Destroyer to walk among the people of Egypt; but he shall stand guard over his own people. The sacrificial blood shall preserve you from harm, when the last plague strikes Egypt; and after that, you shall be a free people. Tell the people also to go to their neighbours, and to those who are staying in their houses, and ask for jewellery of silver and gold and rich clothing, to take for the pilgrim feast which they will hold to Jahweh, when he has brought them out of Egypt. This will be the price of their long slavery in a foreign land, the parting gift for four hundred years of oppression, the spoils of war won, not by men, but by the hand of Jahweh alone. When the lamb has been slaughtered and eaten; when the Destroyer has walked abroad by night; when the cry of mourning rises over the land; then the tribes of Israel will leave Egypt for ever, to take possession of their own land, the land of the promise of Jahweh.' The elders took the words of Moses to the people, and the people bowed their heads and worshipped God. Then they went at once to do as he commanded. They asked the Egyptians for jewellery and clothing; and the Egyptians, who were in awe of Moses, were favourably disposed towards them and gave them all they asked. The Israelites took lambs from their flocks, slaughtered them and smeared the blood on their doorposts, as Moses had said. They waited through that terrible night, while Jahweh brought plague and death over the land.

By midnight the eldest, firstborn, child of every household in Egypt had been struck down. The epidemic was as swift as it was sudden; first came vomiting and convulsions, and death followed almost at once. In every house in Egypt, the last plague brought death; only in the homes of the Israelites, behind locked doors, the people remained untouched. When the King saw his firstborn son fall and die, and heard the grief and terror of his courtiers, he sent to Moses, while it was still night, and said: 'Gather together your people, your dependents and your cattle and sheep, and go from this country. Go to sacrifice to your god, as you wish; and offer sacrifice for me also, that his anger against me and against my people may be appeased. Leave us, and do as you wish; we have endured enough.' The Egyptian people implored the Israelites to leave the country before even worse disasters came upon them, and to take the jewellery and clothes as gifts; for, they said, 'If you stay, we are all dead men'. The tribes had not had time to prepare food for their journey; all they had was dough without leaven, prepared as usual overnight for the following days' baking. So they took the dough as it was, still in their kneading bowls; they gathered together all the possessions they could carry, together with the jewellery from the Egyptians; and, in the first pale dawn after the days of darkness, they set out from Ramesses towards Succoth, in the wilderness. With them went their families, both women and children, all their flocks and herds, and many other people who had been slaves in Egypt. They also took with them the bones of Joseph; for they remembered his dying words: 'God will surely come to you again; then you shall take my bones from this place'. Now at last God had come to free his people; so the mortal remains of the patriarch were brought out of the land of Egypt, to find their last resting place in the country of his people's hope.

Between Egypt and the Sea (Exod. 13, 14)

As the tribes of Israel departed from Egypt, they did not travel North East, directly towards Canaan, because there were many heavily guarded garrisons along that way, who might not hesitate to massacre a straggling horde of unkempt slaves, whether for the sake of their cattle or merely for sport. They turned away from the main trade route, and travelled south into the wilderness. Travelling in haste with their families, their cattle and the many slaves who followed them, they saw before them, outlined alone in the clear sky, a single cloud, rising from the ground like a column of smoke. The whirlwind of sand lay always in front of them as they went, like a beacon marking the way, on the horizon. Moses said, 'It is the messenger of Jahweh, god of the whirlwind and the storm, sent to guard and guide us to the land of promise and plenty'. They travelled all that day, thirty miles into the desert, and camped by the town of Succoth. As darkness came, the cloud column flashed with fire, lighting the desert with warm radiance. The people remembered Abraham's vision of the flaming torch and Moses' story of the thorn bush which burned without being destroyed and they worshipped the god who showed his glory in the radiance of flame and showed the way to freedom in a pillar of fire. The cloud and fire of the glory of God was never from that time to leave his people, by day or night, while they walked in the wilderness.

That night they ate bread without leaven, because, in their haste, they had brought no leaven with them.

Moses said: 'When you come to the land that God has promised you, every year at this time you shall eat bread without leaven for seven days. For that time, there will be no leaven kept in your homes anywhere. For you shall remember this day, in which God brought you out of Egypt with power, and delivered you from slavery. And you shall tell your sons, "This is done because of what Jahweh did for this people, when we came out of Egypt". It shall be recorded in every generation as a tattoo on the right hand and as a charm upon the forehead, so that the name of Jahweh shall be always on your tongue.'

When morning came, the tribes moved on towards Etham, on the edge of the Arabian desert; and the pillar of cloud and fire went before them. At Etham there was an Egyptian garrison fortress; the Lord told Moses to turn back there, travelling Northwards again towards the sea, on the west side of the bitter lakes and reed swamps, which lay between the Mediterranean and the Gulf of Suez. On the third night they camped by Pi-hahiroth, between the border fortress of Migdol and the 'sea of reeds', a vast swampy area which cut off the route to the East. The King of Egypt received couriers from the forts at Etham and Migdol, reporting the movements of the slave column.

'They have had their three days in the wilderness', he said, 'They have had time for their barbaric sacrifice; it is clear they do not intend to return. Now all our labour force has gone; and they have taken our cattle and jewellery. But they have played into our hands; they are unable to find tracks through the wilderness and now they are trapped between our garrisons and the sea of reeds. Let us pursue and destroy them, bringing back those who remain alive to slavery'. So the Lord hardened the hearts of the King and his courtiers for the last time. Even now, the King could have accepted the will of Jahweh, shown by his signs of power, and let his people go. But the ten plagues and the final death of his son had only increased the resentment in his heart, and had produced no inner change in him. He still had no concern for justice, no care for the needs of others, he was still vain and insular; he still nourished a deep hatred for the Hebrew slaves, a poor and ugly and uncultured rabble. So the Lord took the evil that was in his heart and shaped it to lead to his own destruction; he made him the slave of his own rage and resentment, against every prompting of prudence and caution. The King summoned the most feared and effective division of the Egyptian army, the chariot brigade, and commanded them to lead a picked force of cavalry and infantry in pursuit of the slaves.

The Israelites were still camped by the sea of reeds when they saw the dust of the pursuing Egyptian army on the horizon. They were overcome with panic and many of them fell on their faces in the dust and cried to Jahweh to deliver them from death. Others went to Moses and said: 'Is it because there were no graves in Egypt that you have brought us here to die in the wilderness? What have you done to us, in bringing us out of Egypt? When you first went to the King and he increased our daily work, did we not ask you just to leave us alone and let us be slaves to the Egyptians? It would have been better to live as slaves in Egypt than to die as free men in the desert.'

Moses went apart and prayed to God: 'Lord God of fire and storm, of whirlwind and thundercloud', he said, 'it is by your guidance and in obedience to your call that we have come to this place. When you called me on the sacred mountain, I obeyed and you gave me your power to perform signs and miracles before the King. Your people has come out of Egypt, even as you promised; and you have called them to worship before you below the sacred mountain. But now the chariots of Egypt are near us and we are hemmed in by the fortress, the sea and the reed swamps. Where is your power now, Lord God? Where is your strength to deliver us? We have followed you in faith, seeking freedom; but now we are terrified at the approach of our enemies, who have come to seek our death. Save us, O God, by the power of your name; rescue us from our enemies by your strength. Then we will sing of your power and celebrate your love when morning comes; for you are our fortress and our only shelter. We cry to you, for all your hope is founded on your promises.' So Moses prayed and the people cried to God, as they watched with dread the approach of the chariots of Egypt, between Migdol and the sea.

The Sea of Reeds (Exod. 14; cf. Ps. 77)

As Moses sought the guidance of God, his thoughts went back to the time of his first calling on the sacred mountain, to the voice that had enfolded him there and the flame that had dazzled him with morning brightness. He still remembered with perfect clarity the words that had been imprinted then and for ever in his mind – 'I am the Lord; I will redeem my people with an outstretched arm and place them beneath the shadow of my wings; I am the Lord'. As he recalled the words, he seemed to feel again the fear and fascination that had flooded through him on the mountain. The people crying and praying in the camp; the chariots of Egypt coming out of the setting sun; the lonely desolation of the sea of reeds; all these things faded to the margin of consciousness, as he felt his very being dissolve and merge into a reality beyond name or description, beyond knowing and desiring, beyond anything that could be grasped or held by human mind. He no longer had any separate existence; he was one with the whirlwind and the fire, with the pursued and the pursuer, with the Eternal One, for whom all ages of human time are like one unconsidered breath. Yet he remained alone, exhilirated by terror and pierced by love, not comprehending what he most deeply knew, not self sustaining but upheld solely by the One Who Is. And he heard again words from within his heart that he had not spoken, words beyond the possibility of doubt. The God who had united him to himself, from whom he was infinitely apart, placed these words unforgettably within him:

'On this night, at this place, I shall show my presence and my power. The people I have set apart for myself shall escape death. They shall walk through water to the land of promise. By my breath I shall set bounds to the waters of the great deep, as on the first days of creation; and by the flame of my spirit they shall be led to freedom. This night shall be remembered for ever on earth; for by the miracle of this night I declare my will, to bring those who are oppressed to freedom; to bring those who oppress to destruction; and to make the way to my presence open to all who will follow it. Take your staff and hold it high over the sea; I will make a way for you between the waters, and you must take my people through the sea to the other side. I will make the Egyptians foolhardy and they shall pursue you into the middle of the sea. Then I shall show my power before the chariots and horsemen of Egypt, and they shall know that I am the Lord.'

The voice and the presence vanished as quickly as they had come. But Moses did not hesitate; he was certain of God's promises; he called the tribesmen together and said, 'Have no fear; stand firm and see the salvation that Jahweh will bring you this day; the Egyptians whom you see today, you shall never see again. Jahweh will fight for you; you have only to be still'. As he spoke, the sky clouded over and the first stirrings of wind scattered sand lightly through the camp. One moment the sky was a brilliant clear blue, with only the familiar solitary whirlwind of dust on the horizon; the next a strong east wind began to blow, sighing over the reed swamps, showering sand and dust into the air. The people covered their faces to keep out the stinging sand as dark clouds raced towards the setting sun, covering the sky with menace. Where the helmets and standards of the Egyptians had glinted in the sun, a great sandstorm obliterated the light and thunder clouds filled the air. Within half an hour the wind was screaming over the marshes; thunder and lightning flashed and exploded over the desert; torrential rain beat down through the darkness, and the ground trembled with a terrifying sound that seemed to come from the very depths of the earth. There was no sight of the Egyptian army; the worst of the storm lay between them and the Israelites. Moses urged the people forward, into the sea of reeds; and where they walked, the east wind drove the waters before them and made a path for them through the sea. So they walked into the middle of the impenetrable marshes and the waters marked out their way, like borders to the right and to the left, as they walked on dry ground all that night. The terrible dark storm of Jahweh thundered around them, and the wind swept over the waters and divided them, as God led them through the waters of death by the power of his spirit into a new life of freedom.

The Egyptian army came to the camp and saw that the slaves had walked into the sea of reeds and were escaping into the storm. No path was known through those marshes and quicksands; but they saw the tracks leading straight into the sea, through pools of standing water, whipped into fury by the devastating wind. Men, women, children and cattle had all disappeared into the rain and mist. The commander of the force urged his chariots forward. 'If we cannot bring them back, we shall strike them down where they stand,' he said, 'No storm shall save this rabble from the might of Egypt'. So they pursued the Israelites far into the sea, the chariots and horsemen of the King of Egypt, urged on through the darkness and the storm. But as they rode on, the storm increased in violence; the sky flashed with lightning, so that the thick clouds shone with a continuous flickering veil of light; the rain beat down through clothing and armour, blinding the horses and churning the ground into thick mud, clogging the chariot wheels and throwing horsemen to the ground in confusion. The earth trembled beneath them, and at last panic overcame them. 'This is no ordinary storm', they said, 'This is their god fighting against us, the god of plague and storm. We must go back'. Many of them tried to turn and run, while others continued to press forward, until the army was in complete disorder. Then Jahweh said to Moses, 'Stretch out your hand over the sea, and the waters will overwhelm the chariots of Egypt'. Moses did so; and as morning came, the wind veered from east to north west; there was a terrifying cracking sound, as if the earth itself was splitting open; a tidal wave of water, higher than any man, swept over the sea of reeds, obliterating everything in its path. There was no hope of escape. The deep mud dragged the chariots down until they sank without trace; the ground shifted under the soldiers' feet as they desperately fought to keep their balance; the sheer weight of water swept them out into the deep pools and quicksands; when the tidal wave had passed, there was no sign that any man had been there at all. Not one man was left alive; and when the storm and earthquake at last subsided, the Israelites, safe on the further shore of the reed sea, found nothing of the pursuing army of the King except several bodies swept upon the sand, awkward and ugly in the morning light.

On that night, Jahweh saved Israel from the power of Egypt; and the people remembered the words of Moses: 'Jahweh will fight for you: you have only to be still'. They worshipped God and put their trust in him, for they themselves had seen his judgement and his salvation.

The Song of Triumph (Exod. 15)

Miriam, the sister of Moses and Aaron, took her tambourine in her hand and led the women in a sacred dance of victory. In prophetic ecstasy, she sang to the people a song of triumph, a song which was passed down from one generation to another, until at last it came to be written in the sacred records of Israel, a song to Jahweh, god of Israel, who had delivered his people from death:

Sing to Jahweh, mighty in majesty,
Horses and chariots he hurled in the sea.
The Lord is my strength, my defence and deliverance,
He is my god, give glory to him.
God of our ancestors, we will exalt you,
Jahweh the warrior; great is his name.
Sing to Jahweh, mighty in majesty,
Horses and chariots he hurled in the sea.
The army of Egypt he sank in the sea,
drawn to the depths of the boundless deep;
rising in triumph, he routed the enemy,
shattered their strength with the fist of his fury.
Sing to Jahweh, mighty in majesty,
Horses and chariots he hurled in the sea.
At the blast of your breath the waters divided;
the enemy said, "I will seek them and slay them,
I will draw my sword and swiftly destroy them";
You urged the wind and the waters engulfed them.
Sing to Jahweh, mighty in majesty,
Horses and chariots he hurled in the sea.
Who is like Jahweh, highest of gods?
Hidden in holiness, awesome in action?
You stretched out your hand and the quicksand held them,
like lead they sank in the raging sea.
Sing to Jahweh, mighty in majesty,
Horses and chariots he hurled in the sea.
In your changeless love you will lead your people,
Redeemed from death by your glorious deeds;
You will guide by your strength to the sacred city

and bring us at last to the land where you live
Sing to Jahweh, mighty in majesty,
Horses and chariots he hurled in the sea.
Neighbouring nations will hear and tremble,
Edom and Moab and Canaan will cry;
in terror of you they will stand like stone
while the people whom you made your own pass by.
Sing to Jahweh, mighty in majesty,
Horses and chariots he hurled in the sea.
Bring us in peace to the hills of your presence,
land of the promise which you have prepared;
there you will rule and your people will praise you,
King of creation, we live in your care.
Sing to Jahweh, mighty in majesty,
Horses and chariots he hurled in the sea.

Into the Wilderness (Exod. 15)

In the morning, Moses led the people of Israel away from the Bitter Lakes and the sea of reeds into the steppe country of the Northern Sinai peninsula. For three days they travelled over the barren plateau, land without trees or water, bearing just enough thin scrub to feed the sheep and cattle. The straggling column of men, women and children choked in the dust and sweated under the daytime sun; their supplies of food were running low and they found no water on the way. At last, on the third day, they came to a small oasis, a pool of brackish water between a few stunted palms and bushes. Eagerly they ran to drink; but the water was bitter and undrinkable, producing vomiting and violent stomach pains. They called the place Marah, the well of bitterness; at that place many began to regret leaving Egypt. At least in their slavery they had been fed and housed; there was a sort of security in that. Now they were free; but that freedom had thrown them into the wilderness, into an unknown future and a barren, unfriendly world. Canaan, the land they longed for, was occupied by powerful and warlike tribes, so that they were forced to march southwards into Sinai. Moses, the Egyptian prince and shepherd of the wilderness, remained a strange and enigmatic figure, leading them towards a sacred mountain they had never seen, compelling them to accept a freedom they only half desired. He had promised them freedom in the name of Jahweh, the ancient god; that promise had been kept. But beyond that promise lay the well of bitterness, the moment of uncertainty and regret; now came the days without refreshment, the walking in the wilderness, the insistent questioning of doubt.

So the people complained to Moses: 'What are we to drink?' The Lord God tested them with discouragement and their trust began to fail. Moses went apart to pray; and, even as he knelt, he saw a small bush, of a kind he knew well from his long years in the wilderness with Jethro's flocks. Quickly he broke off some branches, stripped the bark from the trunk and went and threw it into the water. Within a short time, the water began to clear; and when Moses tasted it, the bitter tang had gone. The nomads of the desert had long ago discovered the strange ability of certain kinds of vegetation to purify polluted water. The fact that Moses was now applying this knowledge, learned in his shepherd days, made it no less of an answer to his prayer. Eagerly the people drank, and made camp.

Moses brought them together and said: 'If you will obey Jahweh your god and trust in him; if you will hear his commands and keep his laws; then he will keep you from harm and from the plagues of Egypt. For by the wood of a tree in the wilderness he gives life; and turns the bitter waters into a spring of refreshment and healing. Jahweh is your healer; if you hear him, he will preserve you from harm and make you whole.' So Moses told the people the words that Jahweh had given him to say.

The Bread of Life (Exod. 16)

The people travelled slowly south, resting for a long while at Elim, a fertile and beautiful oasis, with twelve springs of water and seventy palm trees, and then on the shores of the Red Sea. One and a half months after the departure from Egypt, they came into the Sinai desert, a country of deep gullies and harsh bare mountains, the landscape twisted into alien shapes, inhospitable and lifeless under the torturing sun. There was nothing here but hard rock; the only tracks were the rough roads to the Egyptian tin and copper mines in the mountains, and they were deserted at this time of year. In every direction, as far as the eye could see, there was only emptiness and desolation. The people became uneasy and began to question the leadership of Moses and Aaron. They looked back to their life in Egypt; in their memories, it seemed to be more desirable than they had thought when they were there; they began to talk of it with nostalgia and fondness. 'It would have been better for us to die in Egypt at God's hand', they said; 'At least we had roast flesh and plenty of bread to eat. Now we have been brought into this desert, where we shall die of hunger'.

When Moses heard what they said, he told Aaron to call the people together and he prayed to God for guidance, to know what he should tell them. Jahweh said to him, 'I have heard the discontent of the people of Israel. Say to them: "At evening you shall know that it was Jahweh who brought you out of Egypt, and in the morning you shall see his glory. For in the evening, between dusk and dark, you shall have flesh to eat and in the morning you shall be filled with bread. Then you shall know that I, Jahweh, am your god, when I give you bread from heaven" '.

Aaron told the people the words God had given to Moses and said, 'Your complaints are not against us; we are nothing. Your complaints are against God, who leads us in the pillar of cloud and fire. He has heard your complaints and tonight and tomorrow he will give his answer'. As Aaron spoke, the people looked out over the desert and they saw the glory of Jahweh flaming in the pillar of cloud. The god of the exodus was with them still, leading them and accompanying them on their way. The people were silent and waited for his will.

That night a flock of quails, flying North on their spring migration, came to ground around the camp. The people were able to trap them quite easily with nets, as they lay exhausted; so that night the Israelites had roast flesh to eat. In the morning, there was a heavy dew lying like mist all around the camp. As it cleared, the ground was covered with small yellowish-white flakes, like coriander seeds, as fine as hoar-frost. The Israelites had never seen anything like it before; but Moses said, 'This is the bread which Jahweh has given you to eat. Each man must gather it for himself and his family, day by day, one day at a time. You must not store it overnight; for Jahweh will give you enough for each day, no less and no more; you must rely solely on him'. Early in the morning, each man gathered the substance in bowls, for it melted away when the sun grew hot. Some gathered more, some less, depending on the number of people in their tents; and when they came to measure it out, they found that each person had just as much as he could eat; there was never too little and never anything left over.

They called it 'manna', from a word in their language meaning, 'What is it?'. They never discovered what it was, though some have thought it was tamarisk-resin, formed from the sting of a tree louse on the leaves of the tamarisk, dropping to the ground in the night. It was very sweet, like wafers made with honey; the Israelites considered it a great delicacy and supplemented their food with it for the whole of the time they lived in the wilderness, until they entered Canaan. Later, they kept a jar of it, about two litres, in the Sanctuary, for future generations to see the bread which God gave in the wilderness, and so to remember his daily care for his people.

Some people disobeyed God's command to gather only enough for one day at a time and tried to keep some overnight; but in the morning it had become maggot ridden and decayed. Moses was angry and said, 'Has God not given you whatever you need, each day? Why do you not trust in him day by day and give up anxiety about what tomorrow will bring? You must accept what God gives, one day at a time; that will be sufficient for all your needs'.

It was at this time that the people of Israel began to observe the Sabbat, the day of rest. For on every sixth day, Moses told the people to gather twice as much bread as usual. He said to the heads of families,

'Each seventh day shall be a day of solemn rest, a sabbat set apart to Jahweh. For when Jahweh created all things, he completed his creation by resting on the seventh day. He blessed and set apart that day and ordained that six days of creative work should be completed by a day of rest. On that day, all shall cease from work; all their days of work shall be completed by being offered to God and all shall rest and be renewed in his strength. You are not even to light a fire in your dwelling; whoever works on that day shall be put to death. God has created man to work and so share in his creation. But he has also created man to rest and rejoice in him. So on each Sabbat, our humanity is fulfilled by being set apart to God alone. Let the people therefore gather bread on six days; on the sixth day there shall be bread for two days and you shall keep all that you have not baked or cooked. On the seventh day, it will not decay and there will be none to gather; let every man stay in his tent on that day, for it is set apart to God.'

Nevertheless, on the seventh day some went out to gather bread; and there was none to be found. God said to Moses, 'How long will my own people refuse to keep my laws? To walk in my law is the way of life; whoever receives in faith the bread that I give enters into my eternal rest. Let my people then take care that they do not lose the promises by which alone they live, and leave the way of life by their own wilfulness.'

Water from the Rock (Exod. 17; Cf. Deut. 25 17-19)

The people of Israel made their way towards the mountain ranges of the Sinai peninsula, camping at Dophkah and Alush. As they neared Rephidim, at the base of a high mountain ridge, weary at the end of a long day's march, a small band of warrior nomads from the tribal confederacy of Amalek, came out of the hills and cut off the rear of the column, which was lagging behind exhausted. They killed the few men who were there and drove off the cattle, leaving the women and children dead by the way. They broke all the customs of desert warfare, attacking the weak and killing the helpless. But they disappeared into the hills as silently and quickly as they had come; the Israelites could only march on to Rephidim, where they could camp and rest.

When they arrived, however, they could find no water anywhere; the children and cattle were exhausted and their way seemed barred by the steep walls of the mountains all around them. Many of the people were anxious and afraid; they had no clear idea of where they were going or of what to do when they got there. They were angry and disheartened at the treacherous raid by the tribesmen of Amalek. The fire and cloud still moved before them and they camped where it halted; but it seemed to be leading them further into the barren mountains, away from the green grazing land they desired. The mysterious manna still surrounded their camp each morning; but they began to tire of its sweet sticky taste and long for fresh fruit and corn from the fields. There was uneasy talking among the tents and some of the tribal elders began to argue publicly with Moses, saying, 'Why did you bring us out of Egypt, to kill us and our children and our cattle with thirst? Find us water to drink, or we will die'. Small groups of tribesmen banded together and talked of stoning Moses to death and making for Canaan on their own. The outcry grew so great that Moses began to fear for his own life. The elders came to him and said, 'Is Jahweh in our midst or not? Will he give us water to drink; or is it his will that we should die in this wilderness?'

Moses replied, 'Jahweh has freed us from slavery and called us to belong to him. I will follow him even to the mountains of death, if that is where he calls'.

'Perhaps that is where he calls you, Moses', they said threateningly, 'And sooner than you think'.

Moses held up his hand; 'Let me pray to God', he said, 'And I will give you his words'.

He went alone into the hills to pray and to seek the word of God. He knew that the limestone rocks of Sinai retained moisture; the problem was to find where it was trapped and release it. In desperation he implored Jahweh for help; and Jahweh heard him. Moses returned to the camp and called some of the elders to him.

'Follow me', he said, 'I will show you water'. He led them through the rocks, bearing his shepherd's staff, which was now his staff of command, until he came to a large crevice in the cliff face. He took his staff and struck at the rock, where it projected from the limestone surface. Nothing happened. He struck it again, and a piece of rock broke away. The elders looked, but saw nothing.

Moses laughed. 'Feel the rock', he said. One of them went up and put his hand on the rock and exclaimed in astonishment, 'It's damp; there's water here'. The others rushed up and started pulling at the stone with their fingers. As pieces of rock broke away, more water began to trickle out from a hidden spring. They took out knives and hacked at the rock in frenzy; and soon a clear strong spring of water gushed out from the hard rock. They drank, gulping the precious liquid greedily; and looked at Moses in awe. 'How did you know?' they asked.

Moses simply said: 'Jahweh showed me the place. From hard rock he has given you the water of life; is anything too hard for the Lord? Now you know that he is in our midst. The staff which turned water to blood in Egypt now draws water from the rock in the desert. Remember this.'

Moses called the spring Massah-Meribah, the place of testing and dispute; because the Israelites had disputed with him and put Jahweh to the test, to see if he was among them.

The Battle of Rephidim (Exod. 17)

The Israelites stayed at Rephidim for over a week, building up their strength. After the first attack by Amalek, they began to forge spears and swords out of the metal objects they had brought with them and to make slings and bows for all the men and older children. They posted sentries around the camp at night; but with such a large and mixed company of people, many tents straggled on the outskirts of the camp, away from the main fires. One evening the Amalekites attacked again, destroying the most isolated tents, killing indiscriminately and again carrying off cattle and sheep in a short bloody skirmish. The Israelites could not stop them, but this time they were able to send men to follow them in the darkness and discover the raiders' camp. They returned to tell Moses where it was, and he called Joshua to him, a young man who was a natural leader, tall and strong.

'Pick your men', he said to Joshua, 'and tomorrow you shall fight for us against Amalek. I will stand on the hilltop which overlooks the valley of their camp, and I shall hold my staff in my hands. As I hold it high, you shall know that Jahweh fights for us. As he delivered us from Egypt by the strength of his arm, so he shall be revenged for the attacks of Amalek on his people. This staff shall be the banner and emblem of Jahweh; as I raise it to his throne in prayer, so he will hear and help us. So may Jahweh deliver us from all our enemies.'

Joshua gathered a picked force of the strongest young men of

Israel, and they set off in the early morning for the Amalekite camp. Moses climbed to the hill top, with Aaron and Hur, an elder of the people; and as the sun rose over the mountain rim, the Israelites saw Moses raise the staff of Jahweh high above his head and they rushed down towards the camp, shouting and brandishing their spears. But the Amalekites were hardened desert warriors, not to be easily overcome by a rabble of poorly armed slaves. Some of them fell at the first charge, taken by surprise. But most of them rallied quickly and formed a tight circle, defended by spear and sword. After some fruitless skirmishing, the Israelites found they were getting the worst of the hand to hand fighting and fell back to the shadow of the hill. The Amalekites were a small foraging party, but well armed and disciplined; as they faced the Israelites across the valley, Joshua knew that this would be no quick victory. The Amalekites drew up in line and marched towards the hill; at its peak Moses stood, his hands held high; with a cry, Joshua urged his men on, and they ran forward, weapons waving wildly in the air, until the two lines met and the hills echoed with the clang of metal and the screams and curses of men. All that day the battle raged to and fro across the valley. Whenever Moses raised his hands, Israel gained the advantage; but when he lowered his hands, their courage waned and Amalek had the advantage. Seeing this, Aaron and Hur took a large stone and put it under Moses; as he sat, they held up his arms, one on each side, so that his hands were steady, raised towards the throne of Jahweh above the firmament of heaven, until the setting of the sun. Again and again Joshua rallied his men, calling them to look to the staff of Jahweh, held high on the hill above them. Again and again they charged the warriors of Amalek, until one by one the Amalekites fell. At sunset, the last man died, cut down by a ring of swords. The Israelites were blooded, and had won their first battle; as darkness came, Amalek was defeated; even the wounded raised the first victory cry for Israel.

Moses recorded the victory in writing, and he recited to Joshua the words he had written: 'I, Jahweh, god of battle and storm, am resolved to erase all memory of Amalek from under heaven'. Moses built an altar and called it Jahweh-nissi, Jahweh is my banner. He offered a sacrifice of thanksgiving on the hill top and said, 'As I place my hand on the staff of God and raise it to his throne, so I swear that Jahweh shall war with Amalek from one generation to another'. The slaves of Egypt had become the warriors of Jahweh; now they lived with a new pride under the protection of their god.

The Priest of Midian (Exod. 18)

In the third month after Israel had left Egypt, on the night of the new moon, they came to the sacred mountain. They had left Rephidim as soon as the wounded were ready to move, winding through narrow passes between high mountain peaks, sometimes in the open glare of the sun, but more often, thankfully, in the shadows cast over the long valleys by the tumbling barriers of stone. Though they had never seen it before, they knew the sacred mountain when it appeared, looming ahead of them in the fading light, brooding over the other peaks around it in solitary grandeur. Without a word, Moses indicated the place where they were to camp, some distance away from the mountain where a multitude of springs scattered over the rocky ground. They pitched their tents in silence, without the usual chatter of voices and noisy bustle of activity; already they felt a sense of foreboding in the great still presence of the mountain, which made speech seem out of place, and filled them with anticipation of the unknown. They had come to the mountain of the god who had torn them from the lives they knew and guided them to himself through the barren desert. Now they waited, in the silence of the mountains, to discover what the end of their journeying would be.

For some days they waited and the mountain was silent and unmoving. Gradually, the people began to establish a familiar routine and to feel more at ease under the towering peaks which surrounded them, like a fortress shielding them from the outside world, leaving them alone and at peace in their broad valley. Then, one morning, a small cloud of dust showed among the further hills; as the day wore on, it drew slowly nearer and four figures could be made out, coming up to the camp. When Moses was told of it, he leaped up in great excitement and went out alone to meet the strangers. For he knew that they were not strangers at all. Jethro, priest of Midian, was coming to his tribal sanctuary; and with him he brought his daughter Zipporah, wife of Moses, and their two sons, Gershom and Eliezer. Moses had sent them out of Egypt when the plagues began, to prevent the King from taking them hostage, and he had not seen them since. He greeted them now with tears of joy, bowing low before his father in law and embracing him. When they came into the tent, Moses told him all that Jahweh had done for Israel and all that he had done in Egypt to deliver his people from slavery. He told him of their journeys through the wilderness; of the doubt and regret by the waters of bitterness; of the dissatisfaction and desire for luxury on the desert plateau; of the challenge thrown to God by the rock of Rephidim; of the testing of courage and endurance in the struggle with Amalek. And he told him how Jahweh had rescued them in their hardships and brought them to worship him on this mountain, as he had promised in the tree of fire.

The priest of Midian rejoiced with Moses at all the good Jahweh had done for Israel in saving them from the power of Egypt. He remembered how he had talked with Moses long ago, and first taught him the ways of the ancient god of Abraham their father; he had listened to his story of the vision on the mountain and given him his blessing to return to Egypt; he had received his wife and children and cared for them when Moses sent them away. He did not know whether he had ever hoped to see him again; one man pitting himself against the mightiest Kingdom in the world. Yet now all the hosts of Israel were camped about the holy mountain; there was no longer room for doubt; his pupil had become his teacher in the ways of God. Jethro praised God and said, 'Blessed be Jahweh, who has saved you from the power of Egypt and her King. Now I know that Jahweh is the greatest of all gods, because he has delivered his people from the arrogance of Egypt'.

Jethro took Moses, Aaron and all the elders of Israel with him to the foot of the holy mountain; there he sacrificed a fire-offering and the ritual sacrifices of Midian to God, as he had come to do. But he offered them not only to the god of the Holy Mountain, who overshadowed the peoples of the desert lands; but to the god whose name was Jahweh, who had chosen an exiled prince to proclaim his will, who had freed a nation of slaves from bondage, who had renewed his ancient promises to Abraham, who waited to declare his will to his chosen people. The priest of Midian knew that his was not the people of the promise; theirs was a destiny they had yet to discern and respond to; he and his people must go their own way. Yet he worshipped Jahweh on the mountain with the elders of Israel; and was filled with awe as they shared bread and wine in the presence of God.

In the following days, Jethro saw that Moses was exhausted, as he sat hearing disputes among the people, from morning until night. He suggested to Moses that he should appoint judges over the people, men of incorruptible fairness, to command groups of ten, fifty, or one hundred families, and to deal with disputes among them. So Moses was relieved of much of the burden of leadership and dealt only with difficult disputes and with the declaration of the Law. Soon afterwards, Jethro left to return to his own people; the Israelites remained, waiting in the shadow of the sacred mountain.

The Ten Words of God (Exod. 19, 20; Deut. 5)

The sacred mountain towered above the little camp that lay under its shadow, where the people established a daily routine for gathering water and food, and began to organize themselves more definitely into tribal units. Moses often left the camp and wandered alone on the mountain, praying or looking out over the jagged hills around, waiting for the voice of Jahweh to echo around the empty rocks. And, in time, it came, that same instantly recognizable yet unspoken language, filling his mind with compelling insistence and quiet irresistible command. When he heard it, he returned to the camp without hesitation and called the elders together. 'Jahweh is coming', he said, his eyes flashing, 'He is coming in glory upon this mountain, in the sight of all the people. He will cover the mountain with the cloud of his glory and will speak his words in thunder, so that all may hear and know that I am his prophet, the speaker of his Law for men. All the people must consecrate themselves to be ready; they must wash their clothes and abstain from sex today and tomorrow; on the third day Jahweh will descend among us.'

Barriers were built between the camp and the mountain, and the people were forbidden to go up the mountain or even to touch it. For three days it was set apart for God alone, and the punishment for anyone who touched it, man or beast, was to be stoned or hurled to his death, for they infringed the absolute barrier between God and men, and their bodies were filled with the danger of divine power, which only death could safely exorcise. For three days the people fasted from dawn to dusk, and silently watched the mountain, high and harsh above them, while all living things around stayed strangely still.

On the morning of the third day, the stillness was suddenly broken by a long shuddering roar which seemed to come from the centre of the earth and spread to the mountain peaks until it rolled like thunder from the hills and through the air. The people threw themselves to the ground in fear. A dense cloud had covered the sacred mountain in the night; lightning flashed and thunder pealed as a great storm gathered over the peak. Then the people saw a pillar of smoke and fire rise from the top of the mountain, until the whole peak was ablaze with flame, while the earth shook; and they heard a great blast, like the noise of a trumpet, from deep within the cloud. Moses called the people to rise and follow him to the foot of the mountain. 'Jahweh has come down to his holy mountain in fire', he said, 'Come up to your god'. But the people were terrified and stayed a good way from the low stone wall which Moses had built at the foot of the mountain, as a barrier. Out of the fire and cloud they heard the voice of the living God; and these were the words he spoke:

I am Jahweh your god who brought you out of Egypt, out of the land of slavery.
You shall have no other gods than me.
You shall not make any sacred object in the form of any star or bird, of any animal or living thing, or any creature of the great deep. You shall not worship such things or serve them. For I, Jahweh your god, am a jealous god, punishing the sins of those who leave my ways, even to the third and fourth generation of their children. But I show steadfast love to untold numbers of

those who love me and keep my commandments.
You shall not use the name Jahweh in conjuring or profanity. I will not leave unpunished the man who misuses my name.
You shall remember the Sabbat and keep it holy. You have six days to do your work; the seventh day is a sabbat to Jahweh your god. On that day you shall do no work – you, your children, your slaves, your cattle or the resident alien with you. For in six days Jahweh made the world; sky, earth and sea and all that is in them; and on the seventh day he rested. Therefore Jahweh blessed the sabbat day and declared it holy. On that day your slaves shall have rest; for you were slaves in Egypt and Jahweh brought you out with strong hand and outstretched arm. For this reason also, all your slaves shall rest on the sabbat of Jahweh.
You shall honour your father and mother, so that you may live long and well in the land which Jahweh shall give to you.
You shall not commit murder.
You shall not commit adultery.
You shall not steal.
You shall not give false testimony against your neighbour.
You shall not set your heart on your neighbour's household; on his wife, his land, his slaves, his cattle or on anything that belongs to him.

When the elders of the people heard the voice of God, they came to Moses and said: 'Jahweh has shown us his glory and his greatness; today we have heard his voice, and know that God may speak with men and they may still live. But if we hear him again we will certainly die and the fire will devour us. You must go near to hear all that Jahweh says to us; we will listen and obey.'

Moses said, 'Do not be afraid. God has come to test your faith in him and to show himself to you, so that you may continue to hold him in awe and be kept from evil. Return to your tents; so must you always fear the Lord and keep his Law.' So the people returned to their tents, while Moses approached the dark cloud which hid the glory of God.

The Covenant at the Sacred Mountain (Exod. 24)

Moses climbed the mountain as it shuddered and thundered under him, and there on the mountain top Jahweh gave him the Law for his people. Then Jahweh said: 'Say this to the house of Jacob, the sons of Israel: you have seen with your own eyes what I did to Egypt, how I carried you on eagle's wings and brought you to myself. Now, therefore, if you will obey my words and keep this covenant, you shall be my own possession among all people. The whole earth belongs to me, but you shall be to me a Kingdom of priests, a holy nation. These words you shall say to the children of Israel.'

Moses went down to the people and set before them all the commands of Jahweh. And they said with one voice, 'Whatever Jahweh has said, we will do'. So Moses wrote down all the laws of God. Early in the morning, he built an altar at the foot of the mountain and erected twelve sacred pillars, one for each of the twelve sons of Jacob, the tribes of Israel. Young men of the tribes came and sacrificed bulls on the altar. Moses took the blood of the sacrifices and put it in basins. Half of it he poured over the altar; then he read the book of the covenant aloud to all the people. They said, 'We will obey, and do all that Jahweh has said'. Moses took the blood and sprinkled it on the book and over the people, saying, 'This is the blood of the covenant which Jahweh has made with you, in accordance with all these words'. By the blood of sacrifice at the foot of the sacred mountain, God and the tribesmen of Israel were inseparably joined in everlasting covenant. Theirs was the Law to obey and delight in, his was the promise to set them apart for himself in a land of their own. On that day and in that place the eternal God bound the people of Israel to himself with his own word and wisdom, set forth in the Law; he bound himself to them through the blood of sacrifice, by which he set before them the promise that they would be his children and share his own eternity.

When the covenant sacrifice had been offered, Moses called Aaron, his two eldest sons Nadab and Abihu and seventy of the elders of Israel, and said: 'This mountain is sanctified by the presence of Jahweh; no man may touch it, or attempt to see the god who shows himself here; if he does so, he will die. Even the priests of the people must keep themselves ritually pure, in case the power of Jahweh breaks out and destroys them. But Jahweh has commanded me to bring Aaron and the elders of the people to him on the mountain, to eat a Covenant meal in his presence.' So Moses and Aaron, Nadab, Abihu and the seventy elders of Israel climbed the mountain of God, while the people watched them with fear. As they climbed, the cloud over the mountain cleared and the elders saw the sky stretching before them like a pavement of glistening sapphire. Above the pavement, even, it seemed, beyond the sky itself, they felt, rather than saw, an awesome presence, the presence of the god of Israel, the god who had showed himself in fire to Abraham and to Jacob. They bowed low to the ground, while Moses went on before them. When he called, they followed; they ate and drank before God and were not harmed. When they returned to the people, they never spoke of what had happened on the mountain. They left only one sentence to record that time, for which they could never provide any description; simply this, 'We stayed on the mountain before God; and under his feet, the sky was spread out like a pavement of blue sapphire'. In that time beyond description, the covenant between Jahweh and his people Israel was sealed.

When the elders had returned, Jahweh said to Moses, 'Come up to me on the mountain and wait'. Moses put Aaron and Hur in charge of the people and told the elders to await his return. He took Joshua with him, and went up the mountain. For six days, cloud covered the mountain top and the glory of Jahweh appeared like a raging fire in the cloud. On the seventh day, Jahweh called to Moses, and he entered the cloud on top of the mountain. He stayed there forty days and nights, and heard the words of God. He hewed two flat pieces of stone out of the rock of the sacred mountain and engraved the ten words, which Jahweh had spoken to all the people out of the cloud, on the front and the back of each stone. In those Words Jahweh declared his Law to Israel; they were written on sacred stone with the finger of God, the imperishable words of the eternal One.

The Golden Bull (Exod. 32)

The people waited below the sacred mountain for five weeks. The cloud still covered the mountain top and Moses and Joshua did not return. In the sixth week they came to Aaron and said, 'This man Moses who brought us out of Egypt, has disappeared; we do not know what has become of him. Let us leave this place and let us have gods to go ahead of us and protect us'. Aaron was afraid of them and said, 'Strip the gold earrings from your wives and daughters, the rings which they took from Egypt, and bring them to me'. They all did so, and Aaron melted them down in a cauldron and made an image in the form of a young bull. He showed it to the people and said, 'These are the gods, O Israel, who brought you from Egypt. The bull is the visible image of the invisible god Jahweh, who rides on the violence of the storm and holds the power of life and fertility in his grasp'. The people bowed down before the image, and Aaron remembered the words of the covenant, that the people should not make gods of gold; he remembered the sprinkling of blood, which bound them to keep these words on pain of death. He was afraid, and built an altar before the image and said, 'This is not Jahweh; it is only the form on which he sits invisibly. Tomorrow there will be a sacred feast to Jahweh, God of Israel'. Nevertheless, he saw that the people worshipped the image and that they were beyond his power to control.

The next day the people rose early and brought animals to sacrifice on the altar before the image of the bull of gold. They sat down to eat and drink, and soon began to laugh and sing for the first time for weeks. They prostrated themselves before the image and danced around it. As they looked at the shining image of fertility and aggression, they felt themselves filled with the power of the smiling bull god, and began to fight and fondle one another, sprawling in the dust, men and women together, arousing their sexual desires, until they called for relief. The bull god remained, smiling impassively, as the people of Israel, the chosen priests of Jahweh, grunted and scrabbled in an orgy of sexual licence, taken over by primitive powers they could not command.

It was on that day that Moses and Joshua returned from the mountain top. Joshua heard the sounds of riot coming from the camp and said to Moses, 'Listen; there is fighting in the camp'. Moses replied, 'That is not the noise of warriors or the crying of a defeated people; it is the sound of singing that I hear'. As they came to the camp, Moses saw the golden bull and the people dancing and making love around it, and he was enraged. He flung the stones, engraved with the words of God, to the ground and they shattered in pieces. Thus the covenant was broken, before they had even left the mountain of its making. Moses took his place at the gate of the camp and said, 'Who is for Jahweh? Who will fight for him? Let him come to my side'. As he called, the Levites, the tribe of Moses and Aaron, came out from the tents where they had stayed, taking no part in the feast, and rallied to him. Moses said: 'Let each one of you take his sword. Go through the camp from gate to gate and back again. You must put to death those who have taken active part in this debauchery.' They hesitated. 'Go', said Moses, 'The way of Jahweh must be kept, even at this terrible price. They have brought their blood upon their own heads, by their own vow, made at this very place. Here they vowed death if they turned from God's Law; so, by the word of Jahweh, God of Israel, and by their own oaths, they stand condemned.' Then the Levites obeyed and swept through the camp, striking down the revellers as they went, whether they were brothers, friends or neighbours.

Moses then said: 'Because you have done this, because you have separated yourselves even from your sons and brothers, for the sake of the word of Jahweh, you have brought upon yourselves a great good. The tribe of Levi shall be consecrated wholly to Jahweh; for, as long ago by the sword, shame was brought on our tribe at Shechem, so now by the sword honour is given to us in defence of the law of our god. For this reason, the children of Levi shall be separated from their families for ever, and given completely to the service of God.'

Moses then took the bull image and destroyed it. He ground the gold to a fine powder and flung it into a torrent of water which flowed down the mountain side. He forced those who had worshipped the bull to drink the water, saying to them: 'This water is a water of judgement; if you have not turned aside from God, your innocence will be established. But if you have turned aside to worship another god, may Jahweh bring judgement upon you; this water, entering your body, will cause you to fall ill and die.'

Aaron said, 'Do not be angry. The people were deeply troubled, that you know. I was afraid; you had been on the mountain so long, and I could not control them; so I gave in to their demands'.

Moses replied, 'Brother, you are weak. Do you not see that you have laid the people of Israel open to the malice of their enemies? They have left the protection of Jahweh and the camp is unguarded. What did the people do to you, that you should have brought this guilt upon them? Now Jahweh himself may take vengeance for what has been done today, from you and from the people. Tomorrow I shall return to Jahweh; perhaps I may obtain forgiveness for your sin.' That night many fell ill and some died, after they drank the water that Moses had cursed. Thus the judgement of God was shown. The people buried their dead in silence. The feast of the bull god was over.

The Prayer of Moses (Exod. 32, 33)

The next day Moses returned to the mountain to pray for his people. As he prayed, it seemed to him that he heard the words of Jahweh: 'I have considered this people and I see that they are wayward and stubborn. They have turned aside from my way and sought again the ancient gods of Egypt. They cannot keep my law, even for a little while. Now, therefore, I will put an end to them and raise up for myself another nation, descended from you alone'.

But Moses said, 'Lord Jahweh, you brought this people out of Egypt with great power and a strong hand. If you slay them, the Egyptians will say, "Their god meant evil when he led them out; he meant only to kill them in the mountains and wipe them from the surface of the earth". Thus they will mock your power to save. Lord, be merciful to your people. Remember Abraham, Isaac and Israel, your servants, to whom you swore: I will make your posterity as numberless as the stars in the sky; and they shall possess the land I give them for ever. These people have sinned greatly; but forgive their sin, that they may yet live to praise you. Or, if you will not forgive, I ask you to blot my name out of the book of the living, that I may die with them.'

Jahweh said, 'It is the man who has sinned against me that I will blot out from my book. Nevertheless, I will hear your prayer and spare the people of Israel, because you have even offered your life for their sake. A time will come when their sins will be punished; but this time they will be spared. Therefore leave this place now and lead the people to the land which I have promised, the land of milk and honey. My angel shall go before you, to drive out those who stand in your way. But I myself will not journey with you; for you are a stubborn people and my presence may destroy you.'

Moses told the people the words of Jahweh; and when they heard that their god would not go with them on their journey, they stripped themselves of all their ornaments, like those who mourn for the dead. From that moment, the Israelites never again wore personal jewellery, because of the anger of God at Sinai. Moses took a tent and pitched it some distance outside the camp; he called it the Tent of Presence, and instructed Joshua to remain there. He said to the people:

'The Lord offered you his love; but you turned away making an image to give you power over the gods. So the anger of Jahweh turned your self seeking love to lust, bringing death and judgement upon you. Yet God is compassionate and gracious; he allows himself to be moved by the prayers of the man of faith, who does not seek his own glory, but offers his life for his people. The Tent of the Presence is now outside the camp, as Jahweh is far from your hearts. If you seek the Lord and worship him, he may yet come among us again.' Moses went daily to the tent; when he went, all the people would rise and stand by their own tents and follow the prophet with their eyes. When Moses entered, the column of cloud came down and stayed by the entrance to the tent while Jahweh spoke with him. Then all the people would prostrate themselves in worship until the cloud ascended and Moses returned to the camp. Everyone who sought the Lord would go out to the Tent of the Presence to worship there. Thus the people mourned for their sins.

Moses said: 'Lord God, you have told me to lead the people on from the mountain of your presence. You have made yourself known to me and blessed me richly. Teach me to know your will and purpose, so that I may lead your own people rightly. Do not send us away, unless you go with us; for if you do not, how shall we remember that we have been chosen out of all nations to serve you and be blessed by you? Do not leave us without your presence.'

Jahweh said, 'I will do what you ask, because of my love for you. I will go with you in person and my peace will be with you, because of your faithfulness.' So the God of Israel answered the prayer of Moses; the waywardness of the people of God was forgiven because of the mourning of repentance and the prayer of faith.

The Final Vision (Exod. 33, 34)

Jahweh said to Moses, 'Cut two slabs of stone, like the two that were broken. Be ready by morning; come up to the mountain peak; but take no man with you; let no man or beast approach the mountain; you alone shall wait for me there'. Early in the morning, Moses climbed to the mountain top and waited. The Israelite camp, far below, was like a nest of desert ants, a huddle of black specks in the brown emptiness of the desert hills. There was no sound, except for sudden gusts of wind around the crevasses of the mountain. The sky, blue and clear as crystal, was unmarked except for one cloud that hovered motionless over the mountain. In the east, the sun flowed over the hills in a sudden river of light, and the mountains changed from black to shining gold in an instant. Moses remembered the thorn tree, which he had never found again; and all the promises of God which he had now fulfilled, in bringing his people out of Egypt to worship him on the mountain. Here Moses had been found by God; now he had to leave and lead the people to a land none of them had seen, putting behind them for ever the sacred mountain, where the presence of God was. He had heard the voice of God; he had seen the vision of fire; he had walked in the cloud of the presence of God and had learned the sacred name. Now he made one final request.

'Lord', he prayed, 'Show me your glory, your inward being, your true self, unhidden and unveiled'.

God said, 'I will make all my goodness pass before you and will proclaim my own self, the One Who Is, before you. For I will be gracious to whom I will be gracious, and I will show mercy on whom I will show mercy. Yet you must hide in a crevice in the rock; for no mortal man may see me and live. I will cover you with my hand while my glory passes by. When I remove my hand, you shall see the departing of my beauty; that is as much as man can bear.'

As he spoke, the cloud grew and covered the mountain top. The sky was blotted out and the cloud began to glow, white and hot like molten metal; fire danced in the cloud, in a cascade of colour, brightening into pain. Moses flung himself into a crevice, etched deeply in the mountain side; but even with his eyes closed, the brightness seared his brain; he heard a roaring, rushing sound, the beating of a thousand wings, a thousand voices shouting together, the fury of wind over the great deep, rising and growing louder moment by moment. He put his hands over his ears and buried his face in the rock. But the colour and the sound became one indistinguishable entity, a feeling running through his whole being, shattering his thoughts, obliterating his personality. He felt himself falling, swirling in a vortex of vast energy that he was unable to control, a beauty that became terrifying in intensity; a truth that overwhelmed his understanding, a goodness that crushed his self esteem. He began to scream, silently and inwardly, as he felt himself torn apart by forces he could not begin to grasp. Then, mercifully, on the edge of annihilation, a great calm came over him, as if some power was shielding him from a reality too immense for human sensation. He remained huddled in the rock, knees drawn up to his chin, arms around his head, sheltered under the hand of God, while the glory of the Almighty passed before him. He heard, from some infinite distance yet as near as his own voice, a cry:

'Jahweh, Jahweh, a god merciful and gracious, patient, full of steadfast love and faithfulness; showing love to thousands; forgiving iniquity, rebellion and sin, not destroying the guilty utterly; but one who punishes sons and grandsons to the third and fourth generation for the iniquity of their fathers.'

Then the hand was taken away, and he saw a clear calm light in the sky, where the glory of God had passed. Faintly and fading, he heard the cry of voices, of laughter and grief, of warfare and love, blending and echoing like the rushing of many waters. He saw an unnumbered throng of faces and figures, twisting and interweaving into one vast tapestry of living forms, a joyful dance of endless life. Beyond and around them, more intricate and complex yet, were worlds of life without beginning or end; and beyond that again, beyond all thought or vision, the still centre of all this measureless immensity. Even as the light faded, rich and subtle in beauty past recall, he understood the infinity of the One Who Is, the Everlasting One. He prostrated himself on the ground and said, 'Lord, if indeed you love me, go with your people; however disobedient and stubborn, forgive us and take us as your own'.

Moses remained on the mountain forty days and nights and Jahweh renewed his covenant with Israel. He said: 'I will perform signs for you that have not been seen in all the world; all people shall fear me when they see my work. I will drive all the inhabitants of Canaan out before you, if only you will observe what I command this day.'

Moses wrote down the words of God on the slabs of stone and came down from the mountain for the last time. As he came to the camp, Aaron and the people were afraid, and he had to call out to reassure them before they would approach him. For the skin of his face shone, because it glowed with the fading splendour of the glory of God.

The Sanctuary (Exod. 30; 31, 25-27, 34-38, Lev. 24)

After the vision on the mountain, Moses covered his face in his robe, so that only his eyes could be seen. He removed the veil only when he entered the Tent of Meeting to pray, because his face shone with the splendour of God and the people were afraid.

He called the people together and said: 'Jahweh has renewed his covenant, to take us to the land of promise. Moreover, when we leave the holy mountain, he will continue to be with us. His presence will rest among us; he has commanded me to make a

Tent of Sanctuary, where he will be; he has shown me what he desires. Now therefore let each man freely offer to Jahweh what he will for the Sanctuary of the Lord. Jahweh has chosen Bezal-El of the tribe of Judah to oversee the work. He has filled him with divine spirit, to inspire his work in wood, metal and cloth. He has chosen Aholiab of the tribe of Dan to help him; and he calls every craftsman who will to help in this holy task.'

Men and women alike brought jewellery, clasps and earrings, yarn and skins, perfumes and acacia wood. The women spun and wove tapestries and coverings; the men forged and moulded the sacred vessels for the Sanctuary. The people brought so much that Moses at last had to ask them to stop bringing gifts; so the Sanctuary of Jahweh was begun.

First, they made the Tent of the Sanctuary. They made three walls of planks of acacia wood, leaving the fourth wall open; they secured the planks with five horizontal bars, slotted through gold rings, and placed them in silver stands; then they overlaid all the woodwork with gold. This framework was covered on its three sides with linked curtains of linen, richly embroidered with cherubim; over this was laid a covering of goatskin and then two weatherproof coverings, one of rams' skins dyed red and one of sealskin. The coverings were then pegged into the ground with bronze pegs. A screen of finely woven linen was hung at the entrance, on five pillars of acacia wood banded with gold, on stands of bronze. Inside the Sanctuary a matching screen, worked with cherubim, was hung on four more pillars, completely plated with gold, on silver stands. This screen marked off the holy place from the Inner Sanctuary, the holy of holies, a perfectly symmetrical space in which only the central mystery of faith was placed.

This was the Ark, a wooden chest made by Bezalel, overlaid with gold, encircled with a band of gold, with two wooden, gold plated poles fastened through rings at the four lower corners, so that it could be carried about. The Ark had a cover of pure gold, with a golden cherubim at each end, a lion with the face of a man, wings outspread and raised to screen the cover. The cherubim faced each other and their wing tips met over the centre of the Ark. In the Ark, Moses placed the stone slabs he had brought from the mountain, the words of the living God. Over the Ark, between the wings of the cherubim, was the place of meeting, where God, the Everlasting One, and man met face to face.

Outside the screen of the Inner Sanctuary there were placed three sacred objects. On the north side was the table for the bread of the presence of Jahweh. It was made of wood, overlaid with gold, with two poles for carrying; on it were placed flagons and bowls, from which drink-offerings were to be poured, and dishes for the bread and incense, all made of gold. Each Sabbat twelve loaves were to be placed on the table, sprinkled with incense; one for each tribe, offered to Jahweh as a food-offering, the holiest of gifts. Week by week the priests were to offer the bread and wine to God and consume the bread with reverence in the holy place; for this bread, offered to God, became the bread of his presence, the memorial of his covenant with man.

On the south side of the Sanctuary stood a seven branched lampstand, formed from a single piece of beaten gold, richly decorated and moulded. The priests were to trim the lamps each morning, fill them with pure olive oil and mount them each evening, so that they burned from dusk to dawn, as a sign of the unsleeping light of Jahweh.

In the centre of the Sanctuary, before the inner screen, was the altar of incense, made of wood and covered with gold, with two carrying poles. Only ritually prepared incense was to be offered upon it, every morning and evening, at the time of the tending of the lamps, as a constant prayer to Jahweh.

One other object stood in the Sanctuary. That was the jar of manna, which Jahweh had commanded Moses to keep as a remembrance for future generations of God's provision in the wilderness.

When the Sanctuary had been set up with all its furnishings, Moses commanded an altar to be built in front of it. A hollow wooden case, covered in bronze with carrying poles, it was to be the place where all the animal and grain sacrifices were offered to Jahweh on behalf of the people of Israel. Between the Sanctuary and the altar, he placed a bronze bowl, made from the mirrors of the women who worked by the sanctuary. It was filled with water, so that the priests could wash their hands and feet before entering the Sanctuary or offering sacrifice, as a ritual purification. Finally, the Court was constructed of rich linen hangings hung on posts, banded with silver and set in bronze stands, in a large rectangle around the Sanctuary. On the east side, towards the rising sun, was the gateway, its screen embroidered in red and purple to match the sanctuary screen, which faced one on entering the Court.

So the Sanctuary of Jahweh was built, exactly as had been revealed to Moses on the holy mountain. Moses inspected the work and saw that all was as God had commanded; and he blessed those who had made it. Now there would be not only the temporary Tent of Meeting, but a permanent shrine, revealed by God himself, in which he would be present with his people in all their journeyings.

The Five Great Sacrifices (Lev. 1-7)

Sacrifices have been offered to God since the earliest recorded time. Cain and Abel brought gifts to God; Noah offered animals on the altar in thanksgiving for his deliverance; Abram built his first altar at Shechem, to claim the land of promise for Jahweh and acknowledge him as the greatest of gods; in obedient devotion to Jahweh, he offered his firstborn son on the unknown mountain. Isaac invoked the Lord at Beer-sheba, where the Lord renewed his promises; Jacob built an altar at Beth-El, where God revealed himself even as he was running away in fear and dishonour; he sealed his covenant with Laban by sacrifice, as he swore an oath; he invoked the god of his fathers as he left Canaan for the last time. Moses himself offered a sacrifice of thanksgiving at the victory of Rephidim; and he sealed the covenant of Sinai with sacrifice. At times of thanksgiving and distress, of pride and shame, of happiness and sorrow, the wandering tribes of the Hebrews remembered their god by offering to him their most valued possessions, an offering of life from those whose own lives were given by God, whose possessions were held on trust from him. On the sacred mountain, Jahweh revealed to Moses the sacrifices by which he willed to be honoured. He laid down their form precisely and so ordained the sacred rites before the

Sanctuary of the Presence, by which his people were to be united to him. These are the five great sacrifices ordained by Jahweh on the sacred mountain:

First, *the fire-offering.* The offerer shall bring a perfect bull, ram or goat. He shall present it before the Sanctuary. If the priest accepts it, he shall lay his hand on its head, so that it will be accepted on his behalf by Jahweh. Then he shall slaughter it himself, skin it and cut it up. The priests shall take the blood, which is the life and so belongs to God, and throw it all around the sides of the altar, returning it to the one who gave it. After washing the legs and entrails, the priests shall arrange the parts of the sacrifice on the altar and burn it completely. The fire on the altar shall never be allowed to go out. The offering shall remain until morning, when the ashes shall be taken outside the camp. The skin of the beast shall belong to the priest. If the offerer is poor, he may bring doves or pigeons; then the priest shall drain the blood against the altar; throw away the crop; tear the body, holding it by the wings, and burn it completely on the altar. Thus the whole offering is burnt, devoted to Jahweh, expressing the dedication of the offerer's own life to God. It shows that he holds nothing back in his obedience and devotion. Jahweh will accept such a sacrifice, offered in sincerity.

Second, *the fellowship-offering.* The offerer shall bring a perfect ox, sheep or goat, either male or female. As with the fire-offering, it shall be killed and its blood thrown around the altar. Then the offerer shall remove all the fat parts of the animal and give them to the priest, who shall burn them on the altar; these are the best parts of the animal and as such are offered to God. The breast and hind leg are given to the priest as his share, when they have been presented to God. The rest must be eaten by the offerer and his companions, on the same day, if it is an offering of thanksgiving; otherwise within two days. For in this sacrificial meal God himself shares with his people in fellowship, and establishes harmony and peace between those who eat together in his presence. Because the meal is holy, anything left over is to be destroyed by fire; otherwise the sacrifice is void and the offender must make atonement. Any flesh which touches a ritually unclean object must be destroyed; any person who eats while himself ritually unclean must be excluded from the community. The fat of no animal shall be eaten, though it may be put to other use; for it is God's share of the fellowship-offering. And the blood of no animal shall be eaten, for it is the life, which belongs to God. Finally, if the sacrifice is one of thanksgiving, unleavened cakes, wafers and dough shall be brought together with leavened bread. One of each shall be presented to God and shall belong to the priest; the rest shall be eaten in the sacrificial meal; there God himself will meet with his people, to unite them with one another and with him.

Third, *the sin-offering.* If a man inadvertently breaks a command of God; or if he refuses to give evidence under oath, or conceals some ritual uncleanness or conceals a rash oath he has made; then he incurs guilt and must make expiation by sacrifice. If he is a priest whose ritual mistake brings guilt on the whole people, he shall bring a perfect bull. He shall lay his hand on its head and slaughter it. Then he shall sprinkle some of the blood seven times before the Inner Screen in the Sanctuary; and smear blood on the horns at the corners of the Altar of Incense. It is this offering of life on the altar and in the Sanctuary which removes guilt. All failure to keep God's Law, however unknowing; and all concealment of truth, however well-intentioned, must be expiated. The expiation is provided by God; it is the life which belongs to him, freely given back, in an act of confession and penitence, by which such sin is forgiven. After that, the rest of the blood shall be poured out at the base of the altar of sacrifice; all the fat meat shall be burned on the altar; the skin and everything else shall be taken outside the camp and destroyed, just as the offerer's sin is taken away and destroyed. If the whole community sins inadvertently – perhaps because of the unexpiated sin of an unknown tribesman – the elders shall sacrifice a bull in the same way, all laying their hands on its head. If a man of standing sins inadvertently, he shall offer a he-goat. The sacrifice is the same, except that the blood is not taken into the Sanctuary; for this is an individual offering, not on behalf of the whole community. The blood is smeared on the horns of the bronze altar; and afterwards, the priest and any man of his family shall eat the remaining meat within the Court. Whatever the meat touches shall be holy; it must be washed, burned or smashed. If a tribesman sins inadvertently, he shall offer a ewe or a she-goat, in exactly the same way. A man must offer the most valuable thing he can afford, and it must be faultless. But if he is poor, he may offer two doves or pigeons. One is for a sin-offering; the head shall be wrenched back, so that some blood can be sprinkled against the side of the altar, and the rest drained out. The other is a fire-offering, according to that rite. If a man cannot afford that, he may offer a measure of flour, without oil or incense. The priest shall burn a handful on the altar; the remainder is for the priest. So even the poorest man may have these sins forgiven him, if he confesses and makes his offering in sincerity.

Fourth, *the guilt-offering.* This may be offered instead of a sin-offering; it must be offered when compensation for sin is involved, or for special occasions of ritual installation or reception into the community. Thus it is offered when one has inadvertently defaulted in sacrificial gifts; and also when one knowingly defrauds a man of property, by lying, theft or extortion; for such offences against men are also grievous faults against God. The offerer shall bring a perfect ram, the value to be determined for the offence by the priest. The sacrifice is that of the fellowship-offering, except that the meat remaining is eaten only by the men of the priest's family in the Court. The offerer shall also make full restitution, adding one fifth to it, on the day of the sacrifice. So he shall be forgiven for any act which brought guilt upon him.

Fifth, *the bread-offering.* This may be of flour or crushed roasted fresh corn, mixed with olive oil, with incense. The priest shall take a little of the flour, with all the incense and burn it on the altar, as a gift to God. One may also offer unleavened cakes or wafers, baked in an oven; or cakes cooked on a griddle or in a pan and broken ready for sacrifice. All such cakes must be unleavened; no leaven or honey which ferments may be offered to God, for they are symbols of corruption; bread made with leaven or honey may only be offered as gifts to the Sanctuary, not presented for sacrifice. All such cakes must be salted, for salt is the symbol of the covenant, establishing community between those who share it. Bread-offerings are normally offered together with offerings of meat; all except the part offered on the altar belongs by right to the priests to be eaten in the Court; flour to be shared by all and cooked cakes to belong to the sacrificing priest. This sacrifice is a perpetual prayer of adoration to the God of Israel. The High Priest of Israel shall present a bread-offering to God each day, half in the morning and half in the evening. It shall be cooked on a griddle, broken and burned in sacrifice; as a priestly offering, it shall be wholly burned and not eaten. All the prayers of Israel shall ascend with it daily to the throne of God.

These are the five great sacrifices ordained by Jahweh on the sacred mountain, to order the worship of Israel in the wilderness, and in her coming to the land of his unchanging promise.

The Installation of the Priests
(Exod. 28, 39, 40; Lev. 8; Num. 7)

On the first day of the first month of the second year after Israel had left Egypt, the Court and the Sanctuary were set up. The twelve tribal chiefs provided six covered wagons and twelve oxen between them, to be used for carrying the Sanctuary and its furnishings. For sacrifice, each chief brought two silver dishes of flour and oil, with one gold dish of incense, as a bread-offering; a bull and two rams, as a fire-offering; a ram as a sin-offering; and two bulls, ten rams and five goats as a fellowship-offering. The chiefs came to present their gifts, one day at a time, so that it took twelve days for the offerings of the Israelites to be presented at the altar, to await the beginning of the sacrificial cult.

On the first day, Moses called Aaron and his four sons; they and their descendants were to serve as the priests of Jahweh for all time. He summoned all the people to meet before the Sanctuary for the installation of the first priests of Israel and the inauguration of the sacrificial rites appointed by Jahweh. He presented the five priests before the Sanctuary and they washed in the water from the great bronze urn. Then Aaron was robed in the sacred vestments of the High Priest, designed to give him dignity and grandeur, woven from the finest materials. He wore four basic garments and four outer garments. Briefs of pure linen were worn, to preserve the cultic requirement that the genital organs should not be exposed before God – a reaction against the religious prostitution and sexual rites used in many Middle Eastern fertility cults. Then there was a chequered tunic of fine linen, with an embroidered sash, in violet, purple and scarlet. The fourth garment was a high headdress of fine linen; these vestments were worn by all the priests.

The outer vestments were unique to Aaron, the High Priest, and they were kept for the use of each succeeding High Priest of Israel. First, a violet sleeveless robe, made in a single piece with a hole for the head. It had a woven hem at the neck and a hem round its skirts, embroidered with pomegranates in violet, purple and scarlet. Between the pomegranates, small golden bells were hung, which sounded as he walked, to announce his presence before Jahweh in the Sanctuary. Second, over the robe was worn a sacred kilt made of gold, worked with violet, purple and scarlet thread, and a waistband of the same material. It had two shoulder straps, with a gold rosette at each shoulder. In the rosettes were set two precious stones, cornelians, finely engraved with the names of the tribes of Israel, six tribes on each stone, in order of seniority. Third, a square pouch, made of the same material as the kilt, worn on the breast. It was a square of folded material, and on it were set twelve precious stones, donated by the chiefs of the tribes, in four rows of three. Each stone, set on a gold rosette, bore the name of one tribe of Israel. So the names of all the tribes of Israel were remembered before Jahweh, born on the shoulders and over the heart of the High Priest, as he ministered at the altar and in the Sanctuary. The pouch had gold rings at each corner; the top two attached by gold chains to the rosettes on the kilt shoulder straps; the lower two attached by violet braid to gold rings just above the kilt waistband, so that kilt and pouch were bound together. Into the pouch were put the Urim and Thummim, two stones by which sacred lots were cast, to give judgements in hard cases brought for decision to Moses. So the High Priest bore the symbols of divine judgement over his heart, when he went before Jahweh. Fourth, a golden diadem was fastened with violet braid to the front of the headdress, and engraved with the sacred letters JHVH, the letters of the name of God. This was a symbol of dedication; if there were shortcomings in the sacrificial rites, it absolved him from blame and made them acceptable to God.

When the High Priest was robed, Moses prepared sacred oil, to be used only for anointing. He consecrated the Sanctuary by anointing it and everything in it. He sprinkled the oil seven times on the bronze altar and anointed the urn. Then he poured oil on Aaron's forehead to anoint him; and anointed his four sons with him. Thus the hereditary priesthood of Israel was inaugurated; the rituals of sacrifice could begin.

The Sacrificial Cult Begins
(Exod. 29; Lev. 8-10; Num. 6)

On the day that Moses consecrated the Sanctuary, when all the people saw Aaron and his sons robed and anointed, Moses instituted the newly consecrated priests in a week long ritual of installation. First, he prepared the bread on the Table of the Presence, mounted the lamps on the lampstand and offered incense on the gold altar within the Sanctuary. Then the priests presented a bull for a sin-offering, to cleanse themselves from all the sins which separated them from the fearful God of the Mountain. The sacrifice was as for a priest, except that the blood was not sprinkled in the Sanctuary, but smeared on the horns of the bronze altar, thereby purifying it by making expiation for it. After that, a ram was presented as a fire-offering, a sign of the dedication of the priestly life to God. A second ram was then presented as a fellowship-offering, to seal the fellowship of God and his priests. Unleavened loaves, cakes and wafers were also offered, in thanksgiving for God's choosing of men to be his priests. In a special rite of ordination, blood was smeared on the right ears, right thumbs and right big toes of the priests; they were to hear the word of God obediently, do his work faithfully and walk in his way unswervingly. A little blood, with anointing oil, was sprinkled over the priests and on their vestments, setting them apart for the service of God. Of the priest's share, the leg was burned and Moses took the breast, after raising it to God, for himself as the sacrificing priest. Aaron and his sons, having raised the fat and bread-offering before the altar, boiled and ate the flesh and bread together before the Sanctuary, destroying all that was left over before morning.

For seven days Aaron and his sons were to keep vigil before the

Sanctuary, while the sacrifices of installation were offered on each day, strictly in accordance with the commands of God. But on the sixth day, the eldest sons of Aaron, Nadab and Abihu, got drunk with wine. They were the heirs of the High Priest; they had been chosen to go with their father and the seventy elders to the covenant meal on the sacred mountain; they were the anointed representatives of God himself to the people. Now they knew themselves to have a power over others which was unique and irrevocable. Theirs was the power to accept or reject sacrifices, and so to give or withhold God's forgiveness. They could claim exemption from work and war and live off the rich offerings of the people. They could declare the oracles of God to those who came for guidance, and receive respect and reverence from all. They were men of dignity and authority in the community. Moreover, as priests they had privileged access to God, his own chosen, separated from the common people for his service. They were the guardians of his honour; without recourse to them, no man of Israel could approach God. They were the hereditary aristocracy of the living God himself, superior in their standing with God, above all harm.

So they drank wine in the sacred court; they took censers and filled them with incense. They could not find the specially prepared incense, but used what they had to hand to burn incense before God. They knew he had not commanded them to do so; but they aimed to accrue merit by their act. While the others slept, they entered the Sanctuary, stumbling and laughing a little as they went in. In the morning, when Aaron went in to trim the lamps, he found his two sons lying dead before the altar. Moses came and saw what had happened and said to Aaron: 'Jahweh has said: "I require holiness in all those who approach me; I will maintain my glory before all the people". Of those whom the Lord calls, he requires much; his judgement upon them is sudden and swift.' Aaron could not say anything. Moses called two of Aaron's cousins to take the bodies out of the camp and said to Aaron and his two younger sons:

'The anointing oil of Jahweh is upon you. You must not mourn, either by letting your hair hang loose or by tearing your robes; you must not leave the sacred court; but you must complete the rituals of sacrifice, today and tomorrow. Today, your brothers, all the people of Israel, shall mourn for the death of your sons before the altar. They shall mourn and remember that God is holy and that all those who come near him must sanctify themselves by obeying his will only. Tomorrow, you shall offer sacrifices for all the people of Israel, as God has commanded.'

On the eighth day, Moses again called all the elders of the people into the Court, commanding them to bring a he-goat for a sin-offering, a calf and a lamb for a fire-offering, a bull and a ram for a fellowship-offering, and an offering of flour. After the priests had offered their own sin and fire-offerings, they prepared the offerings of the people, to make expiation for them. So the people were dedicated to Jahweh, as their priests had been. But Moses saw that the sin-offering for the people had been burnt outside the camp, just as the priests' own offering had been. He was angry with Eleazar and Ithamar, the sons of Aaron, and said: 'Why did you not eat the sin-offering in the court, as you should have done? You know that a sin-offering from the people must be eaten by the priests in the court; if the ritual is broken, their sins will not be borne away.'

But Aaron said, 'All my sons have offered their sin-offerings and fire-offerings; and yet two of them are dead, because they disobeyed God and brought guilt on my family. If we had eaten the people's sin-offering today, bearing this guilt and grief, would it have been acceptable to God?' Moses put his hand on his brother's shoulder and said no more.

Aaron and Moses went together into the Sanctuary; and when Aaron came out, he lifted up his hands towards the people and blessed them, in the words Jahweh had given him: 'May Jahweh bless you and keep you; may Jahweh make his face shine upon you and be gracious to you; may Jahweh lift up his countenance upon you and give you peace'. As he pronounced the name of Jahweh over the people, God drew near to them and blessed them. The cloud of the presence of Jahweh covered the Sanctuary and no one could approach it, because the glory of Jahweh appeared to all the people in the cloud. A brightness like fire came out of the cloud and consumed the offerings on the altar. All the people saw it and shouted and fell on their faces; the God who had freed them from slavery and brought them to the mountain of his glory had come to be present among them for ever.

The Wilderness

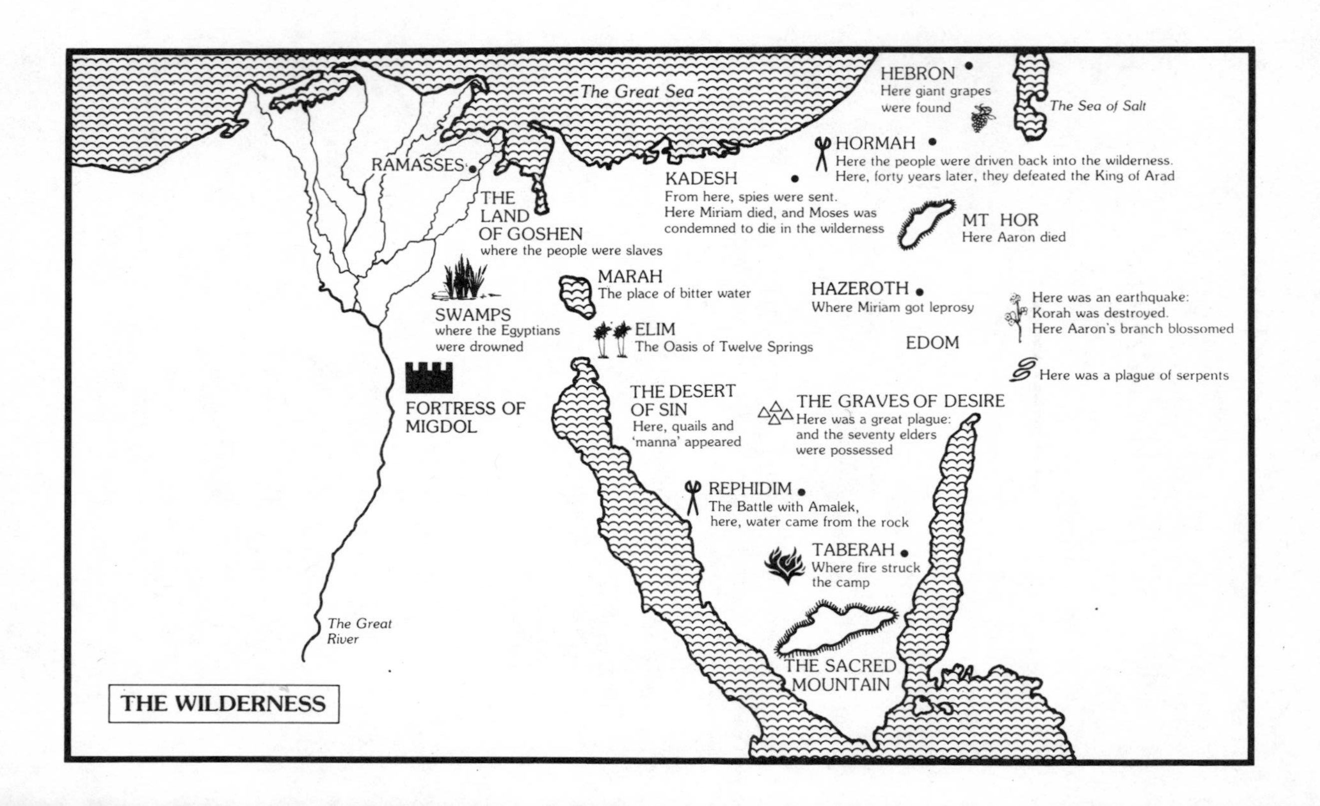
THE WILDERNESS
The Great Sea
HEBRON
Here giant grapes
were found
The Sea of Salt
HORMAH
Here the people were driven back into the wilderness.
Here, forty years later, they defeated the King of Arad
RAMASSES
KADESH
From here, spies were sent.
Here Miriam died, and Moses was
condemned to die in the wilderness
MT HOR
Here Aaron died
THE
LAND
OF GOSHEN
where the people were slaves
MARAH
The place of bitter water
HAZEROTH
Where Miriam got leprosy
Here was an earthquake:
Korah was destroyed.
Here Aaron's branch blossomed
SWAMPS
where the Egyptians
were drowned
ELIM
The Oasis of Twelve Springs
EDOM
Here was a plague of serpents
FORTRESS OF
MIGDOL
THE DESERT
OF SIN
Here, quails and
'manna' appeared
THE GRAVES OF DESIRE
Here was a great plague:
and the seventy elders
were possessed
REPHIDIM
The Battle with Amalek,
here, water came from the rock
TABERAH
Where fire struck
the camp
The Great
River
THE SACRED
MOUNTAIN

The Dedication of the Levites
(Exod. 13, 30; Num. 1, 3, 4, 8, 18)

In the second month of the second year after the people of Israel left Egypt, they prepared to move on from the holy mountain. On the first day of that month, Moses and Aaron, with one chief from each tribe, took a census of all the men over twenty years of age, who were fit for military service. As each man passed by the teller, he had to pay half a piece of silver as a price for his life; for it was believed that to number the people was to set bounds to the extent of God's graciousness, to measure the amount of his love, and so to deserve his judgement. The silver was an offering to God for their lives, and it was devoted to the upkeep of the Sanctuary. Each man, rich or poor, paid the same amount, to signify that wealth could not buy extra privileges from God; his protection was over all the people.

The tribe of Joseph was divided into two – Ephraim and Manasseh – because the tribe of Levi was not registered in this census. The Levites were exempt from bearing arms; those who had defended the Law of God with the sword were now appointed as perpetual servants of his Sanctuary, to care for the sacred things and serve the sons of Aaron the High Priest. No one else was allowed to take down or erect the Sanctuary, and they camped around it, between it and the other tribes, to preserve its sanctity.

Moses said, 'Jahweh claims for his own the first born sons of Israel, all the firstborn males, both man and beast. For when he freed you from Egypt, he claimed all the firstborn of that land; and he asks from you the sacrifice of what you love most dearly, your firstborn, to be dedicated to him. When you take possession of Canaan, you must therefore sacrifice to Jahweh every firstborn animal, and redeem every firstborn son with a lamb. As for donkeys, which are unfit for sacrifice, you shall either buy them back with a lamb or break their necks. When in times to come your sons ask you what this means, you shall say, "By the strength of his hand Jahweh freed us from slavery in Egypt. When the King refused to let us go, Jahweh killed every firstborn male in the land; therefore we sacrifice our cattle and redeem our sons. This is a memorial for ever, a tattoo on the right hand and a charm upon the brow, that Jahweh redeemed us from slavery by his own power". Now, therefore, Jahweh decrees that he will take the tribe of Levi as his own, in place of your sons. They will belong to him, and their cattle will be taken in place of your firstborn cattle; so your sons and cattle will be redeemed.'

Moses commanded that a second census should be taken, of every firstborn Israelite son over one month old. Then all male Levites of one month and older were counted; each Levite redeemed one firstborn Israelite; and there were found to be still two hundred and seventy three Israelites remaining. Moses decreed that they must be redeemed by paying five pieces of silver each to the priests, for the work of the Sanctuary. So all the firstborn of Israel were redeemed by the dedication of the Levites; they were chosen and called by God; the choice was not theirs, but they obeyed his will. The Levites were divided into three clans, after the three sons of Levi, each with its specific duties. The Gershonites were to carry the Sanctuary Tent and all the drapes and curtains of the Court, in two wagons; they camped on the west, behind the Sanctuary. The Merarites were to carry all the frames, posts and stands of the Sanctuary and the Court, in four wagons; they camped on the north of the Sanctuary. Both these clans worked under the direction of Ithamar the priest, and each man was responsible for some specific item and the service connected with it. The Kohathites, the clan of Moses and Aaron, were responsible for everything in the Sanctuary, and for the bronze altar; they camped on the south side of the Sanctuary. All the sacred objects would be wrapped in cloths of blue, red or purple by the priests alone; then the Kohathites would carry the covered objects on their own shoulders; but they were not allowed to enter the Sanctuary or to see the sacred objects uncovered. Eleazar the priest was in charge of the Sanctuary and its contents, and the clan of Kohath were his servants. Moses and the priests camped in front of the Sanctuary, on the east towards the sunrise. Moses took a census of all the Levites between the ages of thirty and fifty;

between these ages they performed full Sanctuary duties, and assisted their colleagues for some years before and after that.

The whole tribe of Levi was dedicated by Moses. Their bodies were shaved all over, so that afterwards their hair, new from their dedication, grew holy and untouched. They were sprinkled with water and their clothes washed. They brought two bulls, one for a sin-offering and one for a fire-offering; all the people laid their hands on the heads of the Levites, and they were presented as a special gift to Jahweh, devoted to the service of his priests, to protect the holiness of his Sanctuary. So the prophecy of Israel was fulfilled, that the sons of Levi were to have no inheritance among the tribes; but their loyalty to Jahweh was rewarded, for they became the servants of his priests, a gift from Israel to God. Without property of their own, they lived on the gifts of the Israelites, the yearly tithe which was taken from herds and crops and of which they in turn gave the best tenth to the Aaronite priests. The Levites became the servants of the servants of the Lord, given to God, born to serve, set apart by the divine will; by their dedication the people of Israel were protected from harm, when they approached the Sanctuary of the Almighty God.

The Journey Home (Num. 2, 9, 10)

On the twentieth day of the second month, in the second year after the people left Egypt, when they had been camped by the holy mountain for almost exactly one year, the cloud of the presence of Jahweh lifted from the Sanctuary. The priests, Eleazar and Ithamar, sounded long blasts on two silver trumpets. One trumpet was used for summoning the elders, and two for calling together the whole community. The sacred trumpets of Israel were used for calling to battle, to announce great feasts and the monthly New Moon festivals, and at every fire-offering and fellowship-offering. They announced the help of God and his deliverance from all enemies. So, at the double call, the whole community gathered around the Sanctuary, and Moses spoke to them:

'You have seen the cloud resting over the Sanctuary by day, and the fire by night. When that cloud rests upon the Sanctuary, we shall stay still, at the Lord's command. But when it lifts, after one night or one year, we shall move on and follow wherever it leads, pitching camp where it comes to rest. So we shall remain at God's command and travel on at God's command; he alone shall lead and protect us. Now the time has come to leave the sacred mountain and travel towards the land which God has promised. He has laid the land open before us; we are to go in and occupy it, the land which he swore to give to our forefathers Abraham, Isaac and Jacob and to their descendants. When short blasts are sounded on the trumpet, the tribes shall march, in due order, each group under its own standard, one group at each trumpet call. First, those who camp on the east of the Sanctuary; the tribe of Judah, with Issachar and Zebulun, marching under the standard of Judah, the royal lion, vanguard of Israel. Then the Levite clans of Gershon and Merari, carrying the Sanctuary in their six covered wagons. After them, those who camp to the south, the tribe of Reuben, with Simeon and Gad, under the standard of Reuben, the human face, the image of the invisible God. Next, the Levite clan of Kohath, carrying the sacred objects on their shoulders. Then those who camp to the west, the tribe of Ephraim, with Manasseh and Benjamin, under the standard of Ephraim, the roaring bull, protector of the weak. Finally, those who camp to the north, the tribe of Dan, with Asher and Naphtali, under the standard of Dan, the flying eagle, guardian of the skies. This shall be the rearguard of all the divisions of Israel. So our warriors will protect our families and herds, and the Sanctuary of Jahweh, as we march where God leads, towards the land of blessing.'

That day the trumpets sounded, and the tribes of Israel left the sacred mountain for ever. Moses raised his arms to the sky, before the Ark of the Covenant, covered by the inner screen of the Sanctuary and wrapped in a cloth of brilliant blue. 'Arise, Jahweh, and scatter your enemies', he chanted; 'Put to flight all those who hate your name'. The acolytes lifted up the Ark, and they led out the tribes of Judah, following the cloud towards the North. Moses watched them move out in their ordered ranks, and he felt the pride of accomplishment as the standards of Israel passed before him. On this mountain, God had commanded him to go alone to Egypt, to liberate an enslaved rabble and forge them into a nation of God's own choosing. Now the impossible had come to be; all the promises of God were reaching fulfilment. God had promised Abraham a great posterity; now the twelve tribes of Israel marched, united and confident. God had promised Abraham to be with his children for ever; now his presence brooded over the camp in cloud and fire. God had given the people his Law to follow, to lead them in the way of life. He had given them the sacrifices to forgive their sin and unite them to himself. He had sealed a Covenant in blood to assure them of his fidelity. Only one promise remained; the possession of a homeland where his people could be rooted and flourish as a free people, where the once alien and oppressed could live at home by honest toil, sovereign in their own country. As the tribes followed the cloud towards the fulfilment of the final promise, the men sang and the children danced and the women laughed aloud in their joy that God, who had set them free, was bringing them home.

The Place of Burning (Num. 10, 11)

For three days they moved northwards, into the great and desolate wilderness. Each morning, Moses chanted before the Ark: 'Arise, Jahweh, and scatter your enemies; put to flight all those who hate your name'; and the Ark journeyed before the people. Each evening, when the cloud came to rest, he chanted, 'Rest, Jahweh, god of the hosts of Israel'; the Ark was lowered reverently to the ground, and the people made camp around it. They took with them Hobab, son of Jethro, priest of Midian, as a guide. At first reluctant, he eventually agreed to throw in his lot with the Israelites. Moses promised him, 'If you come with us, we will share with you all the blessings which Jahweh will give us'.

The first enthusiasm soon began to wilt in the desert heat. Sand and rock stretched as far as one could see on every side. The heat at midday was almost unendurable. The bullock carts got stuck in drifts of sand; the children grew fretful and quarrelled; and everyone was hot, tired and more irritable each day. As Moses forced the people to march on from dawn to dusk, they began to curse and complain. Arguments broke out over the distribution of the small amounts of food they had; between those who lagged behind and those who hurried on; between different families who got in one another's way; between those who talked too much and those who said nothing. There was a mixed group of strangers travelling with the Israelites, and they complained constantly about the lack of meat. 'You have cattle and sheep', they said, 'but all you do is feed your god with them. Why should we not eat them?' Many of the Israelites began to agree, and said, 'In Egypt we had as much fish as we wanted, cucumbers and water melons, leeks, onions and garlic. But now our throats are parched; there is nothing wherever we look except manna, day after day, always the same. At first it tasted sweet and nourishing; but now it is like sawdust, sickly and choking. If only we could have meat for a change'. At the end of the day, the people stood at the entrances to their tents in groups, surly and discontented. Yet all that time, the cloud of Jahweh was leading them; and, where they stopped, it remained with them. Now, as they grumbled and complained, fire flashed from the cloud and burned the tents at the edge of the camp, like lightning striking a tree. The people ran to Moses in fear, and he said,

'This is your warning from the god of fire. To those who approach him with reverence and awe, he will be a flame in the heart and a light in the mind, filling his people with power and love. But to those who are stubborn, who reject his path and seek their own way, he will be a devouring fire. The flame of love will annihilate all who meet it with hatred, whose hearts are hardened in its presence. On the sacred mountain, Jahweh refused to go with you, for fear that his presence would destroy you. But you cried for his presence, and he heard your prayer. Remember then, O Israel, what you have desired, and revere the Lord.' When he had said this, Moses prayed to Jahweh and the fire died away. They called that place Taberah, the Place of Burning, because there the fire of Jahweh had burned among them.

The Graves of Desire (Num. 11)

The people moved on through the wilderness; but, in spite of all that had happened, they continued to complain. Moses was distressed at their constant dissatisfaction. 'Lord God', he prayed,

'Why have you brought such trouble on my head? How have I displeased you, that I am weighed down with the care of all these people? Did I conceive them? Did I bring them into the world, so that I must carry them in my arms, like a nurse with her children, to the land you promised to their ancestors? They pester me with their grumbling and demands for meat. But where can I find meat to give them, without destroying all our cattle which are meant for sacrifice and to be for the inheritance of our children? This whole people is too heavy a burden; I cannot bear it alone. If that is what you want of me, take pity and kill me now, so that I may not live to see my failure.'

Jahweh said, 'Choose seventy elders of Israel, leaders of the people, and bring them into the Sanctuary. I will descend among you, and take the Spirit which I conferred on you, and give it to them, as well as you. Then they will share with you the burden of caring for the people, and you will not have to carry it alone. As for meat, tell the people to consecrate themselves in readiness for tomorrow. For they shall have meat; they shall eat it, not just for one or two days, or five or ten or even twenty days, but for a whole month. They shall eat it until it comes out of their ears and makes them ill, because they have rejected the God who is present among them, and have regretted leaving Egypt at my command. They have chosen anxiety instead of hope; craving instead of contentment; regret instead of gratitude. They shall have what they desire; and they shall pay the price.'

Moses said, 'How can enough cattle be killed to feed the people like that for a month? Would all the fish in the sea be enough? How can they be fed?'

Jahweh answered, 'Is there any limit to the power of God? Today you will see whether or not my words come true'.

Moses told the people the words of Jahweh. He chose seventy elders and called them to the Sanctuary. The cloud descended, and the Spirit took posession of them. Immediately, they fell into a state of ecstasy, calling out in strange words and phrases, dancing and throwing themselves to the ground. Two of them, Eldad and Medad, had not gone to the Sanctuary, being ritually unclean. They were filled with the Spirit, nonetheless, and they fell into an ecstatic trance in the middle of the camp, proclaiming oracles of

God and shouting his praises. A young man ran and told Moses about them, and Joshua said, 'My Lord, they must be stopped'. But Moses said, 'Are you concerned to preserve my authority? I wish that all the people of God were prophets and that Jahweh would pour out his Spirit upon all of them'.

That night the people consecrated themselves, as God had commanded; and the next morning a great wind sprang up, driving from the west. A flock of quail, on their spring migration, were driven over the camp; thousands of birds swarmed around the camp, flying about a metre above the ground, as far as one could see in every direction. For two days and a night the people trapped as many birds as they could, so that even the man who got least had ten donkey loads. The birds were spread out to dry all around the camp; they remembered that a year previously they had caught quail in a similar way, but not in anything like this quantity. Now there was indeed meat for a month's eating. But as the people began eagerly to gorge themselves, almost immediately a terrible plague broke out in the camp; the people's greed received its reward.

At that place, both Moses and the Israelites complained to God; and God answered their complaints. The prophet complained out of a sense of pastoral concern and personal inadequacy, in total dependence on God; and God in answer gave the gift of the Spirit, of new life. The people complained out of gluttony, regret and discontent, rejecting the provision God had made for them; and God in answer gave the satiation of desire which leads to death. They called the place Kibroth-Hatta-Avah, the Graves of Desire; because there they buried many who had craved for meat.

Miriam's Jealousy (Num. 12)

Miriam the prophetess, sister of Moses, had taken a great dislike to his wife Zipporah, who was a foreigner, a Midianite. 'He should get rid of this woman', she said, 'How can he pose as the only mouthpiece of Jahweh to Israel, when he shares his bed with a foreigner, a daughter of the uncircumcised?' She talked with Aaron the High Priest, her brother, and persuaded him to join her in criticizing Moses' absolute authority. 'Is Moses the only one by whom Jahweh has spoken?', they said; 'Has he not spoken by us as well? Why then should he set himself up as the unique mediator between God and men? Such claims to uniqueness can only be a sign of misguided arrogance'. Moses was saddened and angered by his families' jealousy. He knew how reluctant he had been to become God's prophet, and how much he longed to share the burden of leadership with others. If he had a fault, it was excessive humility; for he knew that he owed everything to the power of God. He had endured complaints, disloyalty and threats on his life; but the most painful thing was his own sister's lack of understanding. He could think of no way of justifying himself, so he said nothing.

They had moved on to Hazeroth; and while they were there, Jahweh called Moses, Miriam and Aaron to come before the Sanctuary. Moved by the commanding inward voice that spoke from between the wings of the cherubim over the Ark, the voice that they heard clearly within them, though unheard by those with whom they walked, they approached the Sanctuary together. The cloud descended over the tent, and God called Miriam and Aaron to his presence.

Then God said: 'Hear what I say: if there is a prophet among you, I, Jahweh, make myself known to him in dreams and visions, and speak to him in riddles and occult sayings. It is not so with my servant Moses. I have entrusted him with the care of my people Israel; I speak with him face to face, clearly and not in ecstatic trance; he has seen the form of my glory. I have given these things to no other man. How, then, can you presume to speak against my servant Moses?' The cloud flashed with fire and ascended from the Sanctuary; and as Aaron turned to look at Miriam, he saw that her skin was diseased and disfigured, as white as snow.

'My lord', he said to Moses in alarm, falling to his knees, 'Forgive us; we have been foolish and have done what is wrong. But do not let us suffer this punishment; do not let Miriam your sister walk like a stillborn child, with half its flesh eaten away. Do not let her be excluded from her people and from the presence of Jahweh, because she is no longer whole.'

Moses said, 'Now my sister sees what she has inwardly become; her jealousy has brought about this corruption of her being; and you have followed her, in your weakness. Yet if you truly hear the words of God and repent, he will heal you'. Moses went up to Miriam and placed his hands on her head. Raising his face to heaven, he cried out, 'Heal her, O God'. At once, the disease left Miriam, and her skin was clear and whole again. She was excluded from the camp for seven days, which was the usual punishment for a woman who had brought shame on herself. At the end of seven days, Miriam returned to the camp, and Moses embraced his sister again with joy.

The Land of Promise (Num. 13; Deut. 1)

The Sinai desert is a scorched and desolate wilderness, where the wind has etched deep gullies into the hills and scattered sand and hard flinty stones over the barren rock. The east wind, the Sirocco, sweeps clouds of sand and grit across the plateau, stinging and blinding any who walk there. The sun beats down, reflected from the hills onto the open plain, creating a stifling and oppressive heat where every movement becomes a laborious agony. The tongue becomes swollen and the mouth dry; breathing becomes painful, as the hot air stings the nose and lungs; the skin grows taut and scaled; nothing is seen except bare featureless desert; nothing is heard but faint eddies of wind, scuffing the gritty sand. There is nowhere on earth more hostile to human life; every human sense is attacked and frustrated; the barest necessities of food and water are absent. Through this wasteland the Israelites moved, slowly and painfully, from one oasis to the next, with their cattle and children, living on tamarisk-resin and what little fruit they could find, or on desert scrub raised by the meagre winter rains.

After some weeks they came to the watering place of Kadesh, on the edge of the Mountains of the Negev. There Moses called them together and addressed them: 'This is the frontier of the land which Jahweh our god is giving us. Now we shall begin to take the inheritance which belongs to us. Jahweh has laid the land open before us. We must go forward in fulfilment of his promise to our fathers, and without fear.' The people looked at the forbidding mountain range before them, and were afraid. 'Let us send men to survey the country and report back to us', they said. So Moses chose twelve men, one leading member of each tribe, and sent them ahead to explore the land of Canaan.

For forty days the twelve walked through Canaan, filled with awe as they came to places of which they had only heard in tribal stories, where Abraham, Isaac and Israel had followed God's way and been given his promises. They walked through the Negev into the mountains of Judea, past Hebron, where Abraham, Isaac and Jacob were buried. They watched the sea break on the wide dunes of the coastal plain, where palm and orange groves, fields of corn and melons and great oak forests spread across the fertile earth. They climbed the hills of Samaria and Galilee, where beautiful villages lay cupped in gentle hills, and where streams of clear water splashed and rushed down into cultivated valleys, where fountains and springs watered the hill sides and covered them with clouds of sweet scented flowers. They rested in the valley of Jordan, first a swift flowing river, flowing from the majestic height of Mount Hermon, then twisting lazily down through a deep, rich valley between towering hills on either side, to the strange inland sea from which no river flows, whose still waters glisten under tropical heat. They camped on the green uplands east of Jordan, where sheep and cattle grazed, and where wheat fields and rich vineyards spread out over the table land, up to the very edge of the endless wilderness of the Syrian Steppes. There, between the uncharted sea and the hostile desert, lay a magic land of green trees and cool water under a clear sky, where gentle winds carried the fragrance of herbs and flowers; where figs, apricots and pomegranates refreshed the tongue and delighted the eye, where birds sang in the olive groves and clear water rippled over shaded hillsides; where the sun warmed and the shade soothed, and every moment from sunrise to sunset had its unique and particular beauty. That was the land God had set apart for his people, the enchanted land of Israel.

At the end of forty days they returned to Kadesh, bringing with them some of the fruit which flourished in late July, pomegranates and figs and a single cluster of grapes so large that it had to be carried on a pole by two men.

'These were cut in a valley of the hills near Hebron', they said;

'We named the valley Eshcol — Valley of Clusters; you see what the land is like; it is rich and fertile, flowing with milk and honey. Nevertheless, we found that those who live there are many and strong; their cities are large and well fortified. There are Amalekites, the nomad warriors with whom we have declared blood feud, in the Negev. The Hittite Empire, great and mighty invaders from the North, occupy the hills of Galilee and Samaria. The Jebusite tribe have built fortresses in the Judean hills, around Jerusalem. The Amorites have captured the hill country east of Jordan. The Canaanites control the lowlands, by the sea and in the Jordan valley. Worst of all, around Hebron we saw the descendants of the Necklace People, sons of the Nephilim, the giants of old, begotten by the sons of the gods. Beside those giants we felt like grasshoppers; and so we seemed to them. All these tribes and peoples are constantly at war with one another, so that the country is torn by violence and bloodshed, as one wave of invaders succeeds another. If we enter that land, we shall have no peace; we shall be swallowed up by the violence of the people who will surround us. We are not able to attack these people, for they are stronger than we are.'

Then the whole community cried out in dismay, and wept all that night. On the very border of the promised land, they hesitated, and fear held them back. They stayed weeping in the wilderness, while the land of their longing lay within their grasp.

Return to the Wilderness (Num. 14; Deut. 1)

At Kadesh, on the edge of Canaan, the Israelites turned against Moses and Aaron. 'It would be better to die in Egypt or in the wilderness than to be slaughtered by the giants of this land and imprisoned in their fortified cities', they said; 'Why should Jahweh bring us here, only to die in battle, so that our wives and children will become captives? It will be better to return to Egypt than this'; and they began to talk of choosing a leader to take them back through the desert. Moses and Aaron were in despair; all that they had done to bring the Israelites through the desert had ended in failure; faced with the challenge of danger, the people wanted only to return to slavery. Moses and Aaron threw themselves down on the ground before the people, and wept aloud to God.

Then Caleb, from the tribe of Judah, and Joshua the Ephraimite, who had led the raiding party against Amalek, tore their clothes in grief and anger, and said to all the people, 'We have been through all this land, and it is very good. Surely if God is pleased with us, he will bring us into this land, which flows with milk and honey, and give it to us. You must not rebel against God. For he is with us; he will remove the protection of their gods, and we shall devour them. Do not fear the people of the land. Let us go up at once and occupy the country; for we are easily able to conquer it'. But the people listened to the ten prophets of doom, rather than the two who trusted in God. They picked up stones and were about to stone Joshua and Caleb to death, when suddenly the dazzling light of God's presence appeared over the Sanctuary. The crowd were afraid and dispersed to their tents; and Moses entered the Sanctuary.

God said, 'How long will this people reject me? How long will they refuse to trust me, in spite of all the signs I have shown them? I will disinherit them, and raise up a great nation from you alone'.

But Moses replied, 'Lord, your name must be glorified among men. But if you destroy your people, the Egyptians and the Canaanites will mock your name, saying, "He has killed them in the wilderness, because he was not able to bring them safely into the land he had promised them, even though he led them in a pillar of cloud and fire". Therefore spare them, for the sake of your glory. Now, O Lord, let your power be shown, as you promised when you showed yourself to me on the sacred mountain in the vision of your glory: "Jahweh, patient, full of steadfast love, forgiving iniquity and rebellion, punishing sons and grandsons to the third and fourth generation for the iniquity of their fathers, but not destroying the guilty utterly". Forgive the wickedness of this people, by your great and steadfast love; even as you have forgiven them continually from Egypt until now.' Thus Moses prayed first that God might be glorified; and then, relying on the promises of God, he selflessly asked for the salvation of his people.

God said, 'Because of your prayer, I will forgive them. Yet their continuing faithlessness shall have its due consequence. Say to this people, "As I, Jahweh, live, and as my glory will fill the earth, I will give you what you have wished for. Your dead bodies shall fall in this wilderness. Of all the men who were registered at Sinai, who have seen my glory and the signs I showed in Egypt and in the desert, who have challenged me and disobeyed me ten times, from the first complaint against Moses in Egypt until now; of all those fighting men of Israel who have rebelled against me, not one shall see the land I promised to their ancestors. Only Caleb and Joshua, who have followed me with their whole hearts, shall enter the land and take possession of it, together with the Levites, women and children. Forty days you spent exploring the country; forty years you shall spend bearing your iniquity, one year for each day, until your bones lie in the desert. Your sons shall be wanderers in the wilderness all that time, suffering for your faithlessness; then I shall lead in those whom you thought would be captives, and they shall enjoy the land you have rejected. But, as for you, you shall know what it means to have me against you; this is what I will do to all this corrupt community who have combined against me: here in this wilderness you shall all die. I Jahweh, have spoken".'

Moses told the people the words of God, and they were overwhelmed with grief. That night a plague swept through the camp, and all the men who had walked through Canaan, and brought back their fear, died. Only Joshua and Caleb survived, of the twelve emissaries of Israel. God said, 'Now you must turn back from the land of your desire; tomorrow you must take the way to the Gulf of El Aqaba and return to the wilderness'.

The First Defeat (Num. 14; Deut. 1)

Early in the morning, the Israelites gathered together before the Sanctuary and said: 'We acknowledge our sin before God and repent. We have listened to the prophets of pessimism, and refused to trust God's promises. Now those false prophets are dead, and we can see that we were wrong. Therefore we will fasten on our weapons and attack the hill country, just as Jahweh first commanded us.'

But Moses turned on them and said, 'You do not know what repentance is. You are still disobeying God's command. Is not true repentance to surrender your own plans and desires, and submit to whatever God wills for you? To turn your heart from rebellion to obedience? Yet God has declared that none of you will enter the land, that you must turn back to the wilderness. Therefore do not go out to fight; for Jahweh will not be with you, your enemies will defeat you, and you will die by the sword.'

Nevertheless, the people persisted with their preparations and said, 'Surely it has always been God's will to bring us to this land and give it to us; why else would he bring us out of Egypt and give us his Law on the holy mountain? We confess our sin; we have failed our god many times. Yet he is a gracious god, patient and forgiving. Now if we go to take the country by force he will relent and be with us in battle. God will support the right, now that we show our trust in his help'.

But Moses would not move from the camp, and he refused to let the Ark of the Covenant go before the invading army. 'God has indeed forgiven you,' he said, 'But sin still has its price. At first you would not follow where God called; now you seek to make him follow you. But God, the Almighty, cannot be moved by man, unless he freely accepts the prayer of faith. By such prayer, I have chosen to share in the penalty of your sin, the forty years' wandering, the cost of your rebellion and the test of your faithfulness. If you attack now, you will show yourselves to have regret and not repentance; impetuosity and not obedience; folly and not faith. You will show that you have ceased to follow the Lord, and you will fight without him.'

The armies of Israel marched out, reckless and defiant, their banners flying in the morning light, to take possession of the land of promise. In the hills, the tribesmen of Amalek banded together with the Canaanites from the lowland valleys and the Amorites from east of the Jordan. As the Israelites came out of the desert, the highlanders descended on them like a swarm of bees and the plainsmen pierced their fighting lines with chariot thrusts. Faced for the first time with a trained and organized attack, the ill-disciplined Israelites, without the firm command of Moses or Joshua, broke up in disorder. They were pursued southwards as far as Hormah, in the Negev, and there they were crushed and defeated. That night Moses came and walked among the dead, the torn banners and discarded weapons and the cries of wounded men, and wept for his people. The proud army of Israel was shattered, and the words of God were fulfilled; for thirty eight years the defeated nation was forced to scrape a living from the desert between Kadesh and Eilat, excluded from the cultivated lands and scorned by the surrounding peoples, who had seen them driven back into the desert from which they had come. In the brown hills and rock-strewn plains of the inhospitable waste, a whole generation of the people of God lived and died, because their hearts were corrupt and they could not see the ways of God.

Rebellion (Num. 16)

Many long and barren years passed, and the old restlessness and discontent stirred among the people. Dathan and Abiram, who were descendants of Reuben and wished to see the ascendency of Jacob's eldest son preserved among the tribes, began to spread rumours about Moses' incompetence. Korah the Levite, and a cousin of Moses and Aaron, joined with the Reubenites, and gathered two hundred and fifty well-known leaders of the people to confront Moses and Aaron publicly.

Korah said, 'You have taken too much upon yourselves. All the people are holy, every one of them, and Jahweh is with each one, individually. Why, then, do you exalt yourselves above the community of God?'

Moses prostrated himself before Jahweh and prayed for a long while. Then he turned to Korah and said, 'Is it too small a thing for you that the God of Israel has set you apart from the people to serve him in the Sanctuary, to minister to his people and to be near him, you and your fellow Levites? Do you seek the priesthood also? God has chosen the descendants of Aaron to be his priests; when you murmur against Aaron, you are placing yourselves against God's choice. In the morning Jahweh will show who is his, who he chooses to set apart for himself. Bring the Levites who follow you, and the elders who support them, before the Sanctuary tomorrow. There let every man offer burning incense to Jahweh, and see whose offering God will accept. You will find that it is you who have taken too much upon yourselves.'

Korah and his followers departed, and Moses sent for Dathan

and Abiram, who had been inciting the people to revolt. But they refused to come to him, and said: 'Is it not enough that you have brought us away from the land flowing with milk and honey, to let us die in the desert? Must you also set yourself up as a prince over us? You have failed to bring us into the promised land, to give us our inheritance of green fields and vineyards. Do you think you are going to play some trick on us? We will not come.'

Moses was very angry, and said, 'Lord God, do not accept their sacrificial offerings; I have not harmed anyone, or misused my authority in any way'. That night a great storm sprang up in the Arabah rift valley, where their camp was. The wind howled through the tents, dislodging rock and sand from the cliffs round about; lightning flashed; and the sky took on a lurid and ominous glow, like sulphurous fire. The storm raged all night, and the people were filled with a premonition of fear.

The next morning Moses and Aaron stood by the entrance of the Sanctuary; Korah and his two hundred and fifty followers stood facing them, with the whole community gathered around, summoned by Korah to witness the humiliation of Moses and Aaron. The two hundred and fifty all took censers in their hands, with burning charcoal and incense in them, and offered their incense to God, while the people around them watched in silence. Suddenly the blinding light of God's glory appeared to all the people, and God said to Moses and Aaron, 'Stand apart from this people, that my holiness might annihilate their presumption'.

But Moses and Aaron threw themselves to the ground and said, 'O God, the God of all living things, do not take the lives you have created for the sin of one man.'

So God said, 'Let all the people depart to their tents, except Korah and his followers'.

Then Moses took the elders of Israel and went to the place where Dathan and Abiram were camped. He called out to the people, 'Move away from the tents of Korah, Dathan and Abiram; stand well clear and touch nothing that belongs to them, or you will be swept away with all their sins'. Moses and the elders stood, bracing themselves against the screaming wind, and Dathan and Abiram came to the entrance of their tents, with their families, and faced Moses defiantly. Moses shouted into the wind, 'Now you shall know that Jahweh sent me to do all that I have done, that it was not by my own will. If these men share the common fate of men and die a natural death, then Jahweh has not sent me. But if Jahweh brings judgement upon them, then you shall know that they have despised their god'. As he finished speaking, the wind roared with increased ferocity, blowing dark dust clouds between the two groups of men, enveloping them in suffocating darkness. There was a splitting, cracking sound, and the earth began to move and tremble under their feet. Men ran screaming in terror, as the hard baked surface on which the tents had been set split and disintegrated, revealing the deep lake of liquid mud which lay beneath. As the storm broke up the surface, all the tents of Korah, Dathan and Abiram and their followers slid down into the mud; in a few seconds, the earth had closed over them, and not a trace of them remained. As the dust cloud cleared, the people shouted, 'They have gone down alive to the place of the dead; the earth has swallowed them up'. Then the fire of Jahweh flashed from the altar and destroyed Korah and his followers, who still stood by the Sanctuary, holding up their censers before them in supplication and terror.

Thus Jahweh declared who was his. The men who had seen his glory on the mountain; who had followed him day by day in the pillar of cloud and fire; who had been twice saved from death by the prayers of Moses, still persisted in sin, and at last faced the judgement of the God of storm and fire. Rejecting God's clear choice, seeking to exalt his own status and ignore the way of worship God decreed, destroying the unity of God's chosen people, Korah had led the whole community to challenge the Law of their God. They came before Jahweh for judgement; and his judgement was openly declared.

The High Priest (Num. 16, 17)

The morning after the earthquake and fire, Moses told Eleazar the priest to scatter the ashes from the censers of the two hundred and fifty men of Korah who had offered incense to God, because, having been offered, they were holy, set apart for ever from common use. He told Eleazar to take the bronze from the censers and beat it into plates to make a covering for the altar of sacrifice. Thus when they saw the altar covered in bronze the people would remember the fate of Korah, and know that they could not presume to approach the living God in their own strength, but only through the priesthood and the sacrifices that God himself ordained.

Meanwhile, the people all gathered around the Sanctuary and accused Moses and Aaron of killing God's people by sorcery. Once more the cloud covered the tent, and Moses and Aaron approached it. The voice of Jahweh said, 'Stand apart from this people, for now I will destroy them once and for all'. Moses and Aaron threw themselves to the ground; and a great epidemic fell upon the people; they began to die where they stood. Moses told Aaron to take his censer, put fire from the altar in it, with incense, and make atonement for the people. Aaron took his censer and ran fearlessly into the middle of the assembly; he stood between the living and the dead and interceded for the people, making atonement for them with a pure incense offering. The High Priestly prayer was heard, and the plague stopped. When Aaron returned to Moses at the Sanctuary, one fortieth of the people had died.

The people then said to Moses, 'We shall die, one and all. Everyone who comes near the Sanctuary of Jahweh dies. Must we all then be killed?'

Moses said, 'The sons of Aaron shall be responsible for the altar and the Sanctuary. Theirs alone is the priest's work of sacrifice, and they shall stand within the Sanctuary to protect you from the holiness of Jahweh. The tribe of Levi shall assist them and maintain the Sanctuary; but the Aaronite priests alone shall approach the altar to offer sacrifice to God; any other man who does so shall die. Thus the Law of God shall be upheld and his holiness maintained. Moreover, God will give you a sign to silence your complaints and confirm the authority of Aaron the High Priest.'

Moses told every tribal chief to bring a bare almond branch, with his name on it; then he placed all twelve before the Ark of the Covenant in the Sanctuary Tent. The next day, when he entered the Sanctuary, he found that the branch for the tribe of Levi, bearing the name of Aaron, the tribal chief, had flowered, producing almond blossom and ripe almonds. He brought the branches out to the people, and each chief took his branch; they saw that all the branches were bare, except for one, filled with beautiful almond blossom. The bare tree had blossomed; Jahweh had made his choice plain, and confirmed it by bringing new life from the dead tree. The almond bough was placed in the Inner Sanctuary and kept there. With the Law of God and the bread of life in the wilderness, the flowering almond branch stood to remind the people of Israel that their God had appointed a High Priest whose intercession was acceptable and effective to save them from death, and whose authority was confirmed by the sign of imperishable beauty springing from death. The three symbols of God rested among the people of Israel; there, in the innermost Sanctuary, the tables of the Law showed the call and command of the father of his people; the jar of manna showed the day by day companionship of the one who is the bread of life; and the almond bough showed the hope and promise of new life to be breathed by his spirit upon all his own people.

The Well of Dispute (Num. 20; cf. Num. 21)

In the first month of the fortieth year after the Israelites left Egypt, they came back to Kadesh, where the curse of Jahweh had been laid on them so many years before. For thirty eight years they had been condemned to pitch their tents in the desert between the Negev and the Gulf of Aqaba, moving continually from place to place in search of food and water. While they lived at subsistence level, while the first generation of slaves who had escaped from Egypt died out, Moses and Joshua trained the young men in the skills of warfare, so that they would never again suffer the humiliation that had driven them back into the desert at Hormah. Now at last they were almost ready; the unruly and quarrelsome tribal groups had been forged into a unity by rigorous enforcement of the divine Law and strict adherence to the cult of the central Sanctuary and the elaborate rituals of sacrifice. They were tempered by hardship, fired with the desire to enter and settle the land of God's promise and escape the frugal and uncertain way of life of desert nomads. Moses was a very old man; while they were at Kadesh, his sister Miriam died, and he knew he had not long to live. The attack would have to begin very soon.

They stayed some time, planning and preparing; then the springs began to run dry. The people began to argue with Moses and Aaron, 'If only we had died when our brothers died before Jahweh', they said; 'Why do you keep us in this desert, where men and cattle starve and die? Why did we leave Egypt, to come to this evil place, without wheat or figs, vines or pomegranates? There is not even water to drink; we would be better dead.' As Moses listened to their complaints, he was suddenly overwhelmed with despair and disillusionment. The people had not changed at all; from the first moment he had come to them in Egypt until now, when they stood for the second time on the border of Canaan, they had remained the same, sullen, rebellious and discontented. The last time they had been here they had lost God's promise because of their stupid complaints; and now they were repeating the same old pattern. Moses saw the promised land slipping away, beyond reach for ever, and for the first time he hated this people for whom he had renounced his own happiness and security, to whom he had given his whole life, sharing with them the hardships of the desert when he could so easily have left them to God's judgement. He threw himself down before the Sanctuary, his body in the attitude of prayer but his heart bitter and angry.

The light of God's presence shone from the Sanctuary, and Moses heard the voice of God within him: 'Take your staff; assemble all the people; then, with Aaron your brother, speak to the rock which I will show you; and it will give water for the people and their cattle'. Moses heard; and, with Aaron, he assembled the people before a great rock, a little way from the camp. Moses looked at the people, so quick to complain, so forgetful of God's mercy, and in that moment he saw them as others saw them; not a nation of priests, chosen by God to serve him; but a rabble of timid, querulous gipsies.

'Listen to me, you rebels', he shouted, 'You have been a burden on me since the day I liberated you from Egypt. Whenever anything goes wrong, you complain to me and to Aaron my brother, and expect us to put everything right. Have you got no self reliance or courage? Must we do everything for you? Must we now get water out of this rock for you? Is there no end to your grovelling self pity?' With that, he raised his hand angrily and struck the rock twice with his staff. At once, a stream of water gushed out; enough for all the people and their cattle to drink. Then the people of Israel sang this song, which became a song to celebrate the digging of new wells in Israel: 'Spring up, water from the earth. Greet it with song, the well discovered by the leaders of the people, laid open with the ruler's staff, a gift from the wilderness'.

But God said to Moses and Aaron, 'You have not believed in me, to sanctify me before the people of Israel. You disobeyed my command and your heart was filled with hatred for my people. You struck the rock in anger and did not give me the glory for the things that I have done. You did not trust in the future that I had in store for you, but gave way to despair and bitterness. Therefore even now you have lost the vision of my presence, and you shall not lead the people into the land which I promised to give them.'

So at the last moment, on the edge of the promised land, Moses the servant of God, who talked with him face to face, lost the thing that he had longed for throughout his life, and was commanded to remain in the wilderness. Sadly he accepted the word of God, and called the place Meribah-by-Kadesh, the place of dispute and holiness, because the people disputed there with God, and God showed his holiness among them by bringing water from the dry rock.

The Death of Aaron (Num. 20; Deut. 2)

The Israelites were now ready to leave the desert and begin to settle in Canaan. The army was strong and well trained, and the people were eager to leave the hostile wilderness. The tribal commanders planned to enter Canaan from the East, from the heights across the Jordan, instead of trying to penetrate the heavily defended hill country of the Negev, where they had been defeated thirty eight years before. Moses sent messengers from Kadesh to the King of Edom, who controlled a wide area of desert and mountain territory between the Dead Sea and the Gulf of Aqaba.

They said: 'The people of Israel, descendants of Jacob, brother of Esau, ancestor of your people, send you greeting. You know the hardship that came upon us; how the sons of Israel went to Egypt, and stayed there many years; how the Egyptians took us as slaves;

and how Jahweh heard our cry of distress, and sent an angel to bring us out of Egypt. He delivered us, and we are now at Kadesh, near your borders. We wish to return to Canaan, if you will allow us to pass through your land. We will go along the King's Highway; and we will not turn aside to the right or to the left, until we have passed through your territory. For our eyes are fixed on the promised land'.

But the King of Edom said, 'You shall not pass through; we will resist you with force'.

The messengers said, 'We will not trespass on fields or vineyards; we will stay on the caravan road. We will not take water from your wells, and we will pay for any water we or our cattle need. We do not even wish to ride through; we will go on foot, nothing more'.

But the King still refused. He sent the messengers back and despatched a strong army to the border to guard the main road through Edom. Moses said to the people, 'Old enmities fade slowly; Esau still distrusts his brother Jacob, who once betrayed him and took his birthright. But we shall not fight him. The Lord has told me that he has given this land to the people of Esau, as he has kept a land for the Moabites and Amonites, descendants of Lot. Just as he will drive out the people of Canaan before us, because of their immoral ways, so he drove out the Rephaim, the tall Necklace tribes, before Edom and Moab. Lot and Esau were not chosen to be his covenant people; yet they are still under his hand; outside the Law and the promise, they live under the will and mercy of Jahweh, and we must not invade their land. We will go around their borders.'

The people left Kadesh and made towards the north east, along the border of Edom. But when they came to the mountain called Hor, Aaron knew that he was near death. Moses called Aaron and Eleazar his eldest son, and they climbed the mountain at the command of God, while the assembled tribesmen watched in silence. The evening sun glowed among the mountains, long shadows on jagged peaks, golden and black on the clear sky, as the three figures slowly climbed from sight. It was night when they reached the summit, the first High Priest of Israel with his brother and his son, coming in silence to be gathered to his people and his god. Solemnly, Moses took the priestly robes from the old man and placed them on his son and successor; the tunic and girdle, the robe and kilt, the breastplate and crown; the symbols of priestly care for Israel were passed on for the future. There on the top of the mountain, on the first day of the fifth month of the fortieth year after the exodus from Egypt, Aaron the High Priest died, the golden voiced orator whom God had called to stand with Moses before the King of Egypt; whose weakness had led him to apostasy at Sinai and rebellion at Hazeroth; whose courage had led him to stand among the plague-ridden people to pray for them in the Arabah; whose authority had been vindicated by God in the sign of the flowering almond branch. He did not see the land of promise during his life; but on Mount Hor he was gathered into the arms of his ancestors, and saw the promise which lies beyond all earthly places. In the dawn light, Moses and Eleazar came down from the mountain, to where the people still waited. When they saw that Aaron was dead, they mourned for him for thirty days, and wept for him as for a King.

The Bronze Serpent (Num. 21)

The King of Arad, a walled city in the Negev, had watched the build-up of Israelite military strength with alarm; and when he saw them staying at Kadesh and Mount Hor for six months, he decided that they were preparing for an attack to the north. While they were still in mourning, he attacked their camp by Mount Hor, killing many people and taking a number of prisoners. The Israelite commanders thereupon made a vow to Jahweh, putting the city of Arad and its allies under the Ban. They vowed that, if Jahweh gave them victory, they would hand over everything to him as the real victor, by killing or destroying all the spoils of war. This was the most savage and terrifying form of Israelite warfare, and it was reserved for those who were considered to be the enemies of Jahweh. Once put under the Ban, buildings and fields were destroyed by fire; men, women, children and cattle were consigned to death by the sword; in the holy war of Jahweh, once begun, after due warning, there was no further room for mercy; everything was totally destroyed. The armies of Israel marched north, overtaking Arad's troops at Hormah, and annihilated them. They razed the cities in the area to the ground. Thus they avenged the defeat their fathers had suffered at that place.

The people wanted to go on northwards; but Moses could see that, though they had won their first victory in Canaan, they were still too inexperienced to wage a campaign against the league of city states in the Judean hills. It would still be better to adopt his former plan of attacking across the Jordan, in the north. So he decided to travel in a large circle around the borders of Edom, down to the Gulf of Aqaba and then north along the eastern boundaries of Edom and Moab. They turned south again and made for the Arabah rift valley. But the people were impatient and said: 'We are tired of this worthless manna, and of this miserable life without food or water. Why did our fathers come out of Egypt, only to die in this wilderness?' Thus they protested against God's providence; and a plague of desert snakes overran the camp, inflicting fatal bites on many of the people. They came to Moses and said: 'These are demons of the desert, sent by Jahweh to punish us because we spoke against him and against you. We confess that we have sinned; now pray that Jahweh will take these snakes away from us.' Moses made a bronze serpent and set it on a pole, its coils twisted around the pole, its head resting on a short cross-piece, where everyone could see it. 'Jahweh has told me that if you are bitten by a snake, you must look at this serpent of bronze, and you will live', he said. Lying behind this strange action was the desert tradition that demonic forces could be overcome and their destructive power appeased by venerating an image which represented and expressed them. The serpent was the dangerous earth guardian, protector of the place of the dead, possessor of the power to kill and therefore of the power to heal, implacable enemy of living man, who alone could heal the hurts he brought to the world. The power of Jahweh compelled this demon god to bend to his will, so that the symbol of evil was transformed, by the will of Jahweh, into an instrument of healing and life. The primordial serpent which threatened and killed mankind in the garden, was brought under the power of God, and from the place of death, the final enemy, men found the source of renewed life. But for Israel the serpent was no jinn or demon, with power of its own over men; it was a sign given by the command of Jahweh, with his promise of healing for all who looked towards it in obedience to him alone. The serpent that Moses made was kept by the Israelites; it later came to be worshipped; sacrifices were offered before it and it was called Nehushtan. Even that which is commanded by God may be misused and lead men away from him; and it was eventually destroyed by King Hezekiah, during his religious reforms. But in the desert, the people only had to look towards it, and they lived. At this point, as Israel approached the promised land to claim her inheritance, God gave his people this mysterious symbol of their final destiny: the sign of death, raised up before men so that all who look to it shall overcome death and be healed. The destiny of Israel, God's chosen son, is to be that sign, raised up in the wilderness of the world for its salvation.

The Conquest Begins (Num. 21; Deut. 2, 3)

After a long march around the western border of Edom, the Israelites reached the Gulf of Aqaba. There at last they turned north and made for the eastern bank of the Jordan. Excitement mounted among the people as, day by day, they came nearer to the promised land. They marched through Oboth and Abarim, buying food and water from the Edomites, but being careful not to harass or provoke them. On across the gorge of Zared they travelled, moving more quickly now, with eager songs and a strong step until they came to the river Arnon, flowing westward into the Dead Sea. The *Book of the Wars of Jahweh* speaks of the watershed and the gorges of Arnon that fall away towards the frontiers of Moab; for the Arnon is the dividing line between Moab, where the Israelites were forbidden to go by God, and the Amorite territory. They kept well over to the east, in the trackless wastes of Arabia. But they no longer grumbled or moved dejectedly over the wilderness; for they were marching north to a homeland of their own. And as they moved on, through Beer, Nahaliel and Bamoth, each name was one more milestone towards expected victory. When they finally camped in the valley below the summit of Mount Pisgah, on the edge of the desert, they at once prepared to confront Sihon, King of the Amorites, and provoke him to battle.

Moses sent messengers to the King's Court at Heshbon, saying: 'Let us pass through your territory. We will not turn aside into fields or vineyards; we will not drink from your wells; we will keep to the King's Highway, until we cross the Jordan to the land Jahweh is giving us. We will pay you in full for what we eat and drink, as we did in Edom and Moab.' But Sihon was afraid; he had taken all his territory from the Moabites with the sword, and ruled by terror. God hardened his heart; he called his army together and marched against Israel at Jahaz, on the edge of the desert. There God promised Israel victory; and they utterly defeated the Amorite army. From the Arnon to the Jabbok, the Israelites stormed through the countryside, taking and plundering the cities, killing the inhabitants and setting their nomad tents in the ruins of the walled cities. They avoided only the territory of the Amonites, descendants of Lot, who lived on the upper reaches of the Jabbok and in the hills, according to God's decree. The poets wrote a song to commemorate their victory:

Come to Heshbon, court of the King;
Let us see the city of Sihon restored.
The flame of war had flared from the city
Driving Moab down to the Arnon deeps.
The companies of the Moabite god Kenosh were conquered,
His sons were killed and his daughters captured by the King.
But look now, Heshbon lies in ruin, wailing,
We have fanned a fire of our own as far as Medeba.

Intoxicated by victory, the Israelites pressed on northwards as far as Bashan. There, at Edrei, they fought a great battle with Og, King of Bashan, a giant of the Rephaim, the last survivors of the Nephilim, children of the gods. Jahweh said, 'Do not be afraid; I have delivered him into your hand; you must fight without fear. It will not be easy; you must fight with courage and tenacity to obtain what I have promised'. Jahweh caused a great fear and dread to fall on the defending forces; and Israel slaughtered them mercilessly. The coffin of Og, made of iron, fourteen feet long and six feet wide, was kept at Rabbah for many years. The Israelites took sixty cities in the territory of Bashan after the battle of Edrei, and they then held all the land east of the Jordan from the Arnon to the foot of Mount Hermon. From the high and fertile tablelands of Transjordan they looked over to the hills of Judea and Samaria, and they knew that the time for the fulfilment of the promise was at hand. The conquest of Canaan had begun.

The Wizard, the Donkey and the Angel (Num. 22)

Balak, King of Moab, watched the Israelite conquest of the east bank of the Jordan with alarm. 'This horde of nomads will completely encircle us', he said. 'Even if they do not attack us, they will devour everything around us, as a herd of oxen eats a field bare of grass; and we will be hemmed in for ever'. So Balak consulted with the chiefs of some of the tribes who had been allied with Sihon, whose territory the Israelites now occupied. Together they sent court officials to the north east, to the upper Euphrates, where there lived a sorcerer, famous for the power of his spells, Balaam, son of Beor. The courtiers came to Balaam and gave him the fee for divination.

They said, 'A horde of nomads has come from Egypt, and has camped on our borders; they cover the earth like locusts. King Balak of Moab wishes you to put a curse upon them. They are too strong and numerous to be taken in battle, unless you curse them; for the power of your sorcery is renowned throughout the world'.

Balaam heard what they had to say, and considered. 'Stay here with me tonight', he said; 'I will consult the gods, and tell you what they say'. While they slept, the wizard entered into deep trance, in which occult powers and strange dark forces came into his consciousness and left cryptic signs and omens, for him to decipher. That night, however, it was Jahweh, god of the Hebrews, who came to his dreaming state and spoke to him: 'You shall not go with these men; you shall not curse this people, for they are blessed'. In the morning, Balaam told the courtiers that Jahweh had refused to let him go; so they returned alone to Moab.

Balak said, 'We have not offered him enough'. So he sent more courtiers, of greater rank, with the offer of great riches and honour, if Balaam would curse the tribes of Israel. 'If the King gave me his palace, full of silver and gold, I could not go beyond what I am commanded, to do either less or more', Balaam said. But he asked them to stay the night again, and again consulted the gods.

Once more, Jahweh came to Balaam in the night and said, 'If these men have come for you, go with them; but you must do only what I tell you to do'. In the morning, Balaam saddled his donkey, and set out with the courtiers of Moab. But as he went, he thought of all the King of Moab had offered him, and he determined to do as he wished, and curse the Israelites.

The wizard was riding some way behind the courtiers, with his two servants, when suddenly his donkey swerved from the road, for no apparent reason, and into the field. Balaam struck the donkey, but with no effect. They went along a narrow path between two vineyards, with a wall on either side; then, equally suddenly, the donkey pushed sharply against the wall, pressing Balaam's leg painfully against it. Again he struck the animal, and they went on down the alley way. At a place where the two walls came close together, leaving only a narrow gap, the donkey abruptly lay down on the ground. Balaam tumbled off in a fury, and started beating the stupid beast violently. A moment later he stopped in astonishment, as the donkey opened its mouth and said,

'What have I done to you, to make you beat me these three times?'

Recovering momentarily, the wizard said, 'Because you have been making a fool of me. If I had a sword with me, I expect I should have killed you by now'.

The donkey looked at him, as sorrowfully as only donkeys can, and said, 'Am I not your donkey, on which you have ridden all your life to this day? Have I ever done such a thing before?'

'Well, no . . .' said Balaam; and then his mouth dropped open. For he could see, quite clearly, just in front of the crouching donkey, completely filling the space between the walls of the vineyards, a fiery angel, tall and shining, with a drawn sword in its hand. At once he threw himself to the ground; and the angel said,

'Why have you beaten your donkey these three times? I came to bar your way, because in your mind you had determined to take pay for doing wrong. Three times I stood before you in the way, but in your wilfulness you did not see me and came straight for me. It was your donkey, simplest and most humble of beasts, who saw me and turned aside. If she had not done so, I would have killed you, though she would not have been harmed.'

Balaam replied, 'I have done wrong; for I did not see that you stood in the road against me. Now, if my journey displeases you, I will go back again'.

But the angel said, 'Go on with these men; but you shall say only what I tell you to say'. So Balaam went on his way towards Moab.

King Balak came to the border of Moab, to the Arnon gorge, to meet the great wizard, and said, 'Did I not send to call you? Why did you not come before now? Did you think I would not reward you?'

Balaam replied, 'Here I am now. But I have no power of my own to say anything. Whatever God declares to me, that is what I will say'. Balak and Balaam travelled together to Kiriath-huzoth, south of the Dead Sea, and Balak slaughtered many cattle and sheep to prepare a feast to celebrate the cursing of Israel. But Balaam kept silent and waited for the word of God.

The First Oracles of Balaam (Num. 23)

In the morning King Balak led Balaam up to the heights of Baal, sanctuary of the Lord Kenosh, high god of Moab. From there they could see the southernmost tents of Israel, the nation he had been brought to curse. Balaam said, 'Build seven new altars here and offer on each altar a bull and a ram. Then, as you stay by the sacrifice, I shall go alone to a bare mountain top. It may be that a god will meet me there. Whatever he reveals to me, I will tell you'. Balak did as he was asked, and Balaam went alone in search of omens, and to practise the arts of sorcery. As he both feared and expected, the angel of Jahweh appeared to him and put words into his mouth, saying, 'Return to Balak, and say these words to him'. He returned to where Balak and the Moabite chiefs still stood, by the seven sacrifices, and declared this oracle:

From Aram and the eastern mountains
Balak King of Moab brought me;
'Come', he said, 'Curse Jacob for me,
Cast your evil spell on Israel'.
How can I curse whom Jahweh has not cursed?
How can I bring evil on those to whom God wills no evil?
From these bare heights I see them,
From these high hills I watch;
I see a people who live alone,
Set apart among all nations;
The host of Jacob cannot be counted,
They are blessed with children like the sand of the sea.
May I die as these men will die,
Blessed with honour and fruitfulness.

When he had spoken, Balak said, 'What have you done to me? I asked you to curse my enemies, and you have done nothing but bless them'. Balaam answered, 'Must I not speak only the words that God puts on my lips?' Then Balak took the wizard to a field near the summit of Mount Pisgah, at the northern end of the Dead Sea, well inside the newly acquired Israelite territory. Again he built seven altars and offered seven sacrifices, saying, 'From here you can see the hosts of Israel more clearly; now you may curse them for me more effectively'. Again Balaam went in search of omens, while Balak and his chiefs stayed by the sacrifices. When he returned, Balak asked eagerly, 'What has God said to you?' Balaam said, 'God met me, and put these words into my mouth';

'Rise, Balak, son of Zippor;
Hear what I am charged to say:
God is not man, that he should lie,
A son of man, to change his mind.
Has he spoken and will not do it?
What he proclaims he will fulfil.
I have received command to bless;
He has blessed, I cannot undo it.
He has not seen disaster in Jacob, nor decreed trouble in Israel.
Jahweh the Lord their God is with them,
Acclaimed among them as their King.

The power of God brought them from Egypt,
Like the horns of the wild bull he is their strength.
Israel is immune to magic.
No enchantment ensnares Jacob.
All shall say of Jacob and Israel,
'See the thing that God has done';
A people rising like a lioness,
Rearing like a hungry lion;
It will not rest until it kills its prey
And drinks the blood of its enemies.'

When he heard this oracle, Balak said, 'If you will not curse them, at least do not bless them'. But Balaam answered, 'Did I not warn you that I must do all that God tells me?' So the prophet who came to curse Israel found himself, even against his will, overwhelmed by the power of Jahweh, and compelled to bless the tribes which God had taken to be his own.

The Oracle of the Star (Num. 24)

'Come with me to Mount Peor', said Balak the King; 'From there, you can look out over the barren plain by the Jordan, opposite Jericho, where all the Israelite armies have camped. Perhaps it will please God to allow you to curse them from there'. For the third time, seven sacrifices were offered on seven altars, and Balaam prepared to curse Israel. But he knew in his heart that Jahweh would bless Israel again; he did not go apart to consult the omens, but stood looking out over the plain, where the tents of Israel were encamped, tribe by tribe. As he stood there, the Spirit of God came upon him, and he fell to the ground in ecstatic trance. After a time, he rose to his feet, head raised and with closed eyes, and declaimed in a high sing song voice, almost absurd yet peculiarly impressive:

'This is the oracle of Balaam, son of Beor,
The word of the man whose sight is clear;
Who hears the words of El, the Eternal,
Who understands the knowledge of Elyon, the Most High,

Who sees the visions of the Almighty, El Shaddai,
In ecstasy and with the inward eye:
Desirable are your tents and dwellings, O Israel,
Like rows of palms or gardens by the river,
Like cedars planted by God beside still waters.
Your wells shall overflow and your sowing be fruitful;
Your King shall be greater than Agag, ruler of Amalek.
The power of God has brought you out of Egypt,
Like the horns of the wild bull he is your strength and pride;
You shall break the bones of your enemies and devour them,
You shall lie like a lion and no one will dare to rouse you;
Blessed be everyone who blesses you;
They who curse you will themselves be cursed.'

When he heard this oracle, Balak was enraged, and beat his hands together. 'I summoned you to curse my enemies', he said, 'And now you have blessed them three times. Return to your own country at once, and go empty handed. I promised you great honour; but it is Jahweh, you say, who has kept this honour from you'. Balaam replied, 'I told your messengers plainly, 'Even if Balak gave me his whole palace, full of silver and gold, I could not go beyond what I was commanded to say, either less or more. For I cannot speak of my own will; I say only what the gods tell me. I will return to my people; but first, I will warn you what this people will do to your people in days to come'. Once more, the Spirit fell upon him; his body jerked and stiffened, and words came from his mouth that were not his words, but came from afar, with a hidden meaning that none who heard them could fully grasp, which seemed to speak not only of future time but also of time's end:

'This is the oracle of Balaam, son of Beor,
The word of the man whose sight is clear;
Who hears the words of El, the Eternal,
Who understands the knowledge of Elyon, the Most High;
Who sees the visions of the Almighty, El Shaddai,
In ecstasy and with the inward eye:
I see him, but not now;
I behold him, but not near;

A star shall rise from Jacob,
A royal sceptre from Israel.
He shall crush the head of Moab
And beat down all the sons of strife.
Edom shall be dispossessed; so
Those who corrupt the people of God
And those who bar his way shall fall;
Out of Jacob shall come the Conqueror
Destroying the remnants of the City of Sin.'

Balaam paused; then turned and looked to the south west:

'Amalek, the first of all the nations
Shall end in ruin; nothing shall remain.'

Again he paused; then suddenly he looked towards Jerusalem and spoke again:

'People of Cain, on the mountain crags of Judaea,
You seem secure, but you are doomed to burning;
How long can you live on the hills where I now see you?'

Again a pause; then the strange inspired speech began, but more hesitant and stumbling:

Who shall be living when God brings this to be?
When alien ships from the West come over the sea,
Bringing disaster to Assyria and Persia alike,
Destruction to all who think themselves secure . . .'

Balaam finally stopped, as if his flickering inner visions had stuttered and failed; there was complete silence as he stood, shivering and breathing heavily. Then, as suddenly as it had begun, it was over. The wizard shook his head briefly, turned and walked away. Balak glared balefully after him, and then gestured to his Chiefs to begin the journey back to Moab. The Seer from the land of the two rivers, from the place where God had first called Abram, father of Israel, to seek the promise, had prophesied in the Spirit about the Star of Israel, rising unconquerably in times to come; and, though everything in him resisted the thought, Balak knew with inward dread that all he had said would come true.

The God of Peor Mountain (Num. 25)

Balaam the prophet had come to curse Israel, but God turned his curse into a blessing. Three times Jahweh compelled him to bless Israel, and a fourth time the Spirit showed him the things that were to come. But before he returned to his home, he earned his payment from the King of Moab. 'The God of the Hebrews will not permit me to put a curse on his people', he said, 'But there is another way. Where even magic fails, temptation can succeed. The Israelites are protected by their god from harm by sorcery; but they can be weakened from within, by the strength of their own desires'. So he suggested that the tribeswomen of the occupied territories should seduce the soldiers of Israel and, under the pretext of hospitality, invite them to their sacred feasts. Balaam then departed for Mesopotamia, and the women began to do as he said. The gods of that people were gods of fertility, of blood and soil, and their cult involved ritual prostitution and homosexuality. At their sacrifices, the worshippers aimed to overcome the limitations of human life by intoxication and indulgence in perverse and sadistic sexual acts. In this way, they tried to transcend good and evil and achieve ecstatic unity with the creative and destructive powers which give birth to life in passion and destroy it again in ruthless power. When the women had seduced the soldiers, they invited them to such ceremonies; and before they knew it, the irrevocable step was taken, and they found themselves bowing before the phalluses and obscene masks of the Baal of Peor, Lord of earth and underworld, and binding themselves to serve him. The Israelites began to abandon the hard moral law of Jahweh for the ecstatic life, beyond morality, of Baal; they turned from the intangible promise of a future Kingdom to the present enjoyment of sensual delight; they broke the covenant with the unseen High God, and bound themselves to the felt realities of passion and power. Where neither sorcery nor military might could succeed, the Midianite women triumphed. The unity, determination and discipline of the Israelite troops began to disintegrate, as the sacrificial cult and the Law were increasingly ignored, and the soldiers gave way to sensuality and to religious and moral indifference. After the desert, this life was more than good enough. They revelled in it, unaware that Balak, King of Moab, watched from his northern border, waiting until they were weak and demoralized enough to strike.

But Jahweh commanded Moses to rally the people, and order the judges whom he had appointed to put to death all those who had worshipped the Baal of Peor. The apostate chiefs were flung down from the mountain at sunrise, so that their deaths could atone for Israel's sin. The rest of the people gathered before the Sanctuary, weeping and lamenting for their sin, and praying that the people would be delivered from corruption and death. Even as they wept, Cozbi the daughter of Zur, a midianite chief, persuaded Zimri, son of a Simeonite chieftain, to bring her into the camp. He went with her into the inner chamber of his family tent to have intercourse. Thus he openly flaunted the authority of Moses, ignored the cultic lament and broke the rules of ritual purity which were in force. The people who saw it were shocked and uncertain; could God's law be thus broken with impunity? Phinehas, son of Eleazar the High Priest, burst from the crowd, snatched up a javelin, and rushed into the tent. Zimri and the Midianite woman were lying together on the floor. Hardly pausing, Phinehas raised the javelin high and then thrust it straight through them both, pinning them together. When Moses saw what he had done, he said: 'Now the slaughter of the apostates can stop; the sin of Israel is expiated. As for Phinehas, he has shown zeal for Jahweh, and stoned for Israel's wrongs. He and his descendants shall be priests for ever, and he shall have Jahweh's covenant of peace.' On that day of weeping and destruction, which Jahweh commanded, twenty four thousand men had died, who had worshipped the Baal of Peor. There, in the Valley of the Acacias, the Israelites were given a visible warning of the inward death towards which they were falling. At the very moment of blessing and victory, when they stood firm and strong; then temptation corrupted them from within. But God preserved the lives of all those who held fast to him, because his priest made atonement for them all.

Vengeance on Midian (Num. 26, 31)

Moses said to the people, 'We must take vengeance on the tribes who led us astray to worship idols of lust and greed, whose cunning caused the death of our people and threatened to destroy us at Mount Peor'. Soldiers were taken from each Israelite tribe, and Phinehas, son of Eleazar, led them out with all the sacred vessels from the Sanctuary, the Ark of Jahweh, and the silver trumpets to sound the attack. Thus Holy War was declared in the name of Jahweh; and all the five chiefs of the Midianite tribes – not the Midianites of Sinai, among whom Moses had lived, but a group of tribes living north of Moab, by the Dead Sea, vassals of Sihon, King of the Amorites – all were killed. Zur, the father of Cozbi, who had enticed Zimri to break the law, was among them; and Balaam the prophet, who had instigated the Midianite plot, was killed in his homeland by a small expeditionary force. The women and children were captured, and the cattle, flocks and property were carried back to the camp by the Jordan; the cities and camps were burned.

But when Moses and Eleazar met the returning army outside the camp, they were angry because the women had been spared. 'Was it not they who seduced the Israelites into disloyalty to Jahweh?' they said, 'and who thereby caused the slaughter of so many of our people? They must die, with every male child, so that the tribes of Midian will cease to exist on the face of the earth. Only the virgins may be spared, to be slaves or concubines.' There, outside the camp, the tribes of Midian were ruthlessly massacred; their name disappeared from the land; the vengeance of Jahweh was fearful and complete.

Moses decreed that all who had taken life or touched the dead had to remain outside the camp for seven days, purifying themselves and their captives on the third and seventh days. All property had to be passed either through fire or through water, and all clothes washed, before they could enter the camp. The captured cattle, sheep and women were divided equally between the fighting men and the rest of the people. One five hundredth of the army's share was given to the priests, as an offering to Jahweh;

and one fiftieth of the people's share was given to the Levites, who were in charge of the Sanctuary. When the officers took the roll of their fighting men, they found that not one of them was missing. In amazement and gratitude, they offered to Jahweh all the gold jewellery that they had taken as booty. Moses and Eleazar placed this great treasure of finely worked gold in the Sanctuary, to be a gift in place of the people's lives, and so that Jahweh might remember his people Israel.

After the massacre of Midian, Moses and Eleazar took a census of all the fighting men of twenty years and upwards. Thirty eight years after the census at Mount Sinai, the strength of individual tribes had altered, sometimes considerably. But the hardship of the desert and the judgements their disobedience had brought upon them had taken their toll, and the total number of fighting men was very slightly less than when they had set out. Yet they were harder and tougher, tempered by ruthless discipline and spartan living; and Moses judged that they were ready to cross the Jordan to conquer their promised homeland and at last attain their goal. 'The tribes shall be allotted territory, according to their size at this census', Moses said; 'Each clan shall cast lots for the territory it is to possess, but the size of each territory shall be in proportion to the size of the tribe, as now determined. For your inheritance will be measured by your endurance and obedience in the wilderness wandering.' The Levites, too, who possessed no inheritance – for Jahweh God of Israel is their inheritance – were numbered from one month old. In the list of fighting men, there was not a single person who had been recorded in the first census at Sinai. As God had decreed, they had all died in the wilderness, except for Caleb and Joshua, who had followed God with their whole heart. Now a new generation waited to enter into their inheritance, and follow the call of God to cross over the river to the land of promise.

The Tribal Territories (Num. 32-35; Exod 23)

The chiefs of the tribes of Reuben and Gad came to Moses and said: 'This country east of Jordan, which we have taken by conquest from Sihon, Og and their vassal chieftains, is good grazing land; and our flocks would thrive here. If we have found favour with you, let us have this country for our inheritance, and do not make us cross the Jordan.'

Moses was very angry, and said, 'Are your brothers to go to war while you stay here? You will dishearten the people of Israel, and discourage them from crossing to the land God has given them. Are you going to repeat the sin of your fathers, who refused to enter Canaan and brought judgement on the people for forty years? You are a fresh brood of sinful men to bring God's anger on Israel; if he abandons his people again, you will be the cause.'

But the chiefs said, 'Let us only build walled towns and sheepfolds here, for our dependents and flocks. Then we shall march at the head of the Israelite army, until they take possession of their land. We will not return until every tribe has his inheritance secure; we will claim no share of the land west of Jordan; this shall be our inheritance, where our women and children will remain secure until our return.'

So Moses said, 'If you keep this promise and fight at the head of the army of Israel until its enemies are defeated, then you may return having fulfilled your obligations to Jahweh and to Israel, and this land shall be your inheritance. But if you do not do so, be sure your sin will find you out, and your wish will not be granted. Build cities and sheepfolds, and do as you have promised.'

Moses gave the tribe of Reuben all the land east of Jordan from the Arnon Gorge north to Heshbon; the tribe of Gad was given the land from Heshbon to Mahanaim; half the tribe of Manasseh, which had grown rapidly in the wilderness, joined with the others and was given territory from Mahanaim to the northern border of Bashan. These two and a half tribes had their inheritance beyond the Jordan, east of Jericho, towards the sunrise.

Moses called together all the other tribal chiefs and said: 'Soon you will be entering Canaan. The land which is assigned to you as your perpetual heritage by Jahweh is this: in the south, from the Dead Sea, along the border of Edom, through Kadesh-barnea, to meet the sea at the 'brook of Egypt', the wadi-el-aris. On the west, the boundary is the Mediterranean coast. The northern frontier shall extend from the Mediterranean to the Euphrates. And the eastern boundary shall run south west to Galilee and then along the Jordan River to the Dead Sea. Within this land, Eleazar and Joshua, with one man from each tribe, shall divide the land among you by lot. When you take possession of your territory, you shall drive out all the inhabitants, destroy their sacred monuments, images and hilltop shrines. If you do not do so, those who remain will be like hooks in your eyes and thorns in your sides, continual trouble to you in the land where you live; and Jahweh will do to you as he meant to do to them.

As for the Levites, whose only inheritance is Jahweh their god, they shall have no tribal territory. But forty eight towns shall be set apart for them to live in, with pasture for cattle and sheep. Each tribe shall set aside a number of towns, in proportion to the size of their territory, so that the Levites will be scattered throughout Canaan, and can minister to the whole people, as servants of Jahweh. Six of those cities, three east of the Jordan and three in Canaan, are to be cities of refuge. Those who cause death by accident may flee there, and have sanctuary from the vengeance of the dead man's next of kin, until he can have a fair trial before the community, to decide whether he may stay, or must be delivered for judgement.

Now Jahweh will send the angel of his presence before you, to guard you on the way and lead you to your goal. If you hear and obey him, he will drive out all your enemies before you, and bring you in safety to your destined home.'

The people heard his words, and were filled with longing and excitement; at last the time they had waited for so long had come; the land of the promise lay open before them.

The Law

The Teachings of Moses; The First Exhortation: 'Hear' (Deut. 1-11)

On the first day of the eleventh month of the fortieth year after the Israelites left Egypt, Moses gathered all the people together at the camp east of the Jordan, to proclaim to them all the commands that Jahweh had given them at Sinai and in the wilderness. First he reminded them of their journey through the desert, from Sinai to the border of Canaan; of how Jahweh had guided them despite their grumbling and disobedience, and now set before them the country of the ancestral promise. Then he talked to them of the Law which was to be the basis of their life, the Way they were to walk in for evermore, the Word which God gave to the people of his loving. These were the words he spoke in the days that followed, as he set before them the Law of their God:

Hear, O Israel; the Lord our God is one Lord; you shall love the Lord your God with all your heart, and with all your soul, and with all your might.
You shall keep all the words which I command you this day in your heart.
You shall teach them to your children, and talk of them when you sit and when you walk, when you lie down to rest and when you rise to go to work.
You shall wear them on your hands and on your brows, so that all you do and all you see shall be sanctified by love.
You shall write them on your doorposts and your gates, so that your going out and your returning shall be in the name of God.

Now, O Israel, hear the laws and judgements which I teach you, and do them; that you may live, and take possession of the land which Jahweh, God of your fathers gives you.
You shall not add anything to the word I give you, nor take anything from it; you must keep all the commandments of Jahweh which I give you.
I have taught you laws and judgements, as Jahweh commanded me; these you must keep in the land you are about to enter.

Keep them and do them; thus you will show wisdom and understanding before the nations.
When they hear these laws, they will say, 'It is true that this great nation has wisdom and understanding'.
For what great nation is there that has a god so near to it as Jahweh is to us, whenever we call upon him?
And what great nation has statutes and laws as just as this Law which I set before you today?

Therefore you shall walk in the way which the Lord has commanded you. You shall not turn aside to the right hand or the left.
You shall fear him and keep his laws, that all may go well with you and your children for ever, and that you may live long in the land and multiply and prosper.

This land which you are entering is not like Egypt, where you irrigated the earth by foot, like a vegetable garden.
It is a land of hills and valleys, watered by the rain of heaven, a land which the Lord himself tends; the eyes of the Lord your god are always upon it, from the beginning of the year to its end.
If you love the Lord your God and serve him with all your heart and with all your soul, he will send the rain at its appointed time, in autumn for sowing and in spring for growing, so that you may have grain and wine and olive oil, grass for your cattle and food for men; and live in a land of milk and honey, you and your children for evermore.

When Jahweh gives you the land which he promised to Abraham, Isaac and Jacob
With large and beautiful cities which you did not build
And houses filled with good things which you did not provide;
Water pits dug from rock which you did not dig,
Vineyards and olive groves which you did not plant;
Then, when you eat and are satisfied, do not forget your God, who brought you from slavery to this fertile land.
You shall fear him and serve him and swear by his name;
For he regards his people with jealous love, and punishes those who leave his way.

For you are a people holy to Jahweh; he chose you from all the people of the earth to belong to him only; not because you were

greater or stronger – for you were the least of nations; but just because he loves you and keeps his promise to your fathers.
Know then that the Lord your God is God, the faithful God; he keeps covenant and steadfast love for a thousand generations with those who love him and keep his laws; but he is not slow to destroy those who hate and defy him.

When your sons ask you in time to come, 'What is the meaning of this Law?'
Then you shall say, 'Jahweh our God freed us from bondage and brought us here;
He gave us this Law for our good, to lead us to life, to show us how to be rightly related to him and the world he has made'.

What then, O Israel, does the Lord your God require of you? Only to fear the Lord your God, to walk in all his ways, to love him, to serve the Lord your God with all your heart and with all your soul, and to keep the commandments and laws of the Lord, which I give you this day for your good.

Moses' Second Exhortation: 'Remember' (Deut. 4-9)

Keep the commands of God, walk in his way and fear him;
For God is giving you a good land, a land of rivers, fountains and springs, of clear water in the hills and valleys, a land of wheat and barley, of vines and figs and pomegranates,
A land of olive trees and honey, in which you will eat your fill and lack nothing, rich in iron and copper.
When you have built fine houses to live in, when you have eaten and are full; when your cattle and sheep increase and you store up silver and gold, and prosper in all you do; then bless the Lord your God, who gives you freely all these good things.
Do not forget the god who brought you from bondage through the wilderness, by failing to keep his Law, or by serving other gods, which will surely lead to your destruction.
Do not say in your heart, 'My power and my strength have brought all this'; it is God who goes before you like a devouring fire, and gives you strength to grow rich.
Do not say in your heart, 'Because of my worthiness Jahweh gives

me this land'; you are and always have been a stubborn people; from the day you left Egypt until now, you have defied the Lord.
Many times Jahweh could have destroyed you, but he allows himself to be moved by the prayer of faith, and remains faithful to his promise.
He drives out the Canaanites before you because of their corruption and depravity; if you disobey him, so he will do to you.

Take care; be watchful; do not forget the things your eyes have seen; do not let them leave your hearts as long as you live;
Teach them to your children and grandchildren – how the mountain burned with fire to the heart of heaven, wrapped in cloud;
How Jahweh spoke from the fire of his glory, word without image, the voice of a god without visible form;
For all time past, before our birth, since God created man on earth; from one edge of the world to the other, has anything like this been known?
That the voice of a god should speak from the heart of fire, and the people who heard it should not die, but live?
That a god should forge a people for himself in the furnace of Egypt; and free them by trials, by signs and wonder and by war?
With a strong hand and an outstretched arm, Jahweh brought us out of Egypt by his presence and power, with acts of awe,
That we might know and lay it to heart that Jahweh is God in heaven and earth; there is no other to set beside him.

Remember how Jahweh led you in the wilderness forty years; your feet did not swell nor your clothes wear out;
He humbled you and let you go hungry, that he might feed you with manna, and teach you that man does not gain life by bread alone, but by the word that comes from the mouth of God;
He tested you to know what was in your heart, whether you would keep his laws or not;
He disciplined you as a man disciplines his son, with fatherly patience, to bring you to good in the end;
But until now Jahweh has not given you a mind to understand, or eyes to see, or ears to hear.

Remember what Jahweh did at Peor; he destroyed all those who followed Baal, but saved those who held fast to him;

Remember how you stood before God at Sinai and he said, 'Let the people hear my words, that they may learn to fear me as long as they live, and teach their children so'.

When Jahweh brings you into the land, you will see seven nations more numerous and powerful than you. But you need not fear them; remember what Jahweh did to Egypt; so will he deal with all the people whom you fear. He will spread panic among them, until all who are left or have gone into hiding are destroyed. He will be with you, a great and terrible god, slowly but surely driving all before you. No man shall be able to withstand you; when you defeat them, you must put them to death. You shall make no covenant with them and show no mercy to them. You shall not intermarry with them. If you do, they will lead your children to worship other gods. You shall break down their altars and sacred pillars, hack down their sacred poles and burn their idols; not keeping the silver and gold for yourselves, but destroying it. For they have done everything God hates; incest, perversion and sorcery; even burning their sons and daughters in the fire to their gods; so they shall be placed under the holy Ban. You shall not have any idol in your house, or you yourself shall be put under the Ban also, an abomination devoted to destruction, abhorred by Jahweh.

So when you have children and grandchildren and grow old in the land of promise, do not provoke God by making images and idols, or worshipping the sun and stars;
Nothing in earth or heaven is like the god who has called you to belong to him.
The sun and moon and stars he has given for others to worship, but he has made his covenant with you, his marriage vow;
If you leave his way and worship images, you will be swept away from the land he promised you;
You will be scattered among the nations, few in number, serving gods who neither see nor hear.
Yet if from there you seek the Lord your God, there will be a time of returning;
You will find him, if you seek him with your heart and soul.
When you are in trouble, and these things come upon you, you will return and obey the voice of God,

For Jahweh is a merciful God; he will not fail you nor destroy you
nor forget the covenant with your father which he made;
And all this, because he loves you and chooses you to be his own.

The Blessings and Curses of the Law
(Deut. 7, 28, 29; Lev. 26)

When Moses had reminded the people of their calling by God, and exhorted them to keep the Law, he proclaimed the whole Law in their presence, so that all could hear. Then he recited the blessings and curses which belonged to God's Law:

'If you hear and keep these laws, Jahweh will keep faith with you; he will love you, bless you and give you many children; he will bless the fruit of your body and the fruit of your land, your corn and wine and olive oil, your herds and flocks. You shall be blessed above all people, without sickness or disease or barrenness among man or beast, throughout all the land which he promised your fathers to give you. These are the blessings you shall declare, which shall be yours if you obey the voice of Jahweh:

Blessed shall you be in the city and in the field; blessed shall be the fruit of your body, of your land and of your cattle; blessed shall be your basket and your kneading bowl; blessed shall you be when you come in and when you go out.

Jahweh will defeat your enemies; he will lay the dread of you on all the land; no man shall be able to stand against you; five of you shall chase a hundred, and a hundred shall put ten thousand to flight; the whole land on which you set foot shall be yours, from the Negev to the Lebanon, from the Euphrates to the Western sea.

Jahweh will bless you in your granaries and in all you undertake; you shall reap corn until the grape harvest, and grapes until it is time to sow again; you shall have many fine children, and produce so much that you will have to clear out the old to make way for the new. All the people of earth shall see that Jahweh has named you as his holy people, with whom he has made his home, and they shall fear you.

Jahweh shall make you prosper, giving the rain in its season and blessing all the work of your hands.

You shall lend, but not borrow; you shall be first, not last; you shall be happy, not sad. Jahweh has broken the chains of your slavery, and made you walk upright and proud; he walks among you, and you are his.

These are the curses you shall declare, which shall fall upon you if you do not obey the voice of Jahweh:

Cursed shall you be in the city and in the field; cursed shall be the fruit of your body, of your land and of your cattle; cursed shall be your basket and your kneading bowl; cursed shall you be when you come in and when you go out.

Jahweh will send confusion and frustration in all you try to do; he will send drought and disease on your crops, and fever and plague among your people. He will bring defeat in war; you will go out to battle by one way, and flee seven ways; your enemies shall hound you until you run where there is no pursuit.

If you still do not hear him, he will increase your punishment sevenfold. The skies over you will be like bronze, and the earth below you will be like iron, and the only rain that falls will be fine sand and dust. There shall be famine in your land; he will break your stubborn pride.

If you still defy him, he will punish you a third time, seven times more. Wild beasts shall take your children and cattle and reduce your numbers until your roads are deserted.

If these disciplines do not turn you to Jahweh, he will continue to oppose you as you oppose him, and multiply your ills seven times again. Your enemies will overwhelm you, and when you retreat to your cities, he will send pestilence among you, and you will be forced to surrender. He will cut short your daily bread until ten women can bake their bread in only one oven; it will be rationed out; and when you have eaten your share, you will still be hungry.

If after all this you still refuse to obey God, he will come a fifth time in fury, and increase your woes sevenfold. All the people of earth shall abhor and despise you; your dead bodies will be good for the vultures and wild animals, with no man to drive them away. Jahweh will torment you with diseases of the body, like the plagues of Egypt, for which there is no cure. He will torment you with diseases of the mind, with madness and blindness, so that you shall grope at noonday and fail to find your way. You shall be oppressed and robbed, day in, day out, with no one to save you. A woman shall be pledged to you, but another shall ravage her; you will build a house, but not live in it; you shall plant a vineyard but not eat the fruit of it. You will sow much, but harvest little, for the locust shall devour it. You will have olive groves, but not anoint yourselves with oil, for they will rot. You shall see your cattle killed, but not eat them; your donkey shall be stolen before your eyes, and not given back; your sheep will be given to your enemies, and no one shall help you. The foreigner in your land shall rise higher, and you shall fall lower. He shall lend to you, and you shall not lend to him; he shall be first, and you shall be last.

All these curses shall descend on you and pursue you until you are destroyed; they shall be a sign and an omen to you and your descendants for ever, because you did not serve Jahweh your god with joy and gladness of heart for all the good he gave you, and obey his voice by keeping his Law.

If you do not turn again, to revere the glorious and dreadful name of Jahweh, then he will finally abandon you. He will bring a nation against you from far away, from the end of the earth, who will swoop down like the eagle, swift and pitiless. A people whose language you do not understand, grim-faced, without reverence for age or pity for children, shall put an iron yoke upon your neck; you shall serve them in hunger and thirst, in nakedness and want. They shall strip the countryside and besiege the towns. Your sons and daughters shall be taken into captivity while you look on; your eyes will strain with longing, but you will be powerless to prevent it. You shall be driven mad by the sights which your eyes shall see; for then, in that time of desperation, you will eat your own children, the flesh of your sons and daughters. The most delicate and fastidious man will not share with his brother or his wife any of the meat he is eating, the flesh of his own children. The most pampered and delicate woman, who has scarcely tried to put a foot to the ground lest it gets dirty, will not share with her own husband the afterbirth which she expels, the infants she bears, because she will eat them secretly in her extremity.

Then your hill shrines and incense altars will be destroyed, your dead bodies thrown on your fallen idols. The walls of your cities shall fall, your sacrifices will be rejected by God, and he will scatter you among all the nations, from one end of the earth to the other. There you shall serve other gods, of wood and stone, which neither you nor your fathers have known. The deserted land, its cities in ruins, shall have the sabbath rest which you would not give it when you lived there; it shall be devastated so that even your enemies will be appalled. As God took delight in doing you good and increasing you, so now he will take delight in bringing ruin upon you. You who were as countless as the stars of heaven will be left few in number and scattered. Among all the nations you will find no peace, and there shall be no rest from your wandering. Jahweh will give you an unquiet mind, failing eyes and a despairing heart. Your life shall be continually in danger; fear will be with you night and day; you shall have no security all your life. Each morning you shall say, 'Would it were night'; and each evening you shall say, 'Would it were morning', because of the fear in your heart and the sights that you see.

At last, Jahweh will bring you sorrowing back to Egypt, by the road which he promised you should never take again. There you will offer to sell yourselves to your enemies as slaves; but no one will buy you. You will become a horror, a proverb and a byword to all the people among whom Jahweh scatters you. Travellers will come and see here a burnt-out waste, barren and desolate, with only diseased remnants of a people wandering in a ravaged land. They will say, 'What has afflicted this land? What has caused such destruction?' The answer has always been known to you: 'Because this people forsook the covenant of Jahweh, and worshipped gods they had not known. The curses foretold in the Law came upon them; the anger of Jahweh walked in the land, and they were cast out and scattered, as you see today'. If that day comes, the journey of the children of Abraham will have reached its end.

The Time of Returning (Deut. 29, 30; Lev. 26)

When Moses had foretold the horror which lay before a disobedient Israel, he spoke again to the people, and said:

'Nevertheless, even if all these things come upon you, both the blessing and the curse which I have set before you; if you take them to heart in the far countries to which Jahweh has driven you, and return to him and obey him with all your heart and soul, you and your children, then the Lord your God will restore your good fortune and have compassion upon you. The land must lie desolate until the full penalty for disobedience has been paid; but God will not completely abandon or destroy you. When the time of desolation is fulfilled, he will gather you again from all the countries to which he has scattered you. Even if he were to banish you to the four corners of the world, God will gather you from there and bring you home, to the land which your fathers possessed. There he will make you even more prosperous and numerous than they. God will circumcise your hearts so that you will love him and find life in him. The curses which were upon you shall be put on your enemies who persecuted you. And you shall again keep all God's Law, for he himself shall inwardly renew you. The Lord will again take delight in making you prosper, as he took delight in your fathers, when you turn to him with all your heart and soul. The creator of all will prosper all that you create; the work of your hands, the fruit of your body, of your cattle and of your land; for he gives life to all who keep his laws.'

Then Moses said:

'You stand this day before Jahweh your god; everyone from tribal chiefs to those who hew wood and draw water, that you may accept the oath and enter into the covenant which Jahweh offers you today; that he may take you as his people and that he may be your god; a covenant which will stand for you and your descendants for ever. If there is any man, woman, family or tribe among you whose heart turns away this day from Jahweh, to serve the gods of other nations; such a one will be a root bearing poisonous and bitter fruit. He may say in his heart, 'I shall be safe, even though I follow my own way'; but he will bring everything to ruin. Jahweh will not forgive him, but all the curses of the Law will settle on him and Jahweh will blot out his name from under heaven. For this Law which I give you today is not too hard for you, neither is it far away. It is not in heaven, that you should say, "Who will go up for us to heaven and bring it down, that we may hear it and do it?" It is not beyond the sea, that you should say, "Who will cross the sea for us, and bring it to us, that we may hear it and do it?" But the Word is very near you; it is on your lips and in your heart, so that you can do it.

There are many things hidden, which belong to God alone. But the will of Jahweh is revealed in the Law; it belongs to us and to our children for ever, and it is for us to observe all that it prescribes.

Today I set before you life and good, death and evil. If you obey the Law of God by loving him and walking in his way; if you keep his commandments and ordinances, then you shall live and increase; and Jahweh will bless you in the land you are entering. But if your heart turns away, and you will not hear, but are drawn away to serve other gods, then you shall die; you shall not live long in the land across the Jordan. I call heaven and earth to witness this day, that I set before you life and death, blessing and curse. Choose life, so that you and your children may live, loving the Lord your God, obeying and holding fast to him; for that brings life and length of days, that you may enter into all God's promises.'

The Sealing of the Covenant (Deut. 10, 26, 27; Lev. 19)

When Moses had recited the whole Law before the people, he said:

'When you enter the land of the promise, you must give to God the first fruits of every crop the land gives you. You shall take it to the Sanctuary of Jahweh, and recite: "A wandering Aramean was my father. He went down to Egypt and lived there, few in number. There he became a great nation, mighty and populous. Then the Egyptians treated us harshly, afflicted us and laid upon us hard bondage. We cried to Jahweh the god of our fathers, and Jahweh heard our voice and saw our affliction, toil and oppression. Jahweh brought us out of Egypt with a strong hand and an outstretched arm, with great terror, signs and wonders. He brought us to this place and gave us this land, a land flowing with milk and honey. I declare this day to Jahweh my God that I have come into the land which he promised to my fathers to give me. Now I give to him the first of the fruit of the ground which he has freely given to me." Thus you shall remember your god, and all he has done for you; and you shall rejoice, you, the Levites, foreigners with you and all your family, in all the good he has given you.'

Then Moses, the three priests and the elders stood before the people and said: 'To the Lord your God belongs heaven, even the highest heaven, and earth with all that is in it; yet the Lord set his heart in love upon your fathers, and chose you, their children, out of all nations. Circumcise therefore the foreskin of your hearts and be no longer stubborn; for the Lord your God is God of gods and Lord of lords, the great, the mighty and terrible God. He is no respecter of persons and is not to be bribed; he secures justice for widows and orphans, and loves the foreigner who lives among you, giving him food and clothing. You too must love the stranger; remember that you were strangers living in Egypt. Remember that from the seventy who went down to Egypt, Jahweh has made you as countless as the stars in the sky. You shall therefore love him and keep his laws always; he is your praise and glory.'

All the people of Israel, man, woman and child, kept silence as Moses raised his arms in blessing over them, and said: 'This the Lord declares: I am Jahweh your god; consecrate yourselves, therefore, and be holy, for I am holy. My law gives life, and I make you holy, that you shall be separated from all nations, as I separated light from darkness at creation, and be mine.' The people bowed to the ground, and Moses said:

'This day you have taken Jahweh to be your god; you have promised to walk in his way, keep his laws and obey his voice. This day Jahweh has declared that you belong to him, as he promised; he will raise you high above all the nations he has created, in praise and fame and honour, and you shall be a people holy to Jahweh your god.

When you cross the river Jordan, you shall erect large stone pillars, cover them with plaster, and write on them the words of the Law. You shall set them on Mount Ebal; there you shall build an altar to Jahweh, of stones uncut by iron tools, and offer fire offerings and fellowship offerings to Jahweh and rejoice before him. Thus the covenant, made at Sinai, declared this day in the plains of Moab, shall be sealed in the land of promise, as you enter into your inheritance.

Six tribes shall stand on the slopes of Mount Ebal and six on the slopes of Mount Gerizim, across the valley. The blessings set before Israel will be declared from Gerizim, and the curses set before her will be declared from Ebal. Then the Levites, standing by the sacred oak at Shechem, shall declare the twelve ancient curses of Shechem:

Cursed be he who makes an idol, to worship it.
Cursed be he who dishonours his father or his mother.
Cursed be he who moves a neighbour's boundary mark.
Cursed be he who leads a blind man astray.
Cursed be he who is unjust to foreigners, orphans or widows.
Cursed be he who has intercourse with one of his father's wives.
Cursed be he who has sexual relations with an animal.
Cursed be he who has intercourse with his sister or half-sister.
Cursed be he who has intercourse with his wife's mother.
Cursed be he who secretly commits murder.
Cursed be he who takes money to kill an innocent person.
Cursed be he who does not fulfil this law by doing all it commands.

All the people shall reply, "So may it be".

The Covenant will be sealed.'

The Commissioning of Joshua
(Deut. 3, 31, 32; Num. 27)

When the people had bound themselves to Jahweh and promised to obey his commandments, Moses wrote down the whole Law, from beginning to end, and said to the Levites:

'Place this Law beside the Ark of the covenant of Jahweh, in the Inner Sanctuary of Israel. It shall be a witness for ever against you, when you rebel against God. For I know how rebellious and stubborn your hearts are; even while I have lived with you, you have rebelled against God time and again. Now I am old; I am about to sleep with my fathers, and I know that you will turn aside from the way God has given you. The Lord knows the purposes you are already forming, before he brings you into the land which he promised you. Therefore he has taught me a song of the things which are to come; you will learn it and teach it to your children, that it may live unforgotten in Israel, and that you may know what your end will be, what your God requires and what he will do in the days to come. Lay to your heart all the words I enjoin upon you this day, and teach them to your children, that they may be careful to observe this Law. For it is no empty word; it is your life. Obey it, and you will live long and see good days. Break it, and all the evils of this song shall come upon you. It shall be a witness that these things were known to you from the beginning; and a testimony that finally the purposes of Jahweh shall not fail.'

Moses commanded that the whole Law should be read publicly to the Assembly of Israel every seven years, in the Year of Release at the Feast of Succoth; so that each succeeding generation would hear the Word of God and learn to fear him and walk in the way of the covenant.

Then he went apart to pray, and he pleaded with God: 'Lord God, I have led your people through the wilderness, and given them your Law. You have begun to show your greatness and power; there is no god in heaven or earth who can do the mighty things that you have done. Grant me one thing, Lord; that I may go over and see the good land beyond the Jordan, the beautiful hills of the promised land and the great mountains of Lebanon.'

But God was angry and said: 'You heard my decree at Meribah; that must stand. You have offered your life for this people, and shared their sorrow; but they have not ceased to disobey me, and you must stand under judgement with them. Therefore your prayer shall not be answered; you shall never cross the Jordan. You shall climb to the summit of Mount Nebo, opposite Jericho, city of palm trees, and look out over the land of Canaan. There, when you have seen the land from afar, you shall die on the mountain and be gathered to your people. You shall see the land but never enter it.'

Moses bowed in silent acceptance; he was not to die without sorrow. 'Lord God', he said, 'I am about to die, and can no longer move about as I please. There must be someone to lead the people in peace and war, to lead them out and bring them home, so that the people of God may not be like sheep without a shepherd.' God said: 'Take Joshua, the son of Nun, a man filled with the spirit of wisdom. Lay your hands on him, before Eleazar the High Priest and all the people, so that the people may obey him as they obeyed you. The High Priest, by consulting the Urim and Thummim, shall decide for war and the ending of war, and Joshua shall go out and come in at the head of the community of Israel.'

So Moses took Joshua, and they stood before the Sanctuary. The cloud of the presence of Jahweh descended on the Sanctuary, while the High Priest and all the people watched. Moses commissioned Joshua in these words: 'Be strong and of good courage; for you shall bring the children of Israel into the land which Jahweh has promised them. Jahweh himself will go before you, and dispossess the people, as he did to Sihon and Og, Kings of the Amorites. He will be with you, he will not fail you nor forsake you; do not fear or be dismayed.' Moses laid his hands upon the head of Joshua, and handed on the leadership of Israel. His work was finished; now he had only one thing left to do, before slowly climbing the mountain upon which he was to die.

The Song of Moses (Deut. 32)

This is the Song that Moses and Joshua recited to the people before they crossed to the land of promise, to warn them of things to come, and to turn their hearts to God:

INVOCATION *Let everything in earth and heaven*
Hear the words I have to say;
My teaching shall refresh like rain,
Form on the dust like morning dew;
My words shall fall like rain on grass,
Life giving showers on leaf and bough.

PROCLAMATION *Great is the name of our god, Jahweh,*
In your presence I will praise him;
He is the Rock, the great defender,
Whose works are perfect, whose ways are just;
Faithful and without a fault,
All he does is right and true.

ACCUSATION *But you are perverse and foolish people,*
Your ways unworthy of his children;
Is this how you repay your Redeemer,
Like beings without sense or soul?

Is he not your Father, who formed you?
Did he not make you and mark you out?

THE DIVINE DECREE *Remember the ages of past generations,*
Ask your fathers to tell the tale;
Elyon, the Highest, gave men their inheritance,
Drew out the borders where nations should dwell;
To each Sacred Power he allotted one people,
But the company of Jacob he claimed for his own.

THE FINDING *He found him alone in a desert land,*
In the howling waste of the wilderness;
He cared for him and kept him as the apple of his eye;
Like the wings of the eagle that hovers on the wind,
Carrying its young ones to keep them from harm;
So God carries Israel and keeps him from falling.

THE PROMISED LAND *The Lord will lead him with no god to help him,*
To rule in the Highlands and reap the harvest,
To find wild honey among the hills
And groves of olives in stony ground;
To have milk and meat and herds in plenty
With wine from the vineyards and fields of wheat.

IDOLATRY *Then Israel grew rich and rebellious,*
Fat and sleek and stuffed with food;
He rejected the Rock of his salvation;
With evil rituals arousing God's anger
He sacrificed to strange new gods,
Demons his ancestors never knew.

ABANDONMENT *So they forgot the creator who formed them,*
Left the Lord who had given them life;
God saw and spurned them, his own sons and daughters,
He said, 'I will hide my face from them, and, hidden,
Will watch this wicked and faithless people
To see what their final state will be.'

THE ANGER OF GOD *'They goaded me to jealousy with worthless gods,*

Aroused my anger with unreal idols;
I will rouse them to jealousy with a worthless rabble,
Fire their anger with a nation of fools;
My anger will flame up like fire and devour
The earth and rage down to the world of the dead.'

TERROR *'I will deliver them to disaster,*
Famine and plague and pestilence,
Poisonous snakes and beasts of prey;
The sword will bring death in the streets, and terror
Will strike in the homes; the man of grey hairs
And the child will both die in the day of my rage.'

THE REMNANT *'I could have scattered and struck them down,*
Removed their memory from the earth;
But I could not let their enemies claim
That they had defeated my designs.
If only Israel would understand,
They would see what their end will be.'

THE ENEMY *'They are a nation without wisdom,*
Who cannot see why they come to defeat,
Why Jahweh their god has given them up;
Their enemies know that their own gods are impotent,
Yet they spread like poison vines from Sodom,
Like wine distilled from the venom of snakes.'

SALVATION *'I will remember the acts of these enemies,*
Vengeance is mine and I will repay;
The time shall come when their feet will fall;
The day of their doom shall swiftly dawn.
Then I will come with compassion and justice
To save my people when their own strength has gone.'

AFFIRMATION *'Where are the gods to whom you gave worship,*
To whom you offered food and wine?
Let them rise to your rescue if they can.
No; I am God, there is no other,
I wound and heal, create and kill;
None can escape from my control.'

VENGEANCE *'I raise my hand to heaven and vow*
That, as I live for evermore,
I will sharpen my sword and show my judgement,
I will harry the enemies who hate me;
The shafts from my bow will drip with their blood,
No foe shall be spared who fights against me.'

EPILOGUE *Praise this people, powers of Heaven;*
For God will punish all who oppress them.
The Rock whose strength endures for ever
Will crush his foes and keep his people,
Making atonement for their transgressions,
Washing their land with the water of life.

A Psalm (Deut. 33, 1-5, 26-end)

Jahweh came from Sinai, like the sun
Rising in fire in the desert dawn;
At his right hand ten thousand Holy Ones
Stood as his glory streamed from the mountain's top.
Truly he loves and sanctifies his saints;
He holds them in the hollow of his hand.
They follow in his footsteps, and he guides them,
Giving them the Law of endless life.
He comes to be the King of Israel
When all his people live at one in love.

There is none like the God of the nation of Israel,
Who rides the clouds of heaven to your help,
The Eternal God is your true home and treasure,
Upholding you with arms of ancient love.
He drives your enemies before you and destroys them;
So Israel lives in safety, set apart
In a land of wheat and wine and gentle rain.
Blessed are you, O Israel! Set free
By God, who is your shield and sword to guard you;
By his glory you shall gain the victory.

The Blessing of Moses (Deut. 33; cf. Deut. 18)

Moses looked one last time upon the people he had brought from the Nile to the Jordan through the desert. They were now, as they had always been, a quarrelsome, excitable, fanatical and impatient people. The tribal groups could hardly meet without fighting; blood feuds and interminable arguments over property were commonplace. They were capable of enduring great hardship, of intense loyalty and heroism, and of moments of surprising compassion and hospitality. But it took little to fill them with discontent, and a careless word could destroy the patiently constructed virtues of years. Yet these were the people God had found in the wilderness and chosen to show his own will, in a way which none of them could clearly see. They were the Lord's people; and Moses had spent his life in their care. Now they stood on the threshold of the Promise; and the last act of the man of God was to bless them before he left them for ever. As the tribes passed before him, these were the blessings he gave them:

REUBEN, may you live and not die out, though your numbers will be few.

JUDAH, may Jahweh hear your cry and unite you with your kinsmen, fighting for you and defending you against your enemies.

LEVI, possessor of the Stones of Oracle, who did not fail like your brothers at Massah and Meribah, who disregarded your parents and children in the zeal for God's covenant at Sinai; you shall teach Jacob the precepts and laws of God; you shall burn incense and sacrifice on the altar of God; may Jahweh bless all your being and action, crushing your enemies, that they may rise no more.

BENJAMIN, Jahweh's beloved, you will live in safety; God will shield you all the day long; his temple will lie upon your hillsides.

JOSEPH, the blessing of Jahweh is on your land, the blessings of the sky and of the Great Deep; the choicest fruits of the sun and the due harvest of the months, the finest abundance of the everlasting mountains, and the best gifts of the fruitful earth — all these shall be yours, by the grace of the god of the burning tree. You shall be a prince among your brothers, as strong as the horns of the wild bull, driving nations before you to the ends of the earth. Such will be the thousands of MANASSEH and the ten thousands of the tribe of EPHRAIM.

ZEBULUN and ISSACHAR, you shall rejoice in your homes and in your voyaging, drawing wealth from the trades of the sea and from treasures hidden in sand; people shall flock to Mount Tabor where you offer acceptable sacrifice.

GAD, you are blessed in your wide domain; you lie like a lion who tears its prey limb from limb; you won the best of the land for yourself by force of arms; you will march at the head of Israel's armies, in observance of Jahweh's decrees.

DAN, you are a lion's cub; you will spring from Bashan in time to come.

NAPHTALI, you are richly favoured, filled with the blessings of God; your land shall stretch southward to the Sea of Galilee.

ASHER, you are the most blessed of many sons; favourite among your brothers, your feet bathed in olive oil; you guard the Northern gateway of Israel; may your bolts and bars be of iron and bronze, so that your strength shall last as long as you live.

Only the tribe of SIMEON had no word of blessing; by the ancient prophecy of Jacob, they would be scattered and absorbed into Judah. So Moses declared the rich blessings which awaited the tribes of Israel across the Jordan.

'Now', he said, 'I am leaving you. But Jahweh will raise up a prophet from among you to declare his will; like me, he will pray for you, share your sorrows and speak the words which Jahweh puts in his mouth. Whoever will not hear the words he will speak in the name of God, will be accountable to God. For he will speak in the name of God.' With that last promise, Moses finished blessing the people of Israel.

The Death of Moses (Deut. 34; Ps. 90)

When Moses had blessed the tribes of Israel, he left the camp and travelled alone to Mount Nebo, towards the rising sun from Jericho. In obedience to the insistent inward voice, he slowly climbed the mountain, until at evening he stood on the mountain peak; a solitary figure looking out over the shadowed hills. He looked over the river Jordan, far below, towards the land that he had sought so many years. As he looked, he seemed to see the whole land of the promise spread out before his eyes; the deep valley of the Jordan, its river winding tortuously between densely wooded banks; the barren hills of Judah sweeping out into the hot desert of the South; the gentle green and white of the highlands, terraced with olive groves and vineyards; the scattered houses and clear rushing streams of the North, rising to snow capped Hermon in its rugged majesty; the fertile corn fields of the plain, spreading to the far white waves of the Great Sea. This small and precious country, its hills and valleys golden under the sun and green in the winter rains, was the home he longed for and had never known.

His eyes dimmed as he thought of the long years in the wilderness, walking with the people he had freed from slavery, forging them fiercely into the warrior horde who now stood poised to enter their inheritance. All his life he had followed the call of the god of fire, who had drawn him from the water and revealed his secret name; who had covered him with the cloud of the presence of glory, and written the Law on his heart. He had brought his people from Egypt with great signs and wonders; he had ruled his people with a strong hand and with power; he had given them the Law of everlasting life; he had known God face to face. He had followed the way that was set before him; and now, in the bare hills of the desert and alone, that way was at an end.

As the last light touched the hill tops, and the fire of the sun flared crimson before the dark, Moses wept for himself and for his people. For himself, because he would never walk in the land of his heart's desire. For his people, because he knew them, and he knew the weakness and the wilfulness that would make their way one of sorrow and affliction, before the final breaking of the day.

In his heart he prayed to the God who had called his people on their long journey to seek his promise:

Lord, you have been our home from age to age;
Before the ancient hills were brought to be
Or earth was forged in love's primordial fire,
You were God, unborn, without beginning.
Mankind returns at your command to dust, from which it comes;

A thousand years to you are like the memory of yesterday
Or like an hour in the night, dark and unknown.
Like sleep before the morning you sweep men away;
Like grass that grows in a day and dies when evening comes.
  Your anger overwhelms us
  For all our secret sins are seen in the light of your presence;
  Before your judgement our lives end in futility.
  For seventy years or so we live, in suffering and struggle;
  Soon those years are gone; a moment, and we are no more.
  Yet who considers this and fears your fury?
Lord, teach us to measure our mortality
That we may seek for wisdom.
Draw near, O God; come quickly;
Have pity on those who pray to you.
  Meet us in the morning with your love
  That we may be glad in the presence of your glory;
  Transform our sorrow with your unceasing joy
  And touch our lives with your eternity.
May your majesty be known to us and to our children;
So may we find in you our heart's true home,
And blessed by you the work we have done may endure;
Lord, by your blessing may our work endure.

The small figure knelt on the mountain top; but he was no longer alone. Around him was the sound of many waters and a beating as of a thousand wings, the whispering of the hosts of heaven and the unmistakeable music of ancient laughter, old as the world and distant as the stars, calling him to the end and beginning of his pilgrimage.

There on the mountain peak Moses the servant of Jahweh died. For one month the people mourned him; but to this day no man knows where his body lies. God had taken to himself the one whom he loved.

In the valley by the river, the people waited now with eager expectation. Their journey was over; the time of the promise had come.

Appendix

The Torah

These are all the laws given to Moses at the Sacred Mountain or during the period of the Wilderness wanderings. Together, they make up the Law, the Torah.

The Law is not just a set of rules; it is divine guidance for the life of Israel. In its teachings are enshrined principles which need to be elicited by meditation, discussion and study, and which instruct man how he can live in the way God intended. Many of the laws sound primitive or savage; applied anachronistically and mechanically, they would be. Yet imminent in them, interpreted by the living wisdom of God, is the Way whose following leads to life. This is, then, not so much Law as wisdom or teaching. Its meaning is not open or easy; it emerges only in the wrestling of each soul with the hidden Word, mirror of the heart, light of the mind, guide of those who seek God.

'I have taken your Law as my heritage for ever: for it is the joy of my heart' (Psalm 119).

There are three main collections of laws: the Book of the Covenant (Ex. 20-23); the Holiness Code (Lev. 17-end); and the Deuteronomic Law (Deut. 12-26). In addition, there are Laws of Ritual Purity (Lev. 11-16), the Ritual Decalogue (Ex. 34) and various laws scattered throughout Exodus and Numbers. I have collected these together and listed them under appropriate headings; so that one can see at a glance all the laws on a given topic, with the place they come from.

RULES FOR WAR

These Laws are obsolete, referring only to the conquest of Canaan. They show some concern for conservation; some humanitarian concern; and concern for ritual purity. 'The Ban' is the most ruthless form of concern for religious purity; it was rarely practised; it involves renouncing all plunder and personal benefit from the victory.

Before battle, the priest shall bless the army; then the officers shall release from service all who have built new houses, planted new vineyards or taken a new wife; and also any who are fearful and lack faith. Then commanders shall be appointed, and battle shall begin.

When you attack a city outside Canaan, you shall offer peace. If they submit, you shall take them as slaves. If they fight, you shall kill the men. Women, children, cattle and goods you shall take as plunder.

But in all the cities of Canaan you shall spare nothing that breathes, that they may not corrupt you with their gods. (The Ban)

When laying siege to a city, you shall not cut down fruit trees for siege works. (Deut. 20)

You may take a captured slave to wife. After shaving her head and cutting her nails, to mourn her parents for a month, you may marry her. If you do not like her, she shall go free; you shall not then sell her or treat her as a slave. (Deut. 21)

When in camp, you shall avoid all unclean things; excretions of semen by night must be cleansed by remaining outside camp until evening, then bathing with water.

You shall excrete outside camp, and bury it, that nothing unclean may be in your camp. (Deut. 23)

Kill all the Amalekites (they attacked you in the wilderness). (Deut. 25)

FOOD LAWS

These laws are partly concerned with hygiene and health, but mostly with ritual purity. Some unclean animals were worshipped by other tribes; anything connected with such cults of fertility was banned. Ritually unclean beings may also be those which escape classification, or seem to mix or confuse two different classes — thus they may seem to threaten the precarious orderliness of the world. (Compare the rule about mixing dissimilar things in the section on 'Forbidden Religious Practices'.) The idea of separating clean from unclean is also connected with a visible reminder of the separation of Israel for God. Blood was reserved for sacrificial use. These laws are valid in Orthodox Judaism.

You may not eat any animal with cloven hooves which is not ruminant (pigs); or which is ruminant, but has not hooves (camel, hare, rock badger). You shall not touch them or their carcasses. If you do, you are unclean till evening. If you pick one up you must wash your clothes.

You may not eat fish without fins or scales (eels, shellfish).

You may not eat eagles, vultures, ospreys, buzzards, kites, ravens, ostriches, owls, hawks, gulls, water hens, pelicans, cormorants, storks, herons, hoopoes, bats (roughly birds of prey); or any winged insect or grub. Locusts and grasshoppers may be eaten, however.

You may not eat anything that dies a natural death (you may give them to aliens or sell them to foreigners). If you carry or eat them, you must wash your clothes, bathe and be unclean until evening. (Deut. 14 Lev. 11 Lev. 17).

You shall not boil a kid in its mother's milk. (This is probably an old fertility spell). (Deut. 14, Exod. 23)

You shall not eat blood; it is the life which belongs to God alone. The blood (the life) makes atonement on the altar. (Deut. 12 Lev. 17)

You shall not eat anything killed by wild beasts. Feed it to the dogs. If you eat it, wash your clothes, bathe and be unclean until evening. (Exod. 22, Lev. 17)

All animals without hooves are unclean (dogs, cats, bears).

These are unclean: weasel, mouse, lizard, crocodile, snakes.

Anything an unclean carcass falls on is unclean; it must be rinsed in water, and be unclean until evening. Earthen pots must be broken, their contents thrown away. Food or drink on which water from such a pot is poured is unclean. Stone or clay ovens and stoves must be broken. Springs or cisterns remain clean, as do sowing seeds (unless the seed is water-soaked). (Lev. 11)

Any animal or bird killed in the hunt must have its blood poured on the ground and covered with earth. (Lev. 17)

You shall not eat fat; as the best meat, it belongs to God. (Lev. 7)

A slightly different prohibition is that on eating the muscle on the hip-joint (because Jacob was touched there by the angel: Gen. 32).

TITHES AND FIRST FRUITS

These laws remind us that all things belong to God. They strongly assert the connection between love of God and love of other people — especially of the under-privileged — and also, the connection between love of God and enjoyment of the good things of life. Love of God is costly, but not gloomy.

In Num. 18, all tithes are given to the Levites; whereas in the Deuteronomic Law (Deut. 14), the Levites seem to receive tithes every third year. Deuteronomy also stresses, as usual, the importance of one Central Sanctuary. No doubt there were rules for dividing the gifts up in various ways, which are not included in the Law itself.

The principle of Tithing is still a valid expression of dedication to God.

A tenth of all your produce belongs to God; grain, wine and olive oil. The first born males of all animals belong to God, including first born sons; they must be presented on the eighth day. You shall eat them in a sacrificial feast at the Central Sanctuary, with all your family. (Deut. 14 Exod. 22) Imperfect firstborn shall not be sacrificed; they may be eaten at home by all. (Deut. 15)

If you live far away, you may sell your produce, and take the money to the Sanctuary, to buy food for a feast; there you and your family shall rejoice.

Every third year, the tithe shall be kept in one's town, and foreigners, orphans and widows shall eat it.

The Levites, the country priests, must also be looked after; they shall share in the tithe of every third year. (Deut. 14)

After giving the third year tithe, you shall say: 'I have kept all your laws, and have not transgressed or forgotten any of them. I have not made the tithe impure by eating it in mourning or while ritually unclean or by offering it to the dead. I have obeyed your voice. Look down from heaven and bless your people and the ground which you have given us.' (Deut. 26)

The firstborn of an ass, being unclean, shall be redeemed with a lamb or have its neck broken.

Firstborn sons shall be redeemed. (Exod. 13 Exod. 34)

Grain or fruit tithed may be redeemed at price plus 20%.

One in ten animals belong to God. (Lev. 27)

You shall take your first fruits, cakes, corn and fruit, to the Central Sanctuary each year. There you shall have a feast; you, the Levite, the foreigner and your family. (Deut. 26 Exod. 23 Num. 15)

Priests have all the first fruits (grain, wine, oil, wool) and firstborn (men and unclean beasts must be redeemed after one month); domestic firstborn are not redeemable; the blood is flung against the altar, fat burnt, and the flesh belongs to the priests.

All tithes belong to the Levites, who must give the best tenth in turn to the priests. (Num. 18)

LAWS OF RITUAL PURITY

These laws are concerned with three topics – contagious skin diseases ('leprosy' in a broad sense), and analogous forms of mould in houses and fabrics; discharge from the reproductive organs (including birth); and contact with the dead.

They are partly matters of primitive hygiene; but also connected with ideas of bodily wholeness or intactness, and the need for protection against the mysterious powers of birth and death. They form the most primitive strand of 'taboo' regulations extant in the Law.

Priests shall declare skin diseases which are unclean – sores with white hairs or yellowish thin hairs in the beard, seeming deeper than the skin or being full of puss. Dull white skin sores are clean; but the person shall be quarantined for seven days; then another seven, until the sore fades; after washing his clothes he is clean. But if it spreads he is unclean. A person whose whole body turns white is clean; but if he has an open sore he is unclean. A person with sores in the hair, but only skin deep, shall be quarantined seven days; then he shall shave and wait another seven days. He is clean if the sores have not spread, or if they grow healthy hairs. Reddish-white spots on a bald spot are unclean.

Unclean 'lepers' must tear their clothes, leave their hair uncombed, and cover the lower half of the face, like mourners, calling 'Unclean'. They must remain outside the camp.

Green or red mould or mildew on clothes, if it spreads, is unclean; the object must be burned. After seven days, the object is washed and put away seven more days. Then if it has changed colour, faded, it shall be torn out; after washing again, it is clean. If its colour remains it is unclean. (Lev. 13)

If there is spreading mould in a house, all furniture must be moved out; if green or red spots are eating into the wall, the house must be locked for seven days. Then the rotted stones and plaster must be thrown away. If the rot recurs, the house must be torn down. Anyone entering the locked house is unclean until night; anyone lying down or eating in it must wash his clothes.

Ritual for Purification The priest shall examine the candidate outside the camp. A bird shall be killed, over a bowl of spring water. He shall dip another bird in the blood, and let it fly away. He shall bind a sprig of marjoram to a piece of cedarwood with a red cord, and sprinkle the blood seven times on the house, or the person, who shall wash his clothes, bathe and shave all his hair. He may then enter camp, but must live outside his tent for seven days, then shave again. On the eighth day, he shall go with the priest to the Sanctuary, and offer a lamb and olive oil as a guilt-offering. The blood of atonement shall be smeared on his right ear, thumb and big toe. The oil, for renewal of life, after being sprinkled seven times in the Sanctuary, shall be similarly smeared, and what remains in the priest's left hand is put on the person's head. Then one lamb for a sin-offering, one for a fire-offering and a grain-offering shall complete the rite. A poor man may bring one third of the grain-offering and two pigeons or doves for his sin and fire-offerings; he must bring the guilt-offering. (Lev. 14)

After birth of a male child, a woman shall be unclean, as in menstruation, for seven days; then for thirty three days she shall not touch holy things or enter the Sanctuary. After birth of a girl, the uncleanness shall be for fourteen days and sixty six days respectively.

At the end of purification, she shall bring a yearling lamb for a fire-offering and a pigeon or dove for a sin-offering, to the Sanctuary; the priest shall make expiation for her. A poor woman may bring two doves or pigeons instead. (Lev. 12)

Discharge from the penis makes a man unclean. Any bed, saddle or seat on which he sits is unclean. Anyone who touches him or his bed must wash his clothes, bathe and be unclean till night; so must anyone who sits on what he sat on, or carries it. Anyone who touches what he sits on is unclean till night. If he spits on or touches a man, that man must wash, bathe and be unclean till night. Pots he touches must be broken, and wooden bowls washed.

After the discharge stops, he waits seven days, washes clothes, bathes in spring water; and on the eighth day, he offers two doves or pigeons as a sin and fire-offering.

A man who emits semen must bathe and be unclean till night. Fabrics the semen falls on must be washed and be unclean till night.

After intercourse, man and woman must bathe and be unclean till night.

At menstruation, a woman is unclean for seven days. Anyone who touches her or what she sits on is unclean till night; must wash clothes and bathe. Her bed is unclean for seven days. (Lev. 15)

A man who has intercourse with her is unclean for seven days. (Lev. 15 Lev. 18)

Both man and woman shall be driven out of the camp. (Lev. 15 Lev. 20)

Women with irregular flows of blood are unclean.

When the flow stops, she shall wait seven days, then offer two doves or pigeons for fire and sin-offerings.

— the penalty for breaking these rules is death (caused by God?) (Lev. 15)

Ritual of the Red Cow An unworked red cow shall be killed by the High Priest outside the camp, to the east. Its blood is sprinkled seven times towards the Sanctuary; it is completely burned; cedarwood, marjoram and scarlet thread are put in the fire. (Cf. purification ritual, above). It is a sin-offering. The priest shall wash his clothes and bathe and be unclean until night, as shall the burner. The ashes are kept outside the camp, and used to make 'water of purification'; this water defiles the clean and purifies the unclean.

Anyone who touches a corpse is unclean for seven days; he must be purified with 'water of purification' on the third and seventh days, sprinkled with marjoram; otherwise he is excluded from the camp. All who touch the water are unclean till night; the uncleanness is contagious by touch.

All who enter a tent where a man has died, who touch a human bone or grave, and all open vessels in the tent of a dead man, are unclean. (Num. 19)

All who are unclean with skin diseases, discharges or by contact with a corpse must be excluded from the camp. (Num. 5)

RULES FOR CERTAIN SPECIFIC PERSONS
(Judges, Kings, Levites, Prophets, Nazarites, Priests)

These Laws are dependent upon specific institutions of ancient Israel. They show a concern for justice and a concern to limit the military ambition, pride and wealth of the rulers. They assume that prophecy will continue, but offer a rather simple test of a true prophet — the complexities were realized later. The practice of the temporary calling of some people to special devotion to God is recognized. And the ritual purity of the priests is safe-guarded, with regard to the three main areas of bodily wholeness, contact with death and sex (marriage is, however, the norm). Deut. 18 appears to add to the priestly dues, as set out in Num. 18 and Lev. 10.

You shall appoint judges and officers in all your towns. They shall be just, impartial, and shall not accept bribes. (Deut. 16)

You may set as king over you he whom Jahweh shall choose. He shall not be a foreigner. He must not procure horses for military chariots, or supply Hebrew soldiers to Egypt in return for horses. He shall not have many wives or great wealth, lest he turns from God. He shall possess a copy of the Law; he shall read it every day, so that he may not consider himself greater than his brothers, and that he may fear God. (Deut. 17)

Levites shall have no inheritance — Jahweh is their inheritance.

A Levite from any town may minister in the Central Sanctuary when he chooses, and share in the priestly dues. (Deut. 18)

You shall obey the prophets whom God will raise up. You shall know a false prophet if his prophecy does not come about. He shall die. (Deut. 18)

Nazarites (man or woman) shall abstain from alcohol or anything from the vine. They must not cut their hair or shave; they must not go near any corpse; they are consecrated by vow to God.

If they are defiled accidentally by death, after seven days they must shave their hair, bring two doves or pigeons as sin and fire-offerings, and a yearling lamb, and start their time of dedication again.

When his vow is complete, he shall give an offering – a lamb for fire-offering; ewe for sin-offering and a ram for fellowship-offering; a basket of unleavened bread; corn and wine. His hair shall be shaved and thrown on the sacrificial fire. The priest shall present, and have, a boiled shoulder of the ram, one thick loaf and one biscuit (as well as his normal due). (Num. 6)

These are the priest's dues: (a) 'most holy' gifts, to be eaten by males of his family, in the Sanctuary: animals brought for sin and guilt-offerings; grain-offerings, made into unleavened bread. (b) 'holy gifts', to be eaten by any of his family, at home: the breast and hindleg of all fellowship-offerings; one cake of grain, from thank-offerings. (c) all firstborn animals and first fruits of grain, wine, oil and wool. (d) everything devoted to Jahweh. (Lev. 10 Num. 18)

When animals are sacrificed, the priests shall have the shoulder, two cheeks and the stomach. (Deut. 18)

Priests shall not enter the Sanctuary after drinking alcohol. (Lev. 10)

Priests shall not (a) take part in funeral rites, except for parents, children, brothers and unmarried sisters. They shall not shave their hair, trim their beards or cut their bodies in mourning. (b) they shall not marry a prostitute or divorcee. If a priest's daughter becomes a prostitute, she must be burned.

The Chief Priest must (a) not leave his hair uncombed or tear his clothes or go near the dead, or leave the Sanctuary to mourn, even for his parents. (b) he must marry a Levite virgin.
No blind, lame, disfigured, deformed, crippled, hunchback, dwarf, diseased or eunuch shall offer sacrifice. He may eat the offerings, but must not approach the veil or altar. (Lev. 21)

Priests who are unclean may not approach holy offerings: if they do, they may never serve at the altar. A priest must bathe, and eat the offerings after sunset, if he is temporarily unclean. (Lev. 22)

RELIGIOUS FESTIVALS

The religious festivals are built around moments of harvest in the agricultural year (barley, wheat and fruit respectively), combined with memorials of the exodus from Egypt. They are built around patterns of sevens, regarded as the 'perfect number'. Regulations for Pesech vary between Ex. 12 and Deut. 16 – in the former, lambs are eaten, roasted in the homes; in the latter, they are eaten, boiled in the Central Sanctuary. Deut. also allows cows to be sacrificed, instead of lambs or goats. This seems to arise from the Deuteronomic concern to have a Central Sanctuary for Israel. The rules are not entirely clear, as they stand, and were presumably supplemented by other sources. But the general principle of regular offerings to God of all produce, with rejoicing, and of continual remembrance of God's historical deliverance – ideas connected with creation and re-creation – are clear enough.

The Sabbath shall be kept every seventh day. No work shall be done; you must not leave home; you must not gather wood or make a fire. The penalty is stoning to death. (Gen. 2 Exod. 16, 20; Deut. 5 Num. 15 Exod. 35)

The daily sacrificial offering is doubled on the Sabbath. (Num. 28)

New moons (first day of the lunar month); the silver trumpets are blown, and a special sacrifice offered, of two bulls, one ram, seven yearling lambs and one goat sin-offering. (Num. 10 Num. 28)

Pesech (Passover) On the tenth day of the first month, take a lamb or goat for each house (or one between two families), a yearling male. On the evening of the fourteenth day, roast it and eat it with bitter herbs and unleavened bread (do not boil it). Eat it in haste, with sandals and stick in hand, as if ready for travel. Eat it whole before morning; burn what is left. Smear its blood with a sprig of marjoram on the doorposts and lintels; do not leave the house until morning. Its bones must not be broken, or meat taken outside the house. No foreigner may eat it, but circumcised slaves and resident aliens may. (Exod. 12 Lev. 23)

Those who are ritually unclean or far away may keep Pesech one month later. (Num. 9)

In the month of Abib (April, roughly), sacrifice a sheep or cow at the Central Sanctuary, at sunset. Boil it and eat it, not leaving any until morning. In the morning, you shall return to your tents. (Deut. 16)

Mazzoth (Unleavened bread) This is the first of the three great festivals. It shall last seven days, from the fifteenth day of the first month (full moon), or the evening of the fourteenth day (depending on how one reckons the start of the day). No leavened bread shall be eaten, and there shall be no leaven in your homes. On the first and seventh days there shall be a solemn assembly; you shall do no work; all your men shall come before God, and give as they are able. Sacrifices shall be offered for seven days, the same as for the New Moon festivals. (Exod. 12 Exod. 23 Num. 28)

Day of First Fruits At the end of Mazzoth, offer the first of your barley; the priest shall present it on the day after the Sabbath, with a yearling lamb and double the usual meal and wine offering. Do not eat bread or new corn, raw or roasted, until you do this. (Exod. 23)

Pentecost. (Weeks; Harvest) This is the second of the three great festivals. It comes seven weeks (fifty days) after the Day of First Fruits, at the beginning of the wheat harvest. You shall bring a freewill offering to the Central Sanctuary; all your family, the Levites of your town, the traveller, orphans and widows shall rejoice with you (remember you were slaves in Egypt). The new corn shall be presented, with these offerings: (Lev. 23): two large leavened loaves, seven yearling lambs, one bull, two rams, with grain and wine: one goat as sin-offering, and two yearling lambs as fellowship-offering. It shall be a day of rest and solemn assembly (Num. 28): Two bulls, one ram, seven yearling rams; one goat as sin-offering (as for Mazzoth and New Moon festivals). (Lev. 23 Deut. 16 Exod. 23 Num. 28)

New Year (Trumpets) The first day of the seventh month. The trumpets shall sound; there shall be a day of rest and solemn assembly and an offering of one bull, one ram, seven yearling rams plus one goat for sin-offering, in addition to the New Moon sacrifices. (Lev. 23 Num. 29)

Yom Kippur (Atonement) On the tenth day of the seventh month, you must afflict yourselves, fast and rest from work, both Israelites and foreigners. Only on that day shall the High Priest enter the Inner Sanctuary. He shall wear linen priestly garments only, after bathing in water, and offering a bull, as a sin-offering for himself and family. He shall take a censer of coals from the altar, with two handfuls of incense, and cense the Ark, covering the Place of Atonement, where Jahweh appears in a cloud between the cherubim, so that he shall not see it and die. He shall sprinkle the blood with his finger on the Place of Atonement, and seven times before it. Then he shall bring two goats from the people, and cast lots before the Sanctuary, one for Jahweh and the other for Azalel (demon of the wilderness or 'the precipice'). The goat chosen for Jahweh shall be killed as a sin-offering for the people; its blood sprinkled on the Place of Atonement and in the Inner Sanctuary. The High Priest shall smear blood from the bull and from the goat on the horns of the altar, and sprinkle it seven times. He shall present the goat chosen for Azalel to Jahweh, lay his hands on it and confess all the sins of Israel over it; the goat shall be sent into the wilderness. Finally, the priest shall bathe and put on full priestly dress, and offer a ram for himself and a ram for the people, as whole-offerings. The man who led out the goat, and the one who carries out the remains of the bull and the goat — all but their blood and fat — and burns them outside the camp, shall wash their clothes and bathe and be clean. Thus atonement will be made yearly for the Inner Sanctuary, the Court, the altar, the priests and the people of Israel. There shall be sacrificed one bull, one ram, seven yearling rams and one goat for a sin-offering. (Lev. 16 Num. 29 Lev. 23)

Succoth (Booths, Tabernacles) On the fifteenth day of the seventh month is the third of the three great festivals. At the vintage, the gathering of grapes and olives, you shall hold a Feast for seven days (Deut: at the Central Sanctuary, with your family, Levites, foreigners, orphans and widows). There shall be a Solemn Assembly on the first and eighth days, and rest from work. Take branches of palm and willow, and fruit, and dwell in tents for seven days, to remember the tents of the wilderness. Offerings shall be as follows: on the first day thirteen bulls, two rams, fourteen yearling rams, with one goat as sin-offering. Then one less bull each day, to seven bulls on the seventh day. And on the eighth day, one bull, one ram, seven yearling rams, with one goat as sin-offering. (Lev. 23 Deut. 16 Exod. 23 Num. 29)

All men must come before Jahweh at the three great festivals: no man shall take your land from you when you so appear at the Sanctuary. (Exod. 23, 24)

LAWS CONCERNING SLAVERY AND YEARS OF RELEASE

Slavery is accepted as an institution in the law; but there seems to be some development in a more humane direction between Exodus and Deuteronomy; and perhaps this goes even further in Leviticus. In the Book of the Covenant (Exod.) female slaves are not freed; in Deuteronomy, they are, and both men and women are to be supplied with provisions. In the Holiness Code (Lev.) permanent slavery for Israelites seems to be excluded; selling oneself into slavery is disallowed; and families are to be freed at Jubilee. (It is unclear what the relation between this freeing at Jubilee and the Exod. and Deut. freeing at the Sabbatical year is; does one replace or complement the other?)

The seventh (Sabbatical) year rules also seem to develop between Exod. and Lev.; but the principle of a 'rest' in remembrance of God is clear. The idea that all property belongs to God, and can only be leased by men, is remarkable. It prevents the accumulation of land by one man; but it is fairly impractical, and there is no record of it being practised for long.

Every seventh year your land shall lie fallow; the poor and any wild beasts may eat what grows there. (Exod. 23)

Every seventh year shall be a Year of Release; all debts shall be cancelled, except to foreigners.

Every seventh year all male and female bought Hebrew slaves shall be freed, and given sheep, grain and wine liberally (remember you were slaves in Egypt). If they will not go, pierce their ears, and they shall be your slaves for ever. (Deut. 15)

If a male slave brought a wife with him, she shall go free. But if his master gave him a wife, wife and children shall remain the master's.

A female bought slave shall not be freed in the Year of Release. If her master marries her, then divorces her, she may be bought back by her family; he cannot sell her to foreigners. If she marries his son, she shall be treated as his daughter. If he takes another wife, she shall have her food, clothes and marital rights, as before. Otherwise she shall be freed.

If a man beats a slave to death, he shall die. But if the slave lasts for a day or two, he shall not be punished.

If a man knocks out a tooth or blinds the eye of a slave, the slave shall go free. (Exod. 21)

One who kidnaps an Israelite, to enslave or sell him, shall die. (Exod. 21 Deut. 24)

Slaves escaped from another country shall be allowed to live in your towns; they shall not be returned or enslaved by you. (Deut. 23)

A man who has sex with a slave he has promised to another, but who has not been paid for, shall not die. An enquiry will be held, and he will offer a ram as a guilt-offering. (Lev. 19)

Every seventh year the land shall be uncultivated: you shall not sow, prune or harvest systematically. But its produce may be freely eaten by all.

Every fiftieth year (seven times seven years) shall be the Year of the Ram (Restoration: Jubilee). Blow the trumpets on Yom Kippur and proclaim freedom to all. All shall return to their property. All property shall be returned to its original owner — so property can only be leased, not sold entirely (it belongs to God: you are aliens, allowed the use of it). The price thus decreases as Jubilee draws near. (In the sixth year, the land will produce food enough for two years).

If an Israelite sells himself as a slave, you shall treat him as a hired man. At Jubilee, he and his children shall be free, to return to his property (the Israelites are God's slaves, and must not be sold into slavery or be permanent slaves). But permanent slaves may be bought from foreigners or taken in war or inherited.

If an Israelite sells himself as a slave to a resident alien, he may be redeemed at any time, and must be released at Jubilee (the redemption price is fixed according to a hired man's wages until the Year of the Ram). (Lev. 25)

FORBIDDEN RELIGIOUS PRACTICES

These laws show the rigorous exclusivism of the cult of Jahweh; all fertility, magic and death cults are forbidden; apostasy is ruthlessly punished; they show the lack of respect for personality which is symptomatic of Canaanite religion, and which the cult of Jahweh was trying to root out, in a savage and primitive tribal culture.

You shall destroy all the sacred sanctuaries of Canaan; the hill and tree shrines; the altars, standing stones, wooden poles and images. You shall not serve their gods. (Deut. 12)

You shall not set up poles or pillars by the altars of Jahweh. (Deut. 16)

If a prophet or visionary tempts you away to worship other gods, you shall kill him, even if his predictions come true (then God will be testing you to see if you love him).

If a member of your family tempts you to apostasy, you shall stone him to death; your hand shall be first, then all the people.

If a whole city falls into apostasy, you shall put it under the Ban. All the inhabitants and cattle shall be put to the sword; everything in it shall be burned and destroyed, as a sacrifice to Jahweh. You shall keep nothing; and the city shall remain a ruin for ever; it shall never be built again. (Deut. 13)

Anyone who worships other gods shall be stoned at the gates. (Deut. 17)

Do not invoke or speak of other gods. (Exod. 23)

You shall not put God to the test. (Deut. 6)

You shall not shave your heads or cut yourselves or cut the hair on the sides of your head or trim your beard or tattoo yourselves, for the dead. (Deut. 14 Lev. 9)

You shall not read auguries, or go to mediums or wizards; you shall not sacrifice your children, or practise divination, sorcery, use charms or practise the cults of the dead. (Because of these practices God is driving out the Canaanites before you). (Deut. 18 Lev. 19)

Mediums and witches shall be stoned to death. (Lev. 20 Exod. 22)

Men and women shall not exchange clothing (as in the cults of Astarte). (Deut. 22)

You shall not mix dissimilar things — plough with an ox and ass; wear linen and wool; sow with two kinds of seed (or the whole will be forfeit to the Sanctuary); breed two kinds of animals. (Lev. 19 Deut. 22)

Men and women of Israel shall not be cultic prostitutes; money from them shall not be given to Jahweh in payment of a vow. (Deut. 23 Lev. 19)

You shall not give your children to be sacrificed to Molech: the penalty is death: if it is ignored, God will cut you off. (Lev. 18, 20)

RULES FOR SACRIFICES

Two main stages in the development of sacrificial ritual are mentioned. In the Book of the Covenant, many Sanctuaries are allowed. In Deuteronomy, however, all sacrifices are to be offered at one central shrine (this looks forward to the Temple at

Jerusalem, perhaps). In Deuteronomy, it is explicitly stated that not all animal slaughter is sacrificial whereas in Leviticus what is meant is probably that all animal slaughter must take the form of a fellowship-offering; the Levitical rules perhaps apply only to wilderness conditions, when the Sanctuary was the Tent in the middle of the camp; Deuteronomy again looks forward to the settlement in Canaan.

Num. 15 alters the rule for atoning for inadvertent sin by the whole community, found in Lev. 4; but only very slightly.

It is clear that sacrifice was a central part of Israel's relation to God. But it does not atone for presumptuous sin, for which death is the only penalty.

The main rules for the five main sacrifices are given in Lev. 1-7 — cf. 'The Mountain' p. 175. Sacrifices in fulfilment of a vow or freewill offerings, may be either fire or fellowship-offerings. The following rules are also found in the Law:

Fire-offerings must be male. All offerings must be perfect, and must not be bought from foreigners. Free-will offerings, however, may be stunted or imperfect, but not blind, lame, mutilated, castrated or with running sores. (Lev. 22)

You shall build earth altars, in all places where Jahweh shows himself, causing his name to be remembered in the cult.

If you build stone altars, they shall be unhewn; shaping causes pollution.

You shall not have steps up to the altar; so your nakedness shall not be seen (sex is to have no place in your worship). (Exod. 20)

You shall not let fat from sacrifices remain until morning. (Exod. 23)

The restitution payment for guilt-offerings must be given to the priest, if the victim and his next of kin have all died. (Num. 5)

Grain and wine shall be offered with every animal sacrificed (the amount increases according to whether lambs, rams or bulls are given).

Inadvertent sin by the community requires the sacrifice of one bull (fire-offering) and one goat (sin-offering).

All those who commit presumptuous sin must be killed; sacrifice will not atone for such sin. (Num. 15)

The daily offering shall be one yearling ram each morning and one yearling ram each evening, with grain and wine-offerings. (Exod. 24 Num. 28)

You shall not offer sacrifices at any place, as you see fit. You shall seek the one place which Jahweh will choose, where his Name will live. There all the tribes must bring their sacrifices, first fruits and tithes, to one Central Sanctuary, to preserve the unity of the faith.

You may kill and eat meat anywhere, it is not a sacrifice. (Deut. 12)

If you kill a cow, sheep or goat and do not bring it to the Sanctuary as a sacrifice, blood-guilt will be on you. You shall not sacrifice to goat-demons in the open country. (Lev. 17)

Young animals must be kept with their mothers for seven days; then they can be sacrificed.

Animals and their young must not be sacrificed on the same day.

Any member of a priest's family may eat the 'holy gifts', his slaves and any widowed or divorced childless daughter who has returned to live in his household. But guests, hired men or married daughters shall not eat the offerings.

Anyone who eats an offering by mistake must repay the priest plus a fifth. (Lev. 22)

No one is to go before God without an offering. (Exod. 34)

LAWS CONCERNING THE REDEMPTION OF HOLY GIFTS

These laws make it clear that people and possessions dedicated to God were normally redeemed at their set price, plus a fifth.

A person who has been dedicated to God may be redeemed at a set sum — but priests may set a lower price for the poor.

A man shall not exchange a dedicated or tithed animal; if he does, both animals must be given to God, and cannot be redeemed.

You may dedicate an unclean animal; the priest will set a price for it. To redeem it the price plus a fifth must be paid. So with a house or field. If you sell a dedicated field without redeeming it first, it reverts to the priests at the next Jubilee for ever. Bought dedicated fields revert to the original owners at Jubilee (the price is fixed with this in mind); inherited fields, if not redeemed, remain God's.

No firstborn may be dedicated (they already belong to God). But a firstborn unclean animal may be redeemed at price plus a fifth; if not, it must be sold to someone else by the priests.

Nothing placed under the Ban may be redeemed or sold — land, animal or man. All must be destroyed. (Lev. 27)

RULES FOR THE CULT AND MEMBERSHIP OF THE ASSEMBLY

These rules define who can be a member of the Assembly, and give some positive rules for the cult of Jahweh; together with the food laws, Sabbath-keeping and the sacrificial laws, they provide the cultic requirements of ancient Israel, and to some extent, of modern Judaism. The final law, taken from Moses' farewell speeches, states what is traditionally the 'great commandment'.

No man whose testicles are crushed or whose penis is cut off can join the Assembly of God (for war or the great festivals).

No half-breed can join the Assembly, even to the tenth generation.

No Ammonite or Moabite (descendants of Lot) can join the Assembly, to the tenth generation; you shall not seek their peace or prosperity, because they did not meet you with bread and water when you came from Egypt, and hired Balaam the prophet to curse you.

The children of the third generation of Edomites and Egyptians may join the Assembly; the former are your kin (descendants of Esau); you lived in the latter's land. (Deut. 23)

Boys shall be circumcised on the eighth day, as a sign of the covenant. (Gen. 17 Lev. 12)

Newly planted fruit trees are unclean for three years; the fourth year all fruit is dedicated to God; the fifth year it may be eaten. (Lev. 19)

You shall have tassels on the four corners of your cloak, with a blue thread, to remind you of the Law. (Deut. 22 Num. 15)

Revere the Sanctuary, and consider the priests holy. (Lev. 19)

The Lord our God is one god. You shall love the Lord your God with all your heart and soul and strength. (Deut. 6)

LAWS CONCERNING DEATH OR INJURY

All taking of human life must be expiated by blood. But manslaughter is distinguished from murder, even though the right of blood feud is acknowledged (that the next of kin may kill the murderer).

There shall be three cities of refuge, where one who kills unintentionally may live safely. If your land is enlarged, you shall add another three. (Deut. 19 Exod. 21)

A murderer shall not be safe in a city of refuge. The elders of his town shall fetch him and hand him over to the next of kin of the victim, who shall take revenge. (Deut. 19 Exod. 21)

Murder is: striking with a lethal weapon, striking with malice. The next of kin shall kill the murderer. If the killing is accidental, the murderer shall stay in a city of refuge until the death of the High Priest, then he is free. Until then, he can be killed, if found outside the city.

A murderer's life cannot be redeemed (blood must be expiated by blood). (Num. 35)

A murderer shall be put to death. (Exod. 21 Lev. 24)

A man who kills a thief at night is not guilty of murder. If he kills a thief during the day, he is guilty of murder. (Exod. 22)

Murder by an unknown hand brings blood-guilt on the land. The elders of the nearest city shall take an unworked cow to an uncultivated valley where there is running water. They shall break its neck and wash their hands over it, saying: 'Our hands did not send this blood, neither did our eyes see it shed. Forgive, O Jahweh, your people Israel, whom you have redeemed, and do not place the guilt of innocent blood upon us, but forgive.' So it shall be expiated. (Deut. 21)

A man who injures another in a fight shall not be punished; but he shall pay for his lost time and take care of him until he is well.

If some men are fighting and hurt a pregnant woman, and she loses her child, the offender shall be fined whatever the husband demands, subject to the approval of the judges. If she is injured, the punishment shall fit the crime (lex talionis).

If a bull gores someone to death, it shall be stoned and not eaten, to expiate the blood-guilt. If the owner knew it was dangerous, and had been warned, he shall be put to death also. But he may be allowed to pay a fine to save his life.

If a bull kills a slave, it shall be stoned, and the owner shall pay the slave price, 30 pieces of silver. (Exod. 21)

Any animal which kills a man must be killed. (Gen. 9)

If a woman seizes a man's testicles as he is fighting with her husband, her hand shall be cut off. (Deut. 25)

LAWS CONCERNING PROPERTY

Private property is safe-guarded; but it was not to be treated too exclusively; and the Jubilee laws ensure that appropriation of property by one man cannot occur. The Law distinguishes quite clearly between offences with regard to property and offences with regard to persons; the latter are regarded much more seriously.

You shall not remove your neighbour's boundary stone. (Deut. 19)

If you find a domestic animal which has strayed, you must return it to your brother, and even to your enemy; or keep it until he comes for it. (Deut. 22 Exod. 23)

So you must do with anything that is lost, which you find. (Deut. 22)

You shall not lend at interest to your brother who is poor; you may lend at interest to foreigners. (Deut. 23 Exod. 22 Lev. 25)

You may eat your fill of grapes or wheat from your neighbour's fields; but you shall not use a sickle or take any away in a container, for later use. (Deut. 23)

If a man leaves a pit uncovered, and a bull or donkey falls into it, he must pay for the dead animal, and may then keep it.

If one man's bull kills another bull, they shall sell the live bull, divide the money, and divide the meat of the dead bull; unless the live bull was known to be dangerous, when the owner shall give the victim another bull, keeping the corpse. (Exod. 21)

If a man steals a cow or sheep, and he still has it alive, he shall pay two animals for one; if he has sold or killed it, he shall pay five cows for one or four sheep for one. If he cannot pay, he shall be sold as a slave.

If a man's animals eat crops from another's fields or vineyards, he must make good the loss with his own crops.

If a man starts a fire and it burns his neighbour's corn, he must pay for the damage.

If a man keeps another's goods for him and they are stolen, the thief shall repay double. If he cannot be found, the man shall be brought to a Sanctuary, and swear his innocence on oath, bringing a curse on himself if he is guilty.

All property disputes shall be brought to a Sanctuary; the one judged to be guilty shall pay double to the other.

If an animal given to a man for safekeeping dies, is injured or disappears, the man shall swear an oath of innocence at the Sanctuary; no restitution need be made.

If an animal left for safekeeping is stolen, restitution shall be made to the owner.

If an animal left for safekeeping is killed by wild beasts, he shall show the remains, and need not pay restitution.

If a borrowed working animal is hurt or dies when the owner is absent, a replacement must be provided. If the owner was there, he is responsible, and restitution is not necessary. If it was hired, only the hiring charge is made. (Exod. 22)

A man can redeem his land which he has sold; his next of kin may buy it back, for a price related to the Jubilee, when it returns anyway.

Houses in walled cities can be redeemed within one year; but after that they are never returned, even at Jubilee.

Houses in unwalled villages are like fields — they may be redeemed at any time.

Levite's houses, even in walled cities, are redeemable at any time, and at Jubilee; their land can never be sold at all. (Lev. 25)

Daughters may inherit, where there are no sons; after them the land passes to brothers. But daughters must marry within their own tribe; for every tribe must keep its own patrimony. (Num. 27, 36)

If a man kills an animal, he must replace it. (Lev. 24)

LAWS CONCERNING THE FAMILY

These Laws suppose a society in which extended families live under one patriachal head of the house; polygamy, the possession of concubines and divorce are accepted as normal. The grounds on which divorce is allowable are unclear, and were disputed between various interpreters. Incest and sexual licence were regarded with great abhorrence; in Canaan, sexual practices were often cultic or religious in nature, and so were idolatrous.

The institution of Levirate marriage shows the great importance attached to perpetuating the family name, before a clear doctrine of an after life had been formulated.

Num. 5 gives a primitive form of trial by ordeal, of a very mild nature, depending wholly on psychological pressure, it would seem.

The firstborn son shall have a double share of the inheritance. This may not be changed because of favouritism.

If a son is stubborn, rebellious, a glutton and drunkard, who will not obey his parents, they may bring him to the elders at the city gate; and all the men shall stone him to death. (Deut. 21)

If a man accuses his wife of having not been a virgin, in order to divorce her, then her father and mother may bring her to the elders at the gate, and show the bed sheet, stained with the blood of their wedding night. Then the man shall be whipped and give 100 silver pieces to the bride's father, and he may not divorce his wife ever; for he has given an evil name to a virgin of Israel. But if he is right, the woman shall be stoned to death at the door of her father's house, because she has broken the sacral law, and brought evil on Israel. (Deut. 22)

If a man has sex with another's wife, or a betrothed virgin in the city, they shall both be stoned to death. (Deut. 22 Lev. 18)

If a man has sex by force with a betrothed virgin in the country, only the man shall die. (Deut. 22)

If a man has intercourse by force with a virgin and is discovered, he shall give her father fifty pieces of silver, the bride price; she shall be his wife, and he may never divorce her. But the father has the right to refuse to give her; he still gets the money. (Deut. 22 Exod. 22)

A man shall not marry or have sex with his father's wife. (Deut. 22)

A man who has divorced his wife may not remarry her (he may divorce for 'indecency', giving her a written note of divorce).

A newly married man shall be free from military service or social service for one year. (Deut. 24)

A man shall marry his dead brother's wife, if he had no son; the first son shall bear the dead man's name. If he will not marry her, the wife shall pull off his sandal before the elders at the gate, and spit in his face. His house shall be called 'the house of the unsandled man', because he would not perpetuate his brother's name. (Deut. 25)

A man who hits or places a curse on his father or mother shall be put to death. (Exod. 21 Lev. 20)

One who has intercourse with an animal shall be put to death; the animal shall be killed. (Exod. 22 Lev. 20)

Do not have sex with any kin; mother, sister, step sister, grandchild, half-sister, brother's wife, daughter or granddaughter of a woman you have had sex with; if you do, you will be cast out. For the following, the penalty is death: sex with father's wives, daughter in law. (Lev. 18, 20)

If you marry your uncle's wife or brother's wife, you shall both be childless. (Lev. 20)

You shall not marry your wife's sister, if your wife is still alive.

You shall not have sex with another man; the penalty is death. (Lev. 18, 20)

If you take a mother and daughter as wives, all shall be burned.

You shall not marry your sister or half-sister, or have sex with a woman in menstruation, or you will be driven out. (Lev. 20)

A man who suspects his wife of adultery shall bring her to the priest. He shall give a kilo of plain barley flour to the priest, who shall put it in the woman's hands. Before the altar, he shall pour holy water into a clay bowl, adding earth from the Sanctuary floor. He shall loosen her hair, and make her swear: 'If I am innocent, I will be unharmed. If I am guilty, this bitter water will make my vagina shrink, my stomach swell and my name to be a curse among my people.' The curse will be written by the priest, and washed into the water; he will offer a handful of flour; then they shall wait to see whether the curse takes effect. (Num. 5)

LAWS CONCERNING JUSTICE AND HONESTY

Honesty, justice and promise-keeping had a very high value in the Law (Cf. the story of Jephthah's daughter, Judges 11); perhaps because of the importance of Covenant and trust in the relation established by God between him and Israel.

The 'Lex Talionis' occurs in three contexts, and is probably a picturesque way of saying 'let the punishment fit the crime'.

Though the Law was harsh, often inflicting the death penalty, there is a place for compassion too – and a concern to avoid exploitation of the socially disadvantaged. Perhaps the harshness may be seen as a means of inducing compassion in a primitive and savage society. One may observe the rules of compassion out of fear of punishment; and this may eventually lead to the establishment of a norm of compassion in society.

A man cannot be charged on the evidence of only one witness.

A malicious witness or false accuser shall receive the punishment that would have been inflicted on the accused. (Deut. 19)

You shall take life for life, eye for eye, tooth for tooth, hand for hand, foot for foot, burn for burn, wound for wound, bruise for bruise, fracture for fracture. (Deut. 19 Exod. 21 Lev. 24)

Vows to God must be kept, without hesitation. You need not vow; but all you promise, God will require of you. (Deut. 23)

A man must keep a vow; with women, fathers or husbands are responsible, but must object on the day they hear of it, then it is annulled; otherwise, they are guilty of the vow-breaking, or the vow stands. Widows and divorcees are bound by their vows. (Num. 30)

Each man shall be punished for his own sin; fathers shall not be killed for children, nor children for fathers.

You shall not be unjust to foreigners or orphans. (Deut. 24)

You shall not exploit an alien (you were aliens in Egypt), widows or orphans. (If you do, God will take vengeance, and leave your dependents as widows and orphans). (Exod. 22 Lev. 19)

You shall not curtail the rights of a hired servant, even if a foreigner. If he is poor, you must pay him before night, on the day he earns his pay (remember you were slaves in Egypt). (Deut. 24 Lev. 19)

A man shall be whipped in proportion to his crime; but never with more than forty lashes. (Deut. 25)

You shall possess only one full and just set of weights and measures, so that you may deal honestly. (Deut. 25 Lev. 19)

You shall not curse God, or you shall be stoned; you shall not curse your tribal chiefs. (Exod. 22 Lev. 24)

Do not help a wicked man by giving malicious evidence.

Do not be led into evil by a majority; do not follow them in being unjust.

Do not kill the innocent or acquit the guilty.

Take no bribes; they blind the wise and ruin the cause of the innocent. (Exod. 23)

Do not spread false rumours, or make false accusations.

Do not be partial to a poor (powerful?) man, and do not pervert the justice due to the poor; judge impartially. (Exod. 23 Lev. 19)

Do not steal, cheat or lie.

Do not make a promise in God's name, you do not intend to keep.

Do not oppress your neighbour.

Do not take revenge, or give decisions out of vengeance.

Help those on trial for their lives, if you can. (Lev. 19)

There shall be one law for Israelite and foreigner. (Lev. 24 Num. 15)

Difficult cases shall be adjudicated at the Central Sanctuary, where the priests and judge shall decide. Anyone who does not obey the judgement shall die. (Deut. 17)

CONCERN FOR THE WELL-BEING OF OTHERS

The Law shows a concern for the poor and needy; and takes care to state that foreigners and enemies are to be helped, as well as neighbours. Appeals are frequently made to the past slavery of the Israelites, and to the fact that God freed them and gave them Canaan; this is taken as a model or pattern for their present conduct.

You shall love your neighbour as yourself. Do not hate him or bear a grudge, but settle your differences amicably.

You shall love foreigners as you love yourselves.

Show respect for the old. (Lev. 19)

You shall not glean your cornfields, olive groves or vineyards; do not reap your fields to the borders or gather fallen grapes; all that is left shall be for foreigners, the poor, orphans and widows. (Lev. 19 Deut. 24)

You shall help your brother (and your enemy) to lift an animal which has fallen by the way. (Deut. 22 Exod. 23)

You shall not take a millstone or flour mill in pledge; it is needed for the daily grinding of corn for bread.

You shall not enter your neighbour's house to seek a pledge for what he owes you; you shall wait for him to bring it out. (Deut. 24)

If you take a poor man's cloak as a pledge, you shall return it at night, so that he may sleep in it.

You shall not take a widow's clothing as a pledge. (Deut. 24 Exod. 22)

You must not muzzle an ox on the threshing floor; let it eat the grain. (Deut. 25)

If you come upon a bird's nest with eggs or young, you may take them; but you must let the mother go.

Your house roofs must have parapets, lest anyone falls and brings blood-guilt on your house. (Deut. 22)

You shall not curse the deaf or cause the blind to stumble. (Lev. 19)

You shall open wide your hand to your brother, to the needy and the poor; lend him sufficient for his need. Give freely, without grudging, and the Lord will bless you. (If you obey God, there will be no poor among you; disobey, and the poor will always be with you). (Deut. 15)

If your brother becomes poor, you shall maintain him as you would a hired man; he will live near you; do not give him his food for profit. (Remember God gave you Canaan). (Lev. 25)

Moses said: 'There are many things hidden, which belong to God alone. But his will is given in the Law: it belongs to us and to our children; and we must keep his commands and walk in his way for ever.'